D1423422

SHAKESPEARE SURVEY

SHAKESPEARE SURVEY

AN ANNUAL SURVEY OF
SHAKESPEARIAN STUDY & PRODUCTION

15

EDITED BY
ALLARDYCE NICOLL

Issued under the Sponsorship of

THE UNIVERSITY OF BIRMINGHAM
THE UNIVERSITY OF MANCHESTER
THE SHAKESPEARE MEMORIAL THEATRE
THE SHAKESPEARE BIRTHPLACE TRUST

CAMBRIDGE
AT THE UNIVERSITY PRESS
1962

PUBLISHED BY

THE SYNDICS OF THE CAMBRIDGE UNIVERSITY PRESS

Bentley House, 200 Euston Road, London, N.W. 1
American Branch: 32 East 57th Street, New York 22, N.Y.
West African Office: P.O. Box 33, Ibadan, Nigeria

Printed in Great Britain at the University Press, Cambridge
(Brooke Crutchley, University Printer)

EDITOR'S NOTE

The present volume of *Shakespeare Survey* is largely concerned with his poems, songs and music. For the next, the sixteenth volume, the central theme will be 'Shakespeare in the Modern World', and in it will be printed some of the papers delivered at the International Shakespeare Conference, Stratford-upon-Avon, in August 1961.

To celebrate the fourth centenary of Shakespeare's birth, the seventeenth volume, to be published early in 1964, will depart from *Survey's* usual plan. This volume will be devoted entirely to 'Shakespeare in His Own Age' and will consist of a series of articles on diverse aspects of life in Elizabethan and Jacobean times.

CONTENTS

[Notes are placed at the end of each contribution. All line references are to the 'Globe' edition, and, unless for special reasons, quotations are from this text]

LIST OF PLATES

LIST OF PLATES

TWENTIETH-CENTURY STUDIES IN SHAKESPEARE'S SONGS, SONNETS, AND POEMS

1. SONGS AND MUSIC

BY

F. W. STERNFELD

A consideration of the role that music plays in the dramas of Shakespeare is to be found in reference works of all kinds from the comprehensive encyclopaedia to the brief article in a periodical. General, and specifically English, histories of music include material on Shakespeare, and the forthcoming volume IV of the *New Oxford History of Music* will deal with music for the theatre in Shakespeare's time.

The researches of eighteenth-century scholars provided the basis for subsequent research. It is, perhaps, not generally realized how many musical problems are touched upon in Bishop Percy's *Reliques of Ancient English Poetry* of 1765. His second book 'containing ballads that illustrate Shakespeare' was a pilot study that tried to illuminate the Shakespeare lyrics by reference to sources of the sixteenth and seventeenth centuries. This enthusiasm for the old ballads also distinguishes Thomas Warton's *History of English Poetry* (1774–81). The sympathies of Percy and Warton, harbingers of the coming Romanticism, differed widely from the anti-quarian bent of a Joseph Ritson, yet the latter's *Ancient Songs* (1790; rev. W. C. Hazlitt, 1877) is also a standard source for glosses of later commentators. The general histories of music by John Hawkins (1776) and Charles Burney (1776–89) paid particular attention to manuscript and printed collections. The authors also took advantage of their professional musicianship to reprint some of the music that had hitherto been merely mentioned. In this way Hawkins could add to Percy's discoveries the catch, 'Hold thy peace' from T. Ravenscroft's *Deuteromelia* (1609) mentioned in *Twelfth Night*, II, iii, 67. These collective discoveries were to bear fruit in various annotated editions of Shakespeare's plays, of which Malone's edition of 1790, in ten volumes, is particularly felicitous in its musical glosses. It was Malone's brilliant emendation that connected Pistol's 'calmie custure me' in *Henry V*, IV, iv, 4 with a famous Irish song, recorded in many Elizabethan and Jacobean anthologies. His observant eye also caught in the first line of Desde-mona's Willow Song the erroneous 'singing' as a misprint for 'sighing'[1]. (Boswell's revision of Malone in 1821 contains further emendations and discoveries.)

The roll-call of significant contributions in the nineteenth century begins with Douce's *Illustrations of Shakespeare* (1st edn. 1807) and takes us to Edward Woodall Naylor's *Shakespeare and Music* (1st edn. 1896). The former perpetuates the antiquarian tendencies of his predecessors, but Naylor, the modern scholar, happily puts to good use his competence to transcribe lute and cittern tablatures. Many basic sources were reprinted during the first half of the century, notably in the *Progresses* of Queen Elizabeth and King James, edited by John Nichols (1823, 1828); and the tracts and ballads made available in the *Publications* of the Shakespeare Society (1840–53) as, for instance, J. P. Collier's edition of Robert Armin's *Nest of Ninnies*. Granted that the work of a Nichols or a Collier should in time be revised, with attention paid to modern notions of accuracy, yet the impetus which these publications gave to further studies in the field can hardly be overestimated. When Edward Francis Rimbault published *Who was Jack Wilson?* in 1846, the first sentence significantly read: 'In the second volume of the "Shakespeare Society's Papers", Mr Collier has communicated an article (p. 33) upon "Jack Wilson", the performer of Balthazar in *Much Ado About Nothing*.' Rimbault, along with W. Chappell, was one of the founders of the Musical Antiquarian Society. His publications are too numerous to mention, but the *Musical Illustrations of...Percy's Reliques* (1850) deserves particular notice, with the reservation here, as elsewhere, that modern accuracy is not to be expected. Charles Knight's *Pictorial Edition of Shakespeare* (8 vols. 1839–42) was even richer in its musical illustrations than had been Boswell's revision of Malone. Knight frequently relied on stage tradition at the Drury Lane Theatre, with the result that he provides tunes from the age of Garrick and Sheridan, instead of Marlowe and Shakespeare. Still, his illustrations are sometimes the oldest versions extant, and therefore valuable.

The second half of the century produced a spate of indispensable monographs as well as the bulky editions of Shakespeare, by Halliwell-Phillipps and Furness. Halliwell-Phillipps drew attention to and reproduced in facsimile a musical version of 'Come over the bourn Bessy' from *King Lear*, III, vi, 28 and Furness reprinted the findings of Chappell and others. Chappell opened new fields for the exploration of English balladry. His *Popular Music of the Olden Time* (2 vols. 1855–9), succeeding as it did his earlier collections and editions, was a masterly summary of extant knowledge to which were added many contributions of his own. Here was patient scrutiny of manuscripts at London, Cambridge and Dublin, as well as of early printed editions. When no early source could be found, Chappell searched for oral tradition in collections of the eighteenth and nineteenth centuries, never obscuring or falsifying the pedigree of a tune. His work was revised by H. E. Wooldridge in 1893 (under the title *Old English Popular Music*). Both Chappell and Wooldridge give the original melodies, though with nineteenth-century accompaniments. The main value of their work lies in their lists of extant versions and their ability to detect a Shakespearian tune even when it was veiled below a variety of titles, first lines and other disguises. Chappell (jointly with J. W. Ebsworth) was also the editor of the *Roxburghe Ballads* (9 vols. 1871–99) which, though limited to the texts without music, throw a good deal of light on some of Shakespeare's songs. By contrast John Caulfield's *Collection of the Vocal Music in Shakespeare's Plays* (2 vols. 1864) is almost pointless since the author does not indicate his sources; yet this voluminous collection is very nearly a favourite with theatrical producers. F. J. Furnivall followed in the footsteps of Chappell and Ebsworth with his unbounded enthusiasm for the old ballads. Of his many publications we may single out the edition (jointly with J. W. Hales) of *Bishop Percy's Folio Manuscript*, which contains the earliest known version of 'King Stephen was a worthy peer' from *Othello*, II, iii, 92. Furnivall was also one of the many contributors to the *Publications* of the New Shakspere Society (1874–92). No student of Shakespeare's songs can afford to ignore the many detailed glosses in the Society's *Transactions* or the various musical programmes detailed in the Society's *Miscellanies*. No. 3 of the latter (rev. edn. 1884, ed. by F. J. Furnivall and W. G. Stone) is both the most voluminous (xxxv+ 113 pp.) and the most helpful to the modern student, with its copious index and details of the contents of such earlier collections as J. Playford's *Select Ayres* (1659); J. Vernon's *New Songs* (1762); W. Linley's *Dramatic Songs* (1816); and J. Caulfield's *Collection* of 1864, referred to earlier.

Before the end of the century there were further important contributions in the works of J. F. Bridge, W. Barclay Squire and E. W. Naylor. Bridge's *Songs from Shakespeare: The Earliest Known Settings* (London: Novello, ?1894) together with his later *Shakespearean Music in the Plays* (1923) offers early settings as well as some facsimiles not readily available elsewhere. Barclay Squire (with J. A. Fuller-Maitland) provided a modern edition of the *Fitzwilliam Virginal Book*, one of the most voluminous manuscript collections of the early seventeenth century, and of particular relevance for Shakespearian studies (2 vols. 1894–9). The first edition of Naylor's *Shakespeare and Music* (1896) made full use of the contributions of Chappell, Wooldridge and others, and, moreover, described the background of Elizabethan vocal and instrumental music to a general public.

The twentieth century has witnessed both the blessing and the curse of modern scholarship. One encounters research on the one hand that takes full advantage of bibliographical and photographic facilities, with a resultant degree of accuracy and detail that is novel in modern European history. On the other hand, the exigencies of commercial publishing and marketing have produced a kind of popular book, based on second-hand knowledge and marred by serious inaccuracies. Since both kinds of publications appear in a variety of comprehensive bibliographies, a separation of the sheep from the goats is clearly obligatory. Sir Walter Greg's *List of English Plays...before 1643* (1900), based on authoritative knowledge, is exemplary of its kind. That it should now be superseded by the same author's *Bibliography of Printed English Drama* (4 vols. 1939–59) in no way detracts from its historical importance. Greg's numerous publications are an indispensable tool for musical research on Shakespeare: the chronological and bibliographical judgments are supplemented by many detailed comments on stage directions concerning music and on the different versions of lyrics in quartos and folios. Concerning these matters, the *Editorial Problem in Shakespeare* (3rd edn. 1954) and the *Shakespeare First Folio* (1955) are particularly helpful. But, in contrast to these trustworthy volumes, it must be said that Louis C. Elson's *Shakespeare in Music* (1901) and Charles Vincent's *Fifty Shakespeare Songs* (1906) are typical of glibly popular works, full of inaccuracies. They are neither as learned nor as helpful as Chappell was in 1859, let alone Wooldridge in 1893 or Naylor in 1896. Vincent's volume is a forerunner of several anthologies intended for the singer in quest of material for a recital to be entitled 'Shakespeare in Music'. Vincent's successors have improved somewhat upon his method, notably Vincent Jackson, *English Melodies from the 13th to the 18th Century* (1910) and Frank H. Potter, *Reliquary of English Song* (2 vols. 1915–16, accompaniments by C. Vincent). But none of these publications commands the authority of the best books of the nineteenth century, though Potter's reliquary includes useful facsimiles of the 'Willow Song' and of Jonson's 'Have you seen but a white lily grow'.

The need for authoritative reprints of old music, so forcefully stimulated by Squire's edition of the Fitzwilliam Book, was recognized by Naylor whose researches persevered into the twentieth century and resulted in several standard works. His study of the Fitzwilliam Book (*An Elizabethan Virginal Book*, 1905) was followed by an anthology of Elizabethan music, entitled *Shakespeare Music* (1st edn. 1913, 2nd edn. 1928). Unlike his predecessors, Chappell and Wooldridge, Naylor did not feel impelled to provide modern accompaniments, but reprinted melody and accompaniment as he found them in the original scores. His transcriptions of 'A robyn, gentyl robyn' from British Museum, Add. MS. 31922 and of 'Come over the bourn Bessy' from Cambridge, MS. Dd. 2. 11 are significant steps forward. Of Naylor's later work we may mention here his *Poets and Music* (1928). The chapter on Shakespeare (pp. 89–130) contains a valuable discussion of passages in Shakespeare dealing with concrete musical instruments as well as with the music of the spheres. A revision of *Shakespeare and Music* appeared in 1931 and its excellence is a challenge to later scholars. G. H. Cowling's *Music on the Shakespearean Stage* (1913) is frequently referred to as a supplement to Naylor's standard work. Cowling discriminates nicely between the 'brazen din' of Marlowe and Shakespeare's more economical use of battle signals, but, unlike Naylor, he does not refer to sources where old music may be found. His discussion of the songs, moreover, is marred by his lack of appreciation of their dramatic function. It is fair to say that Naylor's volume remains the most serviceable treatment of the subject, though this is partly due to the fact that some of the most original contributions between the years 1900 and 1960 have appeared in the form of short articles. From a variety of periodical and composite publications which were produced before 1918 we may single out the following nine: The Malone Society was founded in 1906, and its earliest publications appeared in 1907, stimulated by the bibliographical researches of Greg and others. Both its typographical facsimile reprints and the documents contained in its *Collections* make possible a study of lyrics sung and of musical stage directions under conditions which, even in this age of microfilms, are a blessing and a necessity. The fourth volume (1909) of the *Cambridge History of English Literature* contains H. H. Child's chapter on 'Song-Books and Miscellanies' which, though now out of date, should still be consulted.

The first volume of the *Musical Antiquary* appeared in 1909–10, the fourth and last in 1912–13. But its early demise must not obscure its importance for Elizabethan studies: 'Music and Shakespeare', by E. W. Naylor, I, 129–48; 'Early Elizabethan Stage Music', anonymous, I, 30–40 and IV, 112–17; 'Lists of the King's Musicians from the Audit Office Declared Accounts', by E. Stokes, I, 56 *et passim* and IV, 55 *et passim*. Another casualty of the First World War were the polyglot *Sammelbände* of the International Musicological Society containing, among others, a useful article on 'Dances in Shakespeare's England' (vol. XV, 1913–14, pp. 99–102) by Jeffrey Pulver, the author of the valuable *Biographical Dictionary of Old English Music* (1927). Pulver was also one of the contributors to *Proceedings* of the Royal Musical Association which published several articles of interest before 1918 (and continues to do so). G. E. P. Arkwright's 'Elizabethan Choirboy Plays and their Music' (XL, 1913–14, pp. 117–38) is valuable not only for the light it throws on Pistol's 'O death, rock me asleep' but also for his elucidation of the entire tradition as typified by Edwards's *Damon and Pithias* and parodied in Shakespeare's playlet 'Pyramus and Thisbe'. Arkwright belonged to a species, now almost extinct, the gentleman-scholar; his essay of twenty pages, if written today might well have developed into a book of several hundred pages, with caustic footnotes. As it was, his article was supplemented by his labours as editor of the *Musical Antiquary* and of the *Old English Edition* (25 vols. 1889–1902) which reproduced Thomas Campion's *Lord Hay's Masque*. The *Proceedings* of the Royal Musical Association also counted among its contributors Percy Scholes, the well-known author of the *Oxford Companion to Music* and *The Puritans and Music*. His paper 'The Purpose behind Shakespeare's Use of Music' (XLIII, 1916–17, pp. 1–15) illuminates the consistent way in which the poet employed music to make manifest and effective the supernatural element in the plays. The divine interventions in *Pericles, Cymbeline, Winter's Tale,* and *The Tempest* would be wooden without the support of musical accompaniment, and Scholes was the first among musical scholars to explain Shakespeare's method of employing music. If his understanding of the subject was not omniscient, Scholes nevertheless blazed a trail for later writers. The dissolution of the *Musical Antiquary* and the *Journal* of the International Musicological Society in 1914 was, perhaps, the final inducement for the founding in 1915 of the American periodical, *The Musical Quarterly.* It emphasized, as had the earlier *New Variorum Edition* of Furness, the importance of transatlantic publications. Edward Dent's article on the 'Musical Interpretation of Shakespeare on the Modern Stage' (II, 1916, pp. 523–37) is only one of the many contributions on the subject which this doyen of English music historians was to offer. In this article Dent, a man of letters whose interests were by no means restricted to sharps and flats, distinguishes clearly between the roles played by music in spoken drama and in opera, and assesses the differences in kind between Shakespeare's plays and the later adaptations of Dryden and Purcell. Dent deals with the new methods of reviving Shakespeare which William Poel and Granville-Barker initiated, and himself provided Elizabethan music for the Marlowe Society when it produced *Doctor Faustus* in 1910 and the *Knight of the Burning Pestle* in 1911. This passionate enthusiasm of the scholar who helped to shape the policies of Sadler's Wells and Glyndebourne was bound to leave its mark also on musical scholarship in regard to Shakespeare. Of his later works we mention here only his *Foundations of English Opera* (1928) and his chapter on 'Shakespeare and Music' in the *Companion to Shakespeare Studies* (ed. by H. Granville-Barker and G. B. Harrison, 1934). It is an incontrovertible fact that, between them, Naylor and Dent, in the twentieth century, have done more than any other two authors to present a clear and accurate picture of the role of music in the plays. This does not preclude mentioning that subsequent research has modified and revised several details in their accounts. Finally, there remain the shorter articles which appeared in several composite volumes before 1918. These, and a variety of *Festschriften* and *Kongress-berichte* which continue to appear with increasing frequency, are not easily located except in large national libraries and may, therefore, be easily overlooked. J. R. Moore's 'The Function of the Songs in Shakespeare's Plays' appeared in *Shakespeare Studies...University of Wisconsin* (1916, pp. 78–102), and A. C. Bradley's 'Feste, the Jester' in *A Book of Homage to Shakespeare* (ed. I. Gollancz, 1916; republished in Bradley's *A Miscellany,* 1931, pp. 207–17). The author of *Shakespearean Tragedy* scarcely needs an introduction, yet the many fleeting observations on the art of music in Bradley's classic book barely suggest the detail and shrewdness with which the author examines the role of Robert Armin and his songs in *Twelfth Night.* By assigning full credit to Shakespeare (rather than to Armin) for the concluding song of the comedy Bradley joins the minority company of Charles Knight in the nineteenth century, and Richmond Noble and George L. Kittredge in the twentieth, a group which musical scholars of recent vintage are inclined to support. Moore's article is one of several growing out of his doctoral dissertation, which also yielded 'The Songs of the Public Theatres in the Time of Shakespeare' (*Journal of English and Germanic Philology,* XXVIII, 1929, pp. 166–202) and 'The Songs in Lyly's Plays' (*P.M.L.A.* XLII, 1927, pp. 623–40). It is not possible to recount here the well-known controversy in regard to the authenticity of Lyly's lyrics; suffice it to say that no study of *Midsummer Night's Dream* or *Merry Wives of Windsor* can dispense with an examination of the earlier playwright's methods. Another composite publication, *Shakespeare's England* (ed. by S. Lee, C. T. Onions and W. Raleigh, 2 vols. 1917), produced valuable articles by W. Barclay Squire on 'Music', C. H. Firth on 'Ballads and Broadsides' and a 'Glossary of Musical Terms' by C. T. Onions, whose labours on the *Oxford English Dictionary* and the *Shakespeare Glossary* are well known.

The majority of the publications mentioned so far deal, quite properly, with songs and ballads. Serious consideration of instrumental problems begins with the publication of Francis W. Galpin's *Old English Instruments of Music* (1910, 3rd edn. 1932) and Christopher Welch's *Six Lectures on the Recorder* (1911; the first three chapters, including 'Hamlet and the Recorder', reprinted 1961).

In the period between the two World Wars scholarly publications increased with such rapidity that it becomes necessary to exercise an even greater selectivity, in a compilation of this kind. Therefore articles in periodicals, except *in extremis*, must give way to major books and reprints.[2]

No account of the 1920's, however brief, can omit the works of E. H. Fellowes, R. Noble, H. E. Rollins and P. Warlock. Fellowes wrote many books on music, among them monographs on *Byrd* and *Gibbons*, yet his lasting merit consists in his having reprinted the old music in modern editions, thus making it accessible to the ears and the minds of the general public. Recitals of Elizabethan music, whether in the concert hall or over the wireless or gramophone, would be unthinkable today without the industry and daring of Fellowes. There are some minor errors, certain sharps or flats incorrectly placed, some unacknowledged transpositions, some silent emendations. Yet, the details are insignificant compared with the total achievement. The *English Madrigal School* (36 vols. 1913–24) and *Songs...from Beaumont and Fletcher* (1928) were supplemented by the *English School of Lutenist Song Writers* (32 vols. 1920–32), a work that is indispensable to the student of spoken drama. There are two series to this *corpus*, a First Series giving both tablatures and modern transcriptions, and a Second Series giving transcriptions only. The first series includes Dowland, Rosseter and Morley; Campion, Ferrabosco and Jones appear in the second series. To these must be added the *Complete Works of W. Byrd* (20 vols. 1937–50), containing Byrd's keyboard arrangements of popular tunes occurring in Shakespeare. On Fellowes's death in 1951 R. Thurston Dart succeeded him as editor of the *School of Lutenist Song Writers*. Volume 17 of the First Series reprints Giovanni Coperario (alias John Cooper) whose *Songs of Mourning* for Prince Henry and lyrics for Campion's *Somerset Masque* are of great interest. Volume 17 of the Second Series will contain the songs of Robert Johnson whose cardinal importance for *The Tempest* and other plays is well known. A rival and critic of Fellowes, Peter Warlock, nevertheless made an equally important contribution to Shakespeare studies. His taste and emendations were impeccable, his assessment of attributed and anonymous compositions very good indeed. His tantalizingly short book, *The English Ayre* (1926), is the best of its kind to appear so far, and his *English Ayres* (edited jointly with Philip Wilson, 4 vols. 1922–5; 2nd edn., 6 vols. 1927–31) is an indispensable anthology since it includes several important anonymous songs not transcribed by Fellowes. Among these 'I loathe that I did love' is relevant to the gravedigger's song in *Hamlet*. Warlock also edited *Elizabethan Songs... for...voice...and...stringed instruments* (3 vols. 1926) and Ravenscroft's *Pammelia* (1928). That all of these works are now out of print is an indication of the vicissitudes of modern publishing.

Another great editor of the twenties, Hyder E. Rollins, provided a detailed census of relevant musical manuscripts. Rollins's edition of *Tottel's Songes and Sonnettes* (1928–9) brought to completion one of the tasks left unfinished by Bishop Percy in the eighteenth century. The *Analytical Index to Ballad Entries*...(Chapel Hill, N.C., 1924) is an indispensable aid to study of the Stationers' Registers. Of the important contributions in this period there remains *Shakespeare's Use of Song* (1923) by Richmond Noble, whose researches have contributed many a valuable footnote to John Dover Wilson's *New Shakespeare* edition. Noble, after Naylor, wrote the best monograph on Shakespeare and music to date.

The periodical *Music & Letters* was founded in 1920 and from its inception paid heed to Shakespeare research. Before the Second World War it published articles by W. J. Lawrence (1922),[3] H. M. Fitzgibbon (1930), and S. A. Bayliss (1934). Important essays of the period appearing in other periodicals and series were written by E. Law (Shakespeare Association *Papers*, 1920), E. S. Lindsey (*Studies in Philology*, 1924), L. B. Wright (*Studies in Philology*, 1927), E. S. Lindsey (*Modern Language Notes*, 1929) and Ernest Brennecke (*P.M.L.A.*, 1939). Books of the thirties, specifically dealing with musical problems, include J. M. Gibbon, *Melody and the Lyric* (1930), Scholes's *Puritans and Music* (already mentioned) and G. Bontoux's *Chanson d'Angleterre* (1936). Gibbon's book is a useful digest of Chappell, Wooldridge, Naylor and others but, as such, it suffers from its neglect of original sources. Mlle Bontoux's sumptuous volume is to be commended for its facsimiles and other illustrations as well as for its unusually liberal transliterations of lute tablatures. Among general books that throw light on musical topics there are the standard reference works of E. K. Chambers and A. Nicoll, as well as the monographs of G. Wilson Knight.

The harvest of the forties proved more significant for specifically musical studies. Among the important periodical articles R. T. Dart's piece on 'Morley's Consort Lessons of 1599' (*Proceedings of the Royal Musical Association*, 1947–8) brought to the fore one of the most prominent authors, editors and performers of our age. Numerous articles, largely concerned with instrumental music, have appeared over Dart's name in *Music & Letters* and the *Galpin Society Journal*. His *Jacobean Consort Music* (edited jointly with W. Coates, 1955) is an indispensable reprint and equally valuable for the Shakespearian producer are two recent slim editions, the *Suite...Brass Music...James I* and the *Holborne...Suite for an Ensemble* (both 1959).

Otto Gombosi's 'Some Musical Aspects of the English Court Masque' appeared in the *Journal of the American Musicological Society*, I (1948). Gombosi's knowledge of 'passamezzo antico' and 'passamezzo moderno', of Sir Toby Belch's 'passy-measures pavin' in *Twelfth Night*, v, i, 206 remains unchallenged, and his knowledge of early lute books, such as the Giles Lodge Book at the Folger Library in Washington (containing the earliest known musical version of the Willow Song) was equally profound. His untimely death in 1955 deprived music and letters of a first-rate scholar. Other relevant periodical articles are duly recorded in the *New Shakespeare* and the *New Arden* editions of the plays.

The major books of the forties include M. C. Boyd, *Elizabethan Music* (1940), C. L. Day's and E. B. Murrie's bibliography of *English Song Books* (1940), B. Pattison, *Music and Poetry of the English Renaissance* (1948), M. Dolmetsch, *Dances of England and France, 1450–1600* (1949). Of these Pattison's is the most important and should be read in conjunction with his chapters on 'Literature and Music' in V. de Sola Pinto's *English Renaissance* (2nd edn. 1951, pp. 120–138) and 'Music and Masque' in C. J. Sisson's one-volume edition of Shakespeare's *Works* (1954, pp. xlvii–lii). Pattison is one of the few major scholars in the field who followed E. J. Dent in focusing attention on the hybrid and difficult field of words-and-music. Critical evaluations will be found in John Stevens's *Music and Poetry in the Early Tudor Court* and in the review of Pattison's work in the *Journal of the American Musicological Society*, II (1949). The author emphasizes unduly the happy union of poetry and music and minimizes the inevitable conflicts which arise from time to time between these two arts. Nevertheless, his discussion of musical and poetical forms is a *sine qua non* for later research. Of general works bearing on music one may single out G. E. Bentley's *Jacobean Stage*, T. W. Baldwin's *Shakespeare's Small Latin...* and W. A. Ringler's two monographs on *Rainolds* and *Gosson* respectively. The importance of music at the Blackfriars is considered in Bentley's article, 'Shakespeare and the Blackfriars' Theatre' in *Shakespeare Survey* 1, which is supplemented by the studies of Isaacs and Armstrong (*Shakespeare Association Papers*, 1933; *Society for Theatre Research Pamphlets*, 1958). Baldwin's work on the importance of classical sources for Shakespeare's musical passages follows his earlier monograph on the *Organization and Personnel of Shakespeare's Company* (1927) which embarks on, though it does not settle, the all-important question of Robert Armin.

The decade of the 1950's produced the largest number of books either dealing with or reprinting music. W. R. Bowden's *English Dramatic Lyric, 1603–42* (1951) is a carefully documented study of the occasions when Stuart playwrights employed music. Utilizing the material that had been gathered in earlier collections (such as E. B. Reed, *Songs from the British Drama*, 1925; T. Brooke, ed. *Shakespeare Songs*, 1929), Bowden analyses the functions of the lyric and the dramatic purpose underlying the categories most frequently used. His volume contains appendices to all of the songs in the plays of Armin, Beaumont and Fletcher, Chapman, Dekker, Heywood, Jonson, Marston, among others. Catherine Ing's *Elizabethan Lyrics* (1951) gives more consideration to Campion than to Shakespeare, though the section on Shakespeare (pp. 219–30) is valuable, and the general discussion of metrics and music the best to date. Denis Stevens's edition of the *Mulliner Book* (1951, rev. edn. 1954) makes available a collection of keyboard music of great worth for Elizabethan drama. Of an earlier date than the *Fitzwilliam Book* this anthology throws light on the lyrics of Richard Edwards and, in consequence, on 'Where griping grief the heart doth wound', which the clown sings in *Romeo and Juliet*. The *Mulliner Book*, in company with Thurston Dart's *Jacobean Consort Music* (mentioned earlier), is part of a monumental series of reprints of English music which also includes John Stevens's edition of *Mediaeval Carols* (1952, rev. 1958). Both Denis Stevens and John Stevens persevere in their contributions to our knowlege of Tudor music. Walter Woodfill's *Musicians in English Society from Elizabeth to Charles I* (1953) is an indispensable source-book dealing with musicians of the city and of the court; it also offers an excellent bibliography (pp. 315–61). Two valuable reprints of music appeared in 1954, David Lumsden's *Anthology of English Lute Music* and John Ward's *Dublin Virginal Manuscript*, the latter an anthology of keyboard music. Lumsden and Ward are both authorities on lute music and have contributed important articles on that subject to learned journals. Their editions have been supplemented by three further reprints, enumerated below, and altogether the student of today has more music of the sixteenth and seventeenth centuries readily available than his forbears had. Margaret Dean-Smith's edition of *Playford's English Dancing Master 1651* (1957) is a facsimile reprint of one of the main sources of Chappell and Naylor. The author's annotations and cross-references to other English and Dutch collections, as well as to standard reference works (such as Child's *English and Scottish Popular Ballads*) add value to the volume. Andrew Sabol's

edition of *Songs and Dances for the Stuart Masque* (1959) makes available 38 songs and 25 instrumental pieces. The latter are taken from British Museum, Add. MS. 10444, an important
theatrical source, which W. J. Lawrence had described in *Music & Letters* in 1922. The manuscript
presents only treble and bass, so that modern editors must supply the harmony. One does not
always agree with Sabol's solutions, but the edition, including the author's apparatus of notes
and bibliography, is a valuable contribution to scholarship. Sydney Beck's edition of *The First
Book of Consort Lessons, Collected by Thomas Morley* (1959) is one of the finest pieces of scholarly
reconstruction to be reviewed in this survey. It bids fair to supplement Dart's *Jacobean Consort
Music* as a major source of instrumental music for Shakespearian producers. Of its twenty-five
numbers, 'O Mistresse Mine' is of particular interest to students of *Twelfth Night*.

Three further monographs complete the list of books exclusively concerned with music.
John H. Long's *Shakespeare's Use of Music...Seven Comedies* (1955) consists largely of letterpress
but contains thirty-five music examples. Included among these are several of the author's
adaptations of Elizabethan melodies to Shakespeare's lyrics when no specific contemporary
melody was known. Such adaptations are essential in the circumstances and Long's solutions
are, on the whole, musicianly and helpful. Unfortunately, the work is based entirely on the
researches of earlier scholars, such as Chappell and Naylor, and his discussion and bibliography
are marred by serious errors. J. S. Manifold, in *Music in English Drama: From Shakespeare to
Purcell*, casts a wide net and includes a discussion of Restoration music. The author's elucidation
on the associations of 'high' and 'low' music are sound; the contrast between the loud music
of winds and the soft strains of strings is important for Shakespeare and his contemporaries.
Unlike Long, Manifold does not give music examples. By contrast, J. P. Cutts's *La Musique de
Scène de Shakespeare: The King's Men sous le règne de Jacques Ier* (Paris, 1959) contains fifty-three
pieces of music (pp. 1–110) as well as a detailed critical commentary (pp. 111–89). The latter is
most useful since its concordances list many manuscripts scattered in London, Dublin, New York
and Washington. Cutts is a prolific writer, well known in the field, and between 1952 and 1960
he has published two books and some twenty articles. His *Seventeenth Century Books and Lyrics*
appeared in 1959, and the articles are to be found in such standard publications as *Music & Letters*
and *Shakespeare Survey*. Unfortunately, zeal and haste are no substitutes for accuracy, and whereas Cutts's work cannot be ignored, it cannot be trusted either.[4]

Only the briefest selection of periodical articles of the fifties can be offered here. Among
foreign and less easily accessible sources the *English Miscellany*, edited by Mario Praz at Rome,
contains a long and excellent essay by James Hutton (1951). Several symposia, edited by Jean
Jacquot at Paris, include *Musique et Poésie* (1954), *Musique Instrumentale* (1955), *Fêtes de la Renaissance* (1956) and *Le Luth et sa Musique* (1958). These volumes contain much valuable information,
bibliographically and otherwise. The German *Shakespeare–Jahrbuch* contains several pertinent
articles (Prange, 1953; Nicoll, 1958). Of American journals we mention the *Musical Quarterly*
(Vlastos, 1954; Long, 1958); *Shakespeare Quarterly* (Brennecke, 1953; Seng, 1958; Pafford, 1959;
Seng, 1959; Waldo, 1959); *Journal of the American Musicological Society* (Ward, 1951; Ward,
1957); *Renaissance News* (Beck, 1953); and *Musica Disciplina* (Bowles, 1954). In this country the
obvious periodicals are *Music & Letters* and *Shakespeare Survey*. An index to the former is now
in press, and volume XI of the *Survey* contains an index to the first ten volumes, as well as an
article on music by J. M. Nosworthy which supplements his edition of *Cymbeline* for the New

Arden. It is also worth the student's while to check the *Galpin Society Journal* (Lumsden, 1953; Dart, 1958) and the *Lute Society Journal* (Newton, 1958; Spencer, 1958).

Of general works bearing on music three are relevant to boy singers and adult singers. Ronald Watkins (*On Producing Shakespeare*, 1950) agrees with T. W. Baldwin that Shakespeare's brother Edmund is a likely candidate for a singing boy named 'Ned'. Of Alfred Harbage's several books *Shakespeare and the Rival Traditions* (1952) is particularly pertinent to a consideration of the musical resources available at the Blackfriars Theatre where boy singers and instrumentalists so greatly excelled the performers in the adult playhouses. Leslie Hotson's *Shakespeare's Motley* (1952), on the other hand, concentrates on the main adult singer of Shakespeare's company, namely Robert Armin. Several hypotheses advanced by Hotson in this work have found wide acceptance, whereas *The First Night of Twelfth Night* (1954), also touching on Armin, remains highly controversial. Paul A. Jorgensen's *Shakespeare's Military World* (1956) includes a surprisingly detailed and knowledgeable account of battle music.

The major problems of the sixties and seventies will be editorial as well as analytical. Now that the Mulliner and Fitzwilliam books have been reprinted we sorely need editions of the major lute manuscripts in London, Cambridge and Dublin. For the writing of books and articles we are in urgent need of authors who will combine learning in literary and musical matters. Recent developments in international bibliography, as well as the increased availability of microfilms and xerographs, should be of aid.

NOTES

1. Capell had made the emendation in 1768 but Stevens continued with 'singing' in 1785.

2. For sundry relevant articles *Grove's Dictionary of Music* (5th edn. 1954) and the German encyclopaedia, *Musik in Geschichte und Gegenwart* (Kassel, 1949 ff.) should be consulted under such headings as Shakespeare, Byrd, Morley; lute, cittern, cornett, sackbut, tucket; ballad, folk music, ayre, etc. The subject headings of the British Museum and the Library of Congress are likewise useful. The most detailed bibliography is provided by the annual American publication *Music Index*.

3. The many books published by W. J. Lawrence contain several valuable passages on music.

4. For professional criticism see *Library*, 5th ser. x (1955), 55–7; *Shakespeare Quarterly*, IX (1958), 114–15; *Music & Letters*, XLI (1960), 300–3; *Notes* of the Music Library Association, XVIII (1961), 228–9.

2. THE SONNETS

BY

A. NEJGEBAUER

Taken as a whole, the critical writings on Shakespeare's sonnets in the present century, hardly less than in the last, present a mass of varied, often contradictory studies, conjectures and whimsical pronouncements. It is impossible to take them as a whole; only by separating them into sections can their scope be properly surveyed.

THE SONNETS

The bulk of basic editorial work on the sonnets had been completed as early as 1780 by Malone, who also provided the first scholarly commentary, superior to and saner than many a later one. Of the editions published in the twentieth century, several are outstanding for their introductory matter, notably those of H. C. Beeching (1904), Sidney Lee (1905), Knox Pooler (1918), T. G. Tucker (1924) and Tucker Brooke (1936); most important of all are the two variorum editions— R. M. Alden's (1916) and H. E. Rollins's (New Variorum, 2 vols. 1944). After analysing earlier commentary on the subject, Alden stated his own views. He decided that the disputed questions of identification, date and arrangement could not be answered without fresh external evidence, and he distinguished three different approaches to the sonnets—the indifference and neglect of the early editors, the frequent unqualified enthusiasm in the nineteenth century (Wordsworth to Swinburne), and the later tendency to separate sonnets 'of an age', dated by their mannerisms, from those 'for all time'. This was in 1916. The few critical achievements and endless absurdities of the next thirty years have found a worthy monument in Rollins's fourteen extensive appendixes in the second volume of his edition; these are full of grim irony, partly through his own caustic comments and partly through the very juxtaposition of his several résumés. But this makes difficult reading. The combination of non-selective objectivity and personal comment often grants equal space to irresponsible casual remarks and to the well-founded results of scholarly research, obscuring the critical method and the weight of the argument. Apart from original contributions to the textual notes and a conclusive exposure of John Benson's fraud in the 1640 edition, the main importance of the New Variorum lies in its lessons on the failures in criticism of the sonnets, of which it is the best history compiled hitherto.

TEXT, DATE AND ARRANGEMENT

As only two early editions are known, Thomas Thorpe's 1609 quarto (*Shake-Speare's Sonnets*) and John Benson's octavo of 1640 (*Poems: Written by Wil. Shake-speare. Gent.*—a mere piratical reshuffling), bibliographical criticism has had a limited scope; but even so the questions (*a*) whether the 1609 quarto was printed from Shakespeare's own manuscript or from a transcript and (*b*) whether it was authorized and supervised by the poet or not, have never been answered conclusively. Scholars are nowadays inclined to believe that the quarto's title-page and the publisher's dedication indicate a negative answer to the latter question. Nevertheless, other questions have been minutely discussed. The quality of the printing—violently attacked by Beeching (1904), Lee (1905) and Brooke (ed. 1936) and defended, after Wyndham (1898), by J. A. Fort (*A Time Scheme for Shakespeare's Sonnets*, 1929), Stefan George (*Shakespeare Sonette*, 1931) and Denys Bray (1938), with a variety of intermediate opinions—has pivoted mainly on the impression produced by the number of misprints, which varies from about 40 to 100 in a total of 2155 lines, depending on what allowance is made for Elizabethan orthographic practices and different interpretations of individual words.

The basic authenticity of the 1609 text has been repeatedly questioned (e.g. Alden, *Shakespeare*, 1922; J. G. Scott, *Les Sonnets Elisabéthains*, 1929; L. C. Knights, *Scrutiny*, 1934, III). But scholarly doubts must remain within the limits defined by Allardyce Nicoll (*Modern Language Review*,

1927), who wrote that 'the Thorpe Collection professed to be Shakespeare's, and...there is at present no real justification for believing it unauthentic'. Trespasses against this warning have been of two kinds: on the one hand, disintegrating tendencies, culminating with J. M. Robertson (*The Problems of Shakespeare's Sonnets*, 1926), all of them based on subjective aesthetic views about what is too bad to be Shakespeare's (far from defined and mutually contradictory); on the other, groundless hypotheses that somebody else wrote the sonnets—a non-Stratfordian 'Shakespeare', or else Sidney, Barnes, William Warner, Donne, etc. These deserve no attention except as curiosities—any more than does the claim made out for Anne Whately who, according to William Ross (*Story of Anne Whately and William Shaxpere*, 1939), wrote the sonnets, and also the plays, as well as *Hero and Leander* and *The Faerie Queene*.

Although Malone had firmly established the 1609 quarto as the original text, Benson's piratical enterprise, particularly his consciously misleading preface, continued to deceive scholarly opinion as an edition possibly derived from unknown manuscripts. This view was held by Lee (1905) and T. G. Tucker (1924) and refuted, after careful collation, by Alden and K. Pooler (1918). The attempt of G. K. Hinkle (*Shakespeare's Poems of 1640*, 1936) and Stanford (*Abstracts of Dissertations*, 1937) to rehabilitate Benson was based on non-representative textual details and incomplete collation of copies.

The meagre external evidence has provoked a host of critics to use their ingenuity in determining the date of composition of these poems. Much of this activity has been pure guesswork of no consequence. In the search for internal evidence, many an argument has been built upon a preconceived biographical interpretation (e.g. by the Southamptonites Fort, *op. cit.* and T. W. Baldwin, rather apologetically, in *The Literary Genetics of Shakespeare's Poems & Sonnets* (1950) and the Pembrokist E. K. Chambers, *Shakespearean Gleanings*, 1944), fitting the 'dated' sonnets into the respective sonnet stories. Spectres of topical allusions to wars, to peace treaties, to the life and death of sovereigns, to various other unnamed persons, as well as to the mention of solar and lunar eclipses, have been invoked too frequently and too unprofitably to be discussed here. Leslie Hotson's energetically advertised dating venture (*Shakespeare's Sonnets Dated*, 1949), reviving S. Butler's early dating, ensured general mention, but not acceptance. All attempts at dating on the basis of Shakespeare's alleged borrowings from contemporary poets have been equally futile.

Valuable material, however, has been collected as a by-product of unsuccessful comparative studies of Shakespeare's plays, narrative poems and sonnets. Parallels between the sonnets and *Love's Labour's Lost*, *A Midsummer Night's Dream* and *Romeo and Juliet* were studied by C. F. McClumpha (*Modern Language Notes*, XV, 1900; XVI, 1901; *Shakespeare–Jahrbuch*, XL, 1904); Lee (*A Life of William Shakespeare*, 1898; *Sonnets*, 1905) found the parallels with the narrative poems and early plays to be the most numerous and therefore indicative of a closeness in date; A. Wietfield (*Die Bildersprache in Shakespeares Sonetten*, 1916) obtained similar results but wisely refrained from chronological inferences. Beeching (1904) discovered striking parallels with the later plays and suggested that rarely used words in different works indicate simultaneous dates; J. M. Nosworthy proposed Jacobean dates for several sonnets on much the same principle (*Essays in Criticism*, 1952). A. Beatty (Wisconsin *Shakespeare Studies*, 1916) examined 'sonnet-like' passages in the canon and found them distributed throughout. O. F. Emerson's statistical analysis of feminine rhymes and run-on lines in *Venus*, *Lucrece* and the sonnets (*Studies in Philology*, XX, 1923) produced neat percentages of unprovable validity. T. W. Baldwin (*Genetics*) made a profitable study of the variations in the use of figures of speech in the sonnets and elsewhere in Shakespeare, and particularly of parallels within the sonnets themselves; he believed that he could nearly always date any parallel from another, tracing the 'development' of the figure as expansion from, or contracted allusion to, the original use, exercising his own subjective judgements and operating with his own dates for the plays.

The approach to dating through Shakespearian analogues has failed to surmount the difficulty of measuring the closeness of parallels and of finding criteria for their significance—whether they indicate coincidence, precedence, echoes, or merely similar verbal treatment of similar subjects. Other methods, especially arbitrary literal interpretations of words and passages in the sonnets, have produced even less acceptable results.

Little need be said about the vast amount of writings on the arrangement of the sonnets. Thorpe's order has been defended or rejected depending on (*a*) whether it made sense or nonsense of the particular 'story' found by each critic in the series as a whole, and (*b*) whether Shakespeare's authorization and the publisher's concern and responsibility for the arrangement was believed or not. Defenders of the quarto order have offered a variety of divisions of the collection into groups, united with each other by plot, development of ideas, 'sense', 'centre of gravity' and the like, sometimes allowing for a few misplaced sonnets. A belated specimen of a detailed defence of this order is found in Baldwin's *Genetics*, where he undertakes to demonstrate that every sonnet develops out of an earlier, mostly the one preceding, with the aid of literary reminiscences and fresh borrowings. Such thematic connections as Baldwin restates or discovers might be interpreted as indicating a number of different arrangements; besides, he runs out of links half-way through and merely paraphrases some thirty sonnets, while about as many 'continue' or 'develop' the sequence by assertion only. On the other hand, all rearrangements since Benson (or possibly Thorpe) have been purely subjective. M. J. Wolff hit the nail on the head for once (*William Shakespeare*, 1903, p. 39) by observing that all attempts at rearrangement 'must fail, since it is impossible to see in [the sonnets] any sort of complete and logical plot'. Not every critic has remembered that all the sonnets may not refer to one man and one woman only (Reed, 1923, and others). E. K. Chambers's criticism (*William Shakespeare*, 1930) of Bray's 'objective', 'mechanical' regrouping on the basis of rhyme- and word-links shows that even this attempt depends on a number of subjectively selected alternatives; it also separates sonnets linked much more substantially in the quarto order. J. W. Lever's 'third alternative' (*The Elizabethan Love Sonnet*, 1956) of an arrangement based 'on the analogy of scenes in a drama', 'a continuity of poetic thought' and 'iterative images', in which he includes only 97 sonnets, turns out a prop to a neatly progressive, imaginative story with no more justification than can be claimed for previous regroupings. As Alden (1916) and Rollins (1944) have shown, Thorpe's order has little more authority than its numerous substitutes; but as the traditional arrangement of most editions it still remains preferable for the sake of convenience.

THE SOURCES

Although the endeavours to trace the sources of Shakespeare's sonnets go back to the early modern editors, no lasting results were achieved before the present century, except for Massey's demonstration (1866) of a very likely source passage in Sidney's *Arcadia*. A new era in the understanding of Shakespeare's sonnets was opened by Sir Sidney Lee, who came to view them in the larger historical perspective of the Elizabethan sonneteering vogue, in its turn only a naturalized offspring of the earlier French and original Italian sonnet literature. Impressed, however, by the similarities in theme and phrasing, he considered Shakespeare's sonnets merely the best specimens of a purely conventional literary fashion (*Life; Elizabethan Sonnets*, 1904; *Shakespeare's Sonnets*, 1905; *The French Renaissance in England*, 1910). He also overplayed his findings by assuming numerous English and French analogues to be actual sources. In Ovid's *Metamorphoses* he found a wealth of parallels to the sonnets, which throw valuable light on Shakespeare's reading background (*Quarterly Review*, CCX, 1909), but these 'renderings' of Ovid he saw only as the patchwork of a slavish disciple, arrived at mainly through Golding's translation.

Conventionality as the key-word for Shakespeare's sonnets was brought forward even more strongly by Wolff (in a number of studies, of which 'Petrarkismus und Antipetrarkismus in Shakespeares Sonetten', *Englische Studien*, XLIX, 1916 is the most important). Wolff's general thesis is that Shakespeare's sonnets are entirely conventional, since almost every theme can be traced back to his Italian predecessors. He pointed convincingly to significant generic similarities between groups of such themes in Italian Cinquecento sonnets and in Shakespeare's, which he thus placed in part of their historical context, clearly and firmly—too firmly, in fact, for his argument is greatly vitiated by his doctrinaire one-sidedness. In his attempt to reduce Shakespeare's sonnets to a formula of Petrarchism and anti-Petrarchism, with *amor razionale* against *amor sensuale*, he distorted the evidence by accumulating admittedly exceptional, though numerous, analogues and forcing them, often superficially and with highly questionable interpretations, on a biased selection from Shakespeare; he also obscured the issue by substituting his own prose summaries of Shakespeare's 'ideas' and 'motifs' for the verse itself.

Wolff's criticism was the last serious attempt to demonstrate *the* formative influence behind Shakespeare's sonnets. In J. G. Scott's survey of source-hunting the various theories of Shakespeare's borrowings, built up around parallels of enigmatic import, are to be seen shrinking to mere possibilities, save for some passages in Sidney's *Arcadia* and Lyly's general influence. The least satisfactory of Scott's objections are those to Wolff's equations, which she attacks mainly from the biographical point of view, considering the occasion for writing as decisive for the nature of a poem; and her discussion of Shakespeare's originality consists of mere assertions and an enumeration of his technical devices. But she makes some important conclusions: Shakespeare uses current Platonic terms rather than philosophic ideas; the sonnets are largely beyond Petrarchist limitations; they form a collection of a mixed nature, and many passages admit various interpretations.

Apart from a few parallels with the Bible (G. W. Phillips, *Sunlight on Shakespeare's Sonnets*, 1935) and with Thomas Wilson's *Arte of Rhetorique* (E. J. Fripp, *Shakespeare*, 1938) no new Renaissance sources have been seriously suggested, but there has been some progress in the study of Shakespeare's indebtedness to ancient authors. Baldwin (*op. cit.*) has found indications of direct use of the *Metamorphoses*, which Lee would not allow for, and also a few more echoes from the same work (though the actual 'genetics' rather reflect Baldwin's research method than Shakespeare's creative process) and J. E. Hankins (*Shakespeare's Derived Imagery*, 1953) supplements his findings with apparently very close verbal echoes from Palingenius's *Zodiacus Vitae* in B. Googe's translation, a standard textbook with which Shakespeare could well have been familiar. But perhaps it is time to take fully into account the implications of M. B. Ogle's learned study, 'The Classical Origin and Tradition of Literary Conceits' (*American Journal of Philology*, XXXIV, 1913)—that the mere listing of analogues will only too often take us back to the Greeks and leave little to Renaissance literature, and that therefore the *use* of transmitted poetic materials, particularly by a poet like Shakespeare, is a more meaningful object for study. Several good examples of such treatment can be found in Lever's chapter on Shakespeare (*op. cit.*), where the poet is shown as improving on his Ovidian models and defying the rigid Platonic categories of love.

INTERPRETATIONS

Twentieth-century criticism inherited three well-established rival trends in the interpretation of the sonnets, viewing them as (*a*) autobiographical, or (*b*) fictitious, or (*c*) esoteric writings.

(*a*) The biographical theory, launched by Wordsworth and the Schlegel brothers, assumed that the sonnets were sincere records of real events in the life of Shakespeare and the other persons mentioned. Through his critics Shakespeare unwittingly immortalized dozens of men— earls, merchants, actors, and sea-cooks, some of whom may never have lived—and several women. But since none of the suggested identifications and topical allusions are based on factual evidence, they can all be safely discarded.

(*b*) The opposing fiction theory has been held for different reasons. The nineteenth-century concern for Shakespeare's moral reputation, on which some biographical interpretations throw unfavourable light, has continued to crop up occasionally (e.g. Lee, 1905; condemned in L. P. Smith, *On Reading Shakespeare*, 1933); there have also been fresh examples of a sceptical reaction to unsubstantiated biographical claims. But the most impressive attack was made through the application of a comparative historical study of Renaissance sonnets to the problem of interpretation, particularly by Lee (*Life* and elsewhere) and Wolff (*op. cit.*) who declared that the originals of the persons in the sonnets were easy to find—not among contemporaries, but in the conventions of the sonnet literature of the period. This view had many followers, though inconsistently some of them (even Lee himself) were prepared to admit a number of clearly 'personal' sonnets among the 'conventional'. It was, however, soon pointed out (Beeching, 1904; more systematically, E. S. Bates, *Modern Philology*, VIII, 1910; Alden, 1916) that stylized presentation and conventional techniques could be used in writing about real people and events. After all, in his illustrations of conventional Italian sonneteering Wolff gives numerous examples of fully identified patron-friends, mistresses and rival poets. The difficulties and failures of the biographical theory seem to have quickened critical interest in the function of personal experience in the making of poetry. Thus we find conceptions like H. Ord's (*Chaucer and the Rival Poet*, 1921) that the sonnets record Shakespeare's 'Emotions from time to time', 'without any design to work out a revelation', or Hadow's (1907) who considered real events as possible sources, comparable with literary sources, for a poetic development. More specifically concerned with the nature of the sonnet form is G. L. Kittredge's view that 'a good sonnet appears to be a confession' because 'it must seem to express authentic emotion' (*Shakespeare Association Bulletin*, XI, 1936). It should be noted that the term 'literary exercises', used frequently by commentators, is misleading because of its implication that, just as writing out chords on given basses is not composing music, the sonnets are not works of art.

(c) Esoteric interpretations, which have no use for a 'story' or for literary background, fall into a surprisingly repetitive pattern: they either discover a single special meaning for the whole collection or else they identify the persons—as abstractions, of course—to whom allusion is made. Thus they reduce the interest in these poems to one idea or a few personifications, making them appear very dull indeed. For example, we learn from J. E. G. Montmorency (*Contemporary Review*, CI, 1912) that '"the Friend" is Life and Goodness, and "the Dark Lady" is Death and Evil'; to F. J. Forbis (*The Shakespearean Enigma and an Elizabethan Mania*, 1924) the sonnets are Shakespeare's record of his dipsomania and the 'master-mistress' is Wine; he-she is defined as 'the personification of the poet's [i.e. Bacon's] Muse or Genius' by R. L. Eagle (*New Light on the Enigma of Shakespeare's Sonnets*, 1916); and it has occurred to several critics that the Youth is a symbolic fiction. It is more interesting to find the 'straight' story kept but interpreted imaginatively on a deeper personal level as a record of 'bisexual integration' (a diluted modern version of the imputation of homosexuality) and to be reassured that Shakespeare was fortunately in the habit of becoming a *woman* at times and hence could expand his central themes from the sonnets into dramas (G. W. Knight, *The Mutual Flame*, 1955). F. C. Rang (*Shakespeare der Christ*, 1954), similarly preoccupied in spite of the different emphasis, built his whole book towards sonnet 146, or rather on it.

It is a relief to realize that since about 1930 a change may be observed in the general criticism of the sonnets; it has tended to become more cautious, eclectic and sophisticated. An awareness of the complexity and controversial nature of the subject has begun to be felt, even in the most fanciful writings. The increase in knowledge has also brought about an inevitable specialization. Rarely do we now find much attention to the subject in books entitled 'Shakespeare' or in books dealing with the Elizabethan sonnet or poetry in general. Lever's already mentioned chapter is something of an exception, and so is D. L. Stevenson's (*The Love-Game Comedy*, 1946) where the sonnets are related to the comedies on the basis of Shakespeare's emotional acceptance of both the idealization and the reality of love, suggesting the resolution of a long tradition of conflict. Probably the soundest recent general interpretation is E. Hubler's (*The Sense of Shakespeare's Sonnets*, 1952), based on apparent partial meanings (in a sonnet, or a group of sonnets) from which he endeavours to infer the underlying attitudes, although he founds his arguments somewhat too easily upon his own divination of the poet's values and creative intentions.

Formal Elements

The study of formal elements in Shakespeare's sonnets, a rather neglected newcomer to criticism, has so far been either general or fragmentary. The best general survey is found in T. G. Tucker's introduction to his edition (1924). Most attention has been devoted to the historical aspect of the technique of the sonnets. Their dependence on continental Petrarchism and its English equivalents has often been pointed out, but only superficially examined, usually in connection with their alleged sources. Leanings towards the metaphysical style have been seen by J. C. Ransom (*The World's Body*, 1954) as unsuccessful, and by P. Cruttwell (*The Shakespearean Moment*, 1954) as a felicitous new quality in the 'later' sonnets (taking the quarto order for granted).

The differences between the Shakespearian and the Italian sonnet form and their respective merits have continued to provide a subject for lively, if not always fruitful, discussions, marred by some vaguely assumed aesthetic criteria. E. Voege (*Mittelbarkeit und Unmittelbarkeit in der Lyrik*, 1932) and F. Dannenberg (*Shakespeare-Jahrbuch*, LXX, 1934) see a rigid couplet doomed to isolation and weighed down by the mass of the unorthodoxly structured quatrains in Shakespeare's form. As for the metrical qualities, E. Hamer's conclusion that 'the form of Shakespeare's sonnets is invariable' (*Metres in English Poetry*, 1930) is denied by Bray (ed. 1938), who insists on their 'diversity in form', while C. Wood (*Craft of Poetry*, 1929) demonstrates striking variations in the scansion scheme. Whereas Ransom (*op. cit.*) sees too frequent a clash between the metrical pattern and the logical, T. W. Baldwin asks, 'Whose logic?' and quotes sixteenth-century rhetorical forms based on logic as fitting any of the sonnets; unfortunately, he does not give a single illustration.

Alliteration in the sonnets has been examined statistically by R. T. Price (*Studies in Honor of Basil Gildersleeve*, 1902) who found it poetically significant, and by B. F. Skinner (*The Psychological Record*, III, 1939); the latter comes to the opposite conclusion that 'Shakespeare might as well have drawn words out of a hat'. A good reply, supported by an analysis and classification of uses of alliteration and assonance was provided by U. K. Goldsmith (*Journal of English and Germanic Philology*, XLIX, 1950); he shows that this element, mainly ornamental in function, was clearly both used and avoided by the poet for artistic reasons. Quite unlike this in treatment is D. J. Mason's study of 'free phonetic patterns' in the sonnets (*Neophilologus*, 1954: he employs a complicated descriptive terminology and then makes unrelated assessments, attempting to prove that these patterns express the finest shades of meaning. One wonders what sense he would extract from the repetition of patterns like '*m, i/y, n, d/t*' if unassisted by the text.

If this is all (except for Goldsmith's contribution) rather perfunctory and unsatisfactory, the study of the use of figurative speech in the sonnets is almost a blank in criticism. The best studies of Shakespeare's imagery do not contain a single reference to the sonnets and nobody has as yet discussed their imagery as a whole. Hankins's real concern is Shakespeare's use of Pallingenius as a source; images mentioned by Caroline Spurgeon are items in a catalogue and tell us nothing about the sonnets; nor is there much to be gained from G. W. Knight's literary exercise in describing symbols and images; a few penetrating remarks on the subject have been made by L. C. Knights (*Scrutiny*, 1934). Again a fragment, but one from which we desire increase, is M. T. Nowottny's article in *Essays in Criticism*, 1952—'Formal Elements in Shakespeare's Sonnets: Sonnets I–VI'. Another good example in this field is found in Alden's article 'The Lyrical Conceit of the Elizabethans' (*Studies in Philology*, 1917), a study of the nature and kinds of conceits found in Sidney and Shakespeare.

CONCLUSION

The amount of critical writing on the sonnets is second only to that on *Hamlet* in all Shakespeariana. In the present century, however, which has witnessed many an elaboration of old theories on the subject alongside of a much smaller body of fresh treatment, Rollins's edition has provided an imposing reminder: the criticism has been showing a definite decrease in frequency and increase in sobriety since the mid-forties, especially as compared with the period between the two World Wars. On the whole, however, criticism of the sonnets will not stand comparison with that of the plays. The former has not developed anything like the great new ways of approach to the text, the poetic qualities and the dramatic and theatrical values of Shakespeare's dramas; on the contrary, it has largely been amateurish and misplaced, often attempting to answer too many questions at once. Thus the criticism of Shakespeare's sonnets during the last sixty years has left the 'problems' unsolved and many aspects of the poetry incompletely examined; but we can now draw a distinct line between (a) the impossible, and (b) the possible and desirable. Those obsessed by biographical curiosity should try to satisfy it elsewhere. The sonnets make no serious gap in the total chronology of Shakespeare's works: the large body of verbal parallels with his early writings and similarities in ideas and sensibility with some of his later plays point to the mid-1590's as the likely approximate period of composition of the collection. Little hope remains for discovering new sources in the strict sense of the term, though our knowledge of Shakespeare's reading (and listening) background is far from complete; but the interaction between the English Renaissance sonnet tradition and Shakespeare's individual poetic gift seems to be well worth further study. Wholesale interpretations of the sonnets will have to give place to a careful examination of individual sonnets or natural groups of them before new syntheses, based both on historical considerations and on assessments of intrinsic merits, can be profitably attempted. As regards the use of language, stanzaic structure, metre, tropes and imagery, these demand the full tilth and husbandry of criticism.[1]

NOTE

1. Attention should be drawn to J. B. Leishman's *Themes and Variations in Shakespeare's Sonnets* (1961), a book which was published too late for inclusion in this retrospective article.

3. THE POEMS

BY

J. W. LEVER

This survey will be mainly concerned with trends of criticism bearing on three poems whose Shakespearian authorship is generally accepted—*Venus and Adonis, Lucrece* and *The Phoenix and The Turtle*. Like the wood-cutter's three sons, these heirs of Shakespeare's invention have different personalities, and of their fortunes in the modern world different tales must be told. First of all, mention must be made of the outstanding editions and compilations during this period. Early on, Sidney Lee's collotype facsimiles of *Venus and Adonis, Lucrece* and *The Passionate Pilgrim* (1905) afforded useful texts which still do their duty. The 'Arden' *Poems* by C. Knox Pooler (1911) and F. T. Prince (1960) are, each for its day, meritorious productions, while Bernard H. Newdigate's *The Phoenix and The Turtle* (1937) enables Shakespeare's poem to be read conveniently beside other contributions to *Loves Martyr*. A vast range of information and critical comment down to the early 1930's is supplied by H. E. Rollins's 'New Variorum' of *The Poems* (1938), and T. W. Baldwin's *On The Literary Genetics of Shakespeare's Poems and Sonnets* (1950) provides an equally monumental, if at times idiosyncratic, treatment of Shakespeare's way with his sources. Lastly, Geoffrey Bullough's *Narrative and Dramatic Sources of Shakespeare*, I (1957) supplies without interposed comment the primary source-texts in English for both narrative poems, with brief but valuable introductions and a select bibliography. If for these works alone, students of Shakespeare's poems have good reason to be grateful for the scholarship of the past half-century.

1. 'VENUS AND ADONIS'

Modern criticism may well be taken to commence with George Wyndham's Introduction to *Shakespeare's Poems* (1898). Fair attention had been given to *Venus and Adonis* by nineteenth-century writers, but mainly either as a by-product of dramatic genius or as a quasi-biographical document.[1] Rather vague resemblances had been seen to the works of Titian and Rubens. On moral grounds it was deemed too sensual, yet artistically it was considered too cold. Wyndham was out to rehabilitate the poem by its own standards. Clearly influenced by Pater's aestheticism, as well as his impressionist style, he related *Venus and Adonis* to a wider Renaissance outlook. In its qualities of vividness and detachment, the poem was a kind of verbal painting, comparable with the Florentine pictorial treatment of classic myth. Notably it recalled Botticelli's 'Venus' or di Cosimo's 'Cephalus and Procris', 'with its living animals at gaze before a tragedy that tells much of Beauty and nothing of pain'. Yet with this overall clarity and serenity were touches of 'a gaiety not yet divorced from love'; and, permeating the whole work, a faith in Beauty, phenomenal and ideal, as a principle of life.

Wyndham's appreciations were gradually toned down by the Edwardians. In *Shakespeare* (1907) Walter Raleigh conceded that the poem was 'destitute of feeling for the human situation'; the cause, however, lay not in Shakespeare's insensibility, but in his 'preoccupation with art'. This was not quite the earnest aestheticism of Wyndham: it substituted for his positive Renaissance vision the all-absolving password of art for art's sake. With Saintsbury's chapter on the Poems in the *Cambridge History*, v (1910), the plea degenerated, perhaps inevitably, to decoration for decoration's sake. *Venus and Adonis* was mainly praised for its 'melody' of verse and its descriptive 'colour', the aim being 'less to tell a story than to draw a series of beautiful and voluptuous pictures'. As for the voluptuousness, it was of its time and – rather like the allegory in Spenser—would not meddle with anyone who did not meddle with it. Such apologies would hardly convert a determined objector. Samuel Butler in the *Note-Books* and Swinburne in *Shakespeare* (1909) had expressed their distaste, Swinburne frankly preferring *Hero and Leander*. Pooler in his edition (1911) picked out some felicities for praise and defended his author by disparaging Marlowe. He found the subject of Shakespeare's poem 'trifling' and 'certain incidents' 'regrettable'; but essentially the fault lay in 'the intrusion into poetry of the spirit of the epigram'. As the century wore on, such pruderies became infrequent, but antipathies, if anything, more marked. Typical objections were that the poem was 'at once sensuous and sentimental', full of 'conceit' and 'bad taste'. Most damaging in its erudite context was Douglas

Bush's two-edged attack. In *Mythology and the Renaissance Tradition in English Poetry* (1932) Bush found that with regard to this poem Shakespeare 'fiddles on the strings of sensuality without feeling or awakening any such sympathy...for an orgy of the senses it is too unreal, for a decorative pseudo-classic picture it has too much homely realism'. Whether a whole-hogging orgy or a thoroughly 'pseudo-classic' picture would please more is hard to infer. Writing before 1938, Rollins observed with some justice: 'Today scholars and critics scarcely mention *Venus and Adonis* without apologies express or implied.'

An old-fashioned 'aesthete' might have inveighed against philistines—in their dual guise as moral censors and red-blooded sensualists—betraying the fort from within. But at the nadir of the poem's reputation help came in unexpected forms. In *Elizabethan Love Conventions* (1933) Lu Emily Pearson pronounced *Venus and Adonis* 'as didactic a piece of work as Shakespeare ever wrote'. Venus symbolized the destructive agent of sensual love, 'that sullies whatever it touches': Adonis, reason in love, 'all truth, all good'. With the death of Adonis lust triumphed, and chaos ensued. The symbolism overlooked that unequivocally destructive agent, the boar, as well as Venus's endeavour to keep the boy from its way; but Miss Pearson's remarks set the poem in a new, more virtuous light. Less ethically centred were the comments of Kenneth Muir and Sean O'Loughlin in *The Voyage to Illyria* (1937), drawing attention to Shakespeare's 'almost satiric' outlook and his use here, as in *Love's Labour's Lost*, of ironic hyperbole in mockery of 'the exaggerations of love'. Where these writers found subtle irony, Rufus Putney drew up bucketfuls of fun. In two articles for *Philological Quarterly* (1941) and *University of Colorado Studies* (1953), the first suitably entitled '*Venus and Adonis*: Amour with Humor', Putney claimed that Shakespeare was following a tradition of comic eroticism. The idea of a chaste Adonis was 'distinctly funny', and an enamoured Venus, 'frustrated and presently perspiring', was too good a joke to resist. The goddess belonged to the order of Falstaff and Juliet's Nurse; Adonis (with no dramatic counterpart) was 'an Elizabethan Joseph'. The story was ludicrous, even in the later portions, where Venus's lament became 'a diverting parody' to take the sting out of such pathos as the myth contained. Putney did not explain why Shakespeare attached this lament, substantially Bion's, to Ovid's far less pathetic account. Most examples of the comic tradition came later than *Venus and Adonis*, and not all the instances were unquestionably amusing. None the less, this aspect of the poem appealed as much as Miss Pearson's, and a new generation of critics combined the two in a bi-focal vision.

Sharing nothing in common with these attitudes, Hereward T. Price in *Papers of the Michigan Academy* (1945) represented *Venus and Adonis* as essentially a tragic poem. In its theme, its incidents, and especially its patterns of imagery, it gave expression to the pagan vision of a cosmos at war with itself. 'The destruction of something exquisite by what is outrageously vile' was seen by Shakespeare as the central antinomy of life: on this, through a multitude of reinforcing details, the imagery turned. Shakespeare's outlook was closer to Bion than to that of any other writer, and in relation to this vision the much talked-of issues of 'morality' and 'sensualism' were entirely irrelevant. As for the 'outdoor' descriptions, they were more than merely decorative. Animal and bird activity reflected the beauty and horror of nature, a duality of external and inner conflict diffused through the poem in contrasted red and white colour-symbols, until at last reconciled in the flower of the dead Adonis. Combining Wilson Knight's 'spatial' technique with an impassioned scholarship of his own, Price pointed to unconsidered depths in Shakespeare's narrative poem. Whether these depths might be compatible with its surface brilliance was a question left open for others.

Meanwhile symbolism was joining forces with popular trends in more specialized studies. A. J. Hatto in *Modern Language Review* (1946) asked why Venus was jealous of the Boar, and he followed that beast for an answer down long paths of literary allusion. The Boar was proved to be a symbol of 'overmastering virility'; by reversing the usual role of lovers, Shakespeare had made Venus and the Boar into rivals for Adonis. (The rivalry was, however, implicit in an idyll of Theocritus, translated in 1588, where the Boar declared his love for the young shepherd.) The Horses came up for scrutiny by Robert P. Miller in *Journal of English Literary History* (1952), their archetype being found in the dark, mis-shapen allegorical horse of Plato's *Phædrus*. By 'conditional parallelism' equine conduct was made to suggest the human situation while allowing Venus and Adonis a moral choice. Shakespeare's 'position' was thus equated to 'conventional Renaissance morality', though managing at the same time to be 'delightfully humorous'. Miller's Horses, shown by their points as 'by Putney out of Pearson', met with D. C. Allen's approval in a contribution to *Elizabethan and Jacobean Studies* (1959), and Wat the Hare joined the symbolistic troupe as a fertility emblem. Allen's main concern, however, was to show hunting and courtship as traditionally cognate themes. 'Venus...hunts with her strong passions; the hunted Adonis lives to hunt the boar; and the boar is death, the eternal hunter.' These sombre implications are not taken to mar the playfulness of the poem; Venus is again 'the frustrate lady, flushed and sweating'; 'a forty-year-old countess'; and after the death of Adonis, 'a fluttery and apprehensive Doll Tearsheet'. In the course of this article Allen touched on a number of analogues or possible sources to the poem which will be noted later.

Venus and Adonis passed in these years from virtual disregard to no small degree of critical interest and acclaim. It stood rehabilitated as a highly moral, even highly didactic poem, once Renaissance conventions were understood. Furthermore, it was good entertainment, once Shakespeare's meaning was grasped. Those who liked virtue, and those who liked amour-with-humour, especially those who liked both, might find here the right kind of reading. Nevertheless, some writers have questioned the current trends. C. S. Lewis in *English Literature in the Sixteenth Century* (1954) reasserted the attitude of Bush. If the poem was 'by a young moralist', 'against lust', the story did not point the moral at all well. As erotic incitement, however, it failed. Allusions to such physical reactions as satiety, sweating and the like aroused disgust— a dangerous ally to virtue. And the flushed, over-ardent Venus bore no resemblance to the golden Aphrodite. Franklin M. Dickey in *Not Wisely But Too Well* (1957), though admirably schooled in the proper 'conventions', also showed truant tendencies over the moralized Venus. Yes indeed, she was Plato's *Aphrodite Pandemios*, and Ficino's *amor vulgaria* too; but somehow she was 'more than ordinarily attractive'. Her arguments for passion were not wholly destructive, but creative as well. But she was displeasing to 'the Renaissance God', who was a rationalist; those who took her side would also find Milton's Satan more sympathetic than his God. (Milton's Adam had suffered for eating forbidden fruit; Shakespeare's Adonis died for abstaining.)

Lastly, there are critics who, though dissociated from the new trends, give their approval to the poem. In *Shakespeare and Elizabethan Poetry* (1951), M. C. Bradbrook saw *Venus and Adonis*, with other Ovidian romances, as inspired by a Lucretian conception of nature. His vision of an 'unregenerate but lovely' world of fecundity, presided over by Venus Genetrix, had been transmitted to men of the Renaissance, including Shakespeare and Marlowe. Venus and Adonis inhabited an innocent pastoral world 'freshly and naturally observed'; they were 'purely instinctive creatures'; even their physical reactions—'feeling presented in terms of flesh, its moistness, its texture'—were wholesome and good. Bullough (1957) declared the poem to be 'anything but a Platonic piece'. Shakespeare's sympathies were primarily with Venus and the coupling animals, though he allowed a 'Spenserian' viewpoint to be stated. The poem as a whole, like the plays to follow it, provided 'an explanation of love's urgencies, perversities and contrarieties'. F. T. Prince (1960) related the mood of *Venus and Adonis* to that of the romantic comedies, with 'their delight in human energies and emotions, their keen savour of everyday life mixed with abundant poetry, and their undertones of deeper seriousness'. Possibly, after the barometric changes of sixty-odd years, the atmosphere to be discerned in the poem may become again, as it was for Wyndham, 'not oppressive, but eager and pure and a part of an immense serenity'.

2. 'Lucrece'

Very different has been the sober, unspectacular progress of *Lucrece* through the twentieth century. Its incidental merits have been pointed out, its obvious faults somewhat repetitively noted. Defenders have come forward, but in all the changes of taste and approach it has neither won enthusiastic support nor been heatedly condemned. For Saintsbury (1910) *Lucrece* was 'a school exercise', for Bush (1932) 'a museum piece', and for Prince (1960) 'as a whole... a failure'. This general estimate has by no means deprived the poem of critical interest. Its place in literary tradition and its significance in Shakespeare's development remain matters of serious concern.

By many writers of last century the two narrative poems had been thought of as companion studies, presenting a kind of diptych which, in Dowden's words (*Poems* 1903), contrasted 'female lust and boyish coldness' with 'male lust and womanly chastity'. Yet the second poem disappointed; and it was by the standards of dramatic realism, as learnt from Coleridge and Hazlitt, that this failure was explained. The too-ample rhetoric of Lucrece was said to impede the action and supersede characterization; its moral purpose, commendable as this might be, was over-explicit and gave an effect of artificiality. In defence of the poem, Wyndham saw here good grounds for protest. Narrative poetry, he insisted, was to be judged on its own merits. Much of human experience lay outside the range of the dramatic medium, constituting a 'monodrama' such as the romantic narrative of the nineteenth century set out to explore. *Lucrece* was rightly concerned, not so much with characters in action, as with the study of moral passions, mental debates and physiological perturbations. Wyndham (1898) did the poem a service by clarifying the functions of narrative, but his contemporary analogies were unhelpful. The highly vocal hero of *Maud* was not, after all, in the position of a Tarquin; Keats's Madeleine, on the other hand, did not declaim hundreds of lines on awaking to find Porphyro in her bedchamber. The co-presence of tense situation and expatiatory rhetoric belonged to another literary tradition.

Pooler (1911) effectively dealt with the theory of the narrative poems as 'companion studies'. *Venus and Adonis* was not, in his view, a very serious treatment of female lust; Adonis's plight was really more comic than tragic; in contrast, *Lucrece* was concerned with 'irreparable agonies' and 'unforgiveable cruelty'. Unlike Ovid, who softened the effects, or Livy, who was concerned with teaching a political lesson, Shakespeare chose to dwell on suffering and wrong. Hence the lengthy soliloquies, which purposed to leave nothing of the truth untold; hence the elaborate account of the picture of Troy, an objective projection of Lucrece herself. The dramatic analogy, however, was less easily dismissed. In *Words and Poetry* (1928) Rylands observed how Shakespeare's talents as a dramatist were at work in *Lucrece*, and how here more than in the earlier poem he was seeking to realize the sensations of the protagonists. Bush too (1932) saw the poem as primarily dramatic: Shakespeare was leaving mythology behind him to deal realistically with 'historical' personages in a tragic situation. This did not, however, suit the narrative form or justify the rhetorical trappings; Shakespeare had sacrificed Chaucer's irony, emotion and depth for an 'undramatic drama' which sometimes suggested an unconscious burlesque of Elizabethan plays. It was for Esther C. Dunne in *Literature of Shakespeare's England* (1936) to explain the anomaly. *Lucrece*, she thought, should be viewed as a 'borderline' piece, half-narrative, half-dramatic, and as such characteristic of its time. Seneca's dramatic poems and *Titus Andronicus* were hardly nearer to what we would regard as true plays; *Lucrece* was in theme another 'lamentable tragedy' much on these lines. Using the narrative form, it employed two kinds of technique: the 'morality' presentation of Tarquin and Lucrece as opposed types of evil and good; and, for the exploration of personality, the rhetorical devices of *débat*, invocation and lament, already well developed in this medium. Typically in an indecisive phase of Elizabethan literature, *Lucrece* fell half-way between narrative and drama; on the other hand, Shakespeare would soon learn to convert rhetorical self-expression into effective dramatic soliloquy.

Other writers were to suggest more personal reasons for Shakespeare's change of manner from *Venus and Adonis* to *Lucrece*. Muir and O'Loughlin (1937) noticed that imagery drawn from reading and town life had largely replaced observations of nature: this might well have been the effect of closer association between Shakespeare and his patron. 'Heraldic imagery and that connected with page-boys, servitors, rich fabrics and paintings came naturally to a middle-class provincial newly introduced to the splendours of a nobleman's town mansion.' Even, it was suggested, the picture of Troy might have been inspired by some painting that belonged to Southampton. No one, of course, can prove or disprove such guesses. Similarly, A. H. R. Fairchild in *Shakespeare and the Arts of Design* (1937) suspected that a likely pictorial 'source' for *Lucrece* lay in the celebrated 'Triumph of Chastity' tapestries, with suggestions for incidental themes 'undoubtedly' available in 'Troy' and the 'Triumph of Time'. Another result of the Southampton connection, more didactic than artistic, was detected by E. P. Kuhl, who pointed out (*Philological Quarterly*, 1941) that many political maxims from *Lucrece* were included with non-literary matter in *Englands Parnassus*. The dedication of *Venus and Adonis* had promised 'some graver labour', and that of *Lucrece* had referred to the poem as a 'Pamphlet'. This second offering should therefore be seen as an attempt to indoctrinate Southampton with Shakespeare's own political and moral ideals, notably his rather radical objections to 'royal tyranny' at this time. Were Shakespeare indeed so minded (there seems little evidence to confirm it) he would have done better, one feels, to have kept closer to his source in Livy. It is also hard to believe that *Lucrece* was undertaken in 1594 'to impress Southampton's mind and soul' and to serve as a 'Godlike guide' without believing too, that *Venus and Adonis* was concocted in 1593 with other designs on the young earl's mind and soul, perhaps to serve as a less godly aphrodisiac.

More central to literary concern is the place of *Lucrece* in Shakespeare's artistic development. Parallels with *Macbeth* and *Cymbeline* in situation, language and imagery had been observed as far back as Whiter and Malone. Further affinities with *Macbeth* were listed in Muir's 'Arden' edition (1951), while for M. C. Bradbrook (1951) the soliloquies of Tarquin were 'like a first cartoon' for the study of this play. Muir and O'Loughlin (1937) had noted the use of bird and beast symbolism as in the great tragedies, and seen the description of the Troy picture as anticipating *Troilus and Cressida* and the 'Hecuba' speeches in *Hamlet*. Time and food images, Muir was later to remark (*Shakespeare Survey*, 1955), carried similar associations in *Troilus* and *Lucrece*. Ranging more widely, Price (1945) traced a pattern of tragic imagery in the poem, with juxtaposed symbols of fire and darkness, red and white, flowers and weeds, creatures of innocence and slaughter, which gave expression, as in *Venus and Adonis*, to Shakespeare's profound sense of cosmic dualism. In his total view of reality evil was universal, though envisaged in diverse forms. 'Tarquin is one with the force that destroyed Romeo and Juliet, with the boar that slew Adonis.' As in the analysis of the earlier poem, new troubled depths were intimated. And here too it was left for others to distinguish between undercurrents of authentic tragedy and the very different look of things on the poem's surface; not in this case calm and serene, but lurid with those rather managed storm-effects which Shakespeare, with most of his generation, still thought fitting for 'lamentable tragedy'.

No writer has come forward to claim that *Lucrece* was a conscious parody, or very tragical mirth. Clifford Leech, however, dwelt in *Shakespeare's Tragedies* (1950) on the co-presence of comedy with tragedy and took as an example the incident of Lucrece's blushing groom. 'It is not comic, in the sense of laughter-provoking, yet it...nearly succeeds in making us question the basis of tragic dignity.' Implicit in such effects Leech discerned Shakespeare's 'strong suspicion that cosmos was chaos and man a blind beggar'. Different as were the aspects of the poem which caught their attention, it would seem that Leech and Price were not far apart in their basic estimate of Shakespeare.

M. C. Bradbrook (1951) showed more interest in the poem's relation to conventional forms. Like *Titus*, *Lucrece* was a 'tragical discourse', affording moral emblems of beauty and virtue, 'mirror images' of grief and deceit, and figuring *Lucrece* as Chastity personified. Such traditional methods had their part in Shakespeare's development, and were never entirely given up. Yet here without doubt the sententious and over-explicit moralising and the elaborate rhetorical patterning had an artificial effect, bordering on parody; they were closely bound up with the contemporary notion of tragedy as 'the blind senseless horror of purely physical outrage'. C. S. Lewis (1945) recognized the shortcomings of *Lucrece*, but also found qualities deserving of praise. It was heroic poetry of the kind inspired by Lucan and Ovid rather than Virgil, and far better than most 'tragedies' of the *Mirror for Magistrates* order. If medieval rhetoric and 'gnomic amplification' were uncongenial to our age, there were also fine verbal effects, and frequently our sympathies too were engaged.

Prince's estimate of the poem (1960) may serve to conclude. *Lucrece* was found to be formally defective in its turn from the narrative manner of Ovid and Chaucer to a semi-dramatic, semi-rhetorical mode. Narrative in appearance, it was substantially 'tragic' in the style of *Titus Andronicus*. But the essential weakness was not one of form: rather it lay in the choice of this kind of tragic theme by a writer whose natural inclination at this period drew him rather towards comedy. Further to Prince's last remark, it may perhaps be said that tragedy for the younger Shakespeare seems to have had two connotations. One was a literary formula for combining 'moral heraldry' with physical horror; the other an intuitive response to the duality of things, the omnipresence of beauty and destruction, which found expression in a complex interweaving of imagery. When the formula for tragedy was consciously followed, convention and sensibility were apt to inhibit one another. When, however, romance was the chosen medium, with less call for violent actions and explicit morality, Shakespeare's tragic intuitions found their own level. Hence, it may be, the complex appeal of *Venus and Adonis*, as compared with the mainly historical interest evoked by *Lucrece*.

3. 'The Phoenix and the Turtle'

'Its very concinnity and restraint', Grosart observed, 'compared with the fecundity of *Venus and Adonis* and *Lucrece*, differentiate it from all other of Shakespeare's writings.' Yet for many readers *The Phoenix and The Turtle* has seemed to contain in its eighteen terse stanzas the quintessence of Shakespeare. Its literary and philosophical affinities have not altered the uniqueness of its position. Allusive, abstract and incantatory, with 'a certain far-withdrawn and heart-conquering tenderness', the poem beckons and eludes.

Early in the century two kinds of approach were already apparent. One was to explore the evidence for a 'personal allegory' and discover what occasion, and what persons, the poem celebrated. Its connection with Chester's patron Sir John Salusbury and his wife seemed rather tenuous, while Grosart's speculations on an Elizabeth–Essex significance (in his 1878 edition of *Loves Martyr*) were clearly far-fetched. More plausibly, von Mauntz (*Shakespeare–Jahrbuch*, 1893) had argued that the poem was a kind of sequel to the sonnets, expressing Shakespeare's estrangement from Southampton. The alternative approach was to seek in *The Phoenix and The Turtle* a revelation of Shakespeare's major artistic concerns. In Charles Downing's article in *The Shrine* (1902) the poem was said to recall, not only the themes of the sonnets, but such dramatic relationships as those of Orsino and Viola, Ferdinand and Miranda, Florizel and Perdita. Shakespeare was not just 'a tranquil mirror of nature', but had long reflected on the 'all-comprehensive, absolute ideal of the human spirit'. Downing may have been addicted to rather hazy abstractions,[2] but the substance of his interpretation was in accord with the more imaginative trends in later criticism.

There was, thirdly, a strictly formal approach to the poem. Fairchild in *Englische Studien* (1904) set the pattern by tracing its literary antecedents back, in part to the Court of Love poetic tradition with its bird-symbolism, in part to sixteenth-century emblem literature with its epigrammatic and Platonic modes of expression. As for the work in itself, Fairchild saw no more in it than an occasional exercise. No recondite meanings, biographical significances or metaphysical profundities need be sought. This pragmatic dismissal was enough for Carleton Brown, who in his edition of *The Poems of Salusbury and Chester* (1913) classed Shakespeare's poem as 'an ingenious exercise'. Other editors of this period were equally impervious to the poem's profounder qualities: C. H. Herford in the 'Eversley' Shakespeare (1899) took it as 'a trifle', and W. C. Hazlitt in *Shakespear* (1912) as 'inferior even to the *Sonnets*' (for Ridley in 1935 it was still 'a trifle', for Baldwin in 1950 'a most charming little poem'). In contrast, John Masefield in *William Shakespeare* (1911) responded to the 'mystery and vitality' and saw 'spiritual ecstasy' as the keynote, while Saintsbury (1910) remarked on its 'extreme metaphysicality'.

In the 1920's, however, a transformation in taste hoisted the poem to celebrity. Milton and Shelley were being dislodged, Donne and the Metaphysicals canonized, and *The Phoenix and The Turtle* became a hero of the literary revolution. Frank Mathew's *An Image of Shakespeare* (1922) found in it affinities to Donne's 'brooding austerity' and likened it to *The Relic* and *The Funeral*. In the same year J. Middleton Murry's note to *The Problem of Style* contrasted its Phoenix imagery to that of Milton's 'reminiscence' in the last chorus of *Samson* (to Milton's detriment) and in *Discoveries* (printed 1924) set the poem against Shelley's *The Sensitive Plant* (to the disadvantage of Shelley). On the actual merits of *The Phoenix and The Turtle* Murry was more evocative than explicit. It was 'mysterious' yet 'crystal clear'; it was also 'obscure, mystical and strictly unintelligible'. 'Pure' poetry it was indeed, providing 'heightened awareness', yet it was 'too personal and too esoteric to gain the general ear'. Perhaps, Murry hinted, it was a little too refined for Shakespeare himself: in comparison, 'even the most wonderful poetry of his dramas' might appear '"stained with mortality"'—a revealing misquotation.

But other, more positive appreciations were to follow in the thirties. R. J. Shahani ('Ranjee') has been tendentiously presented by Rollins. In *Towards The Stars* (1931) he alluded to the poem's 'academic aroma', its 'elusive Platonism', and the resemblance of its diction to the language of Trinitarian theology. *The Phoenix and The Turtle* was characterized as 'a *brave* poem', with its vision of the divinity of love and constancy made immortal in death, its sense of the cosmic tragedy of love, and its note of 'resignation yet triumph'. Perversely, the poem's author was identified with Fletcher; a lapse which J. Wilson Knight deplored in reviewing the book for *The Criterion* (1931). Knight was, however, deeply impressed by Shahani's critical estimate. Preoccupied himself with the poetic qualities of Shakespearian drama, and out of sympathy with Murry's conception of 'pure' poetry, he found here a very relevant approach. In *The Imperial Theme* (1931) 'A Note on *Antony and Cleopatra*' acknowledged the debt and took the play and the poem as 'reciprocally illuminating', presenting, both of them, a vision of love and death as 'synchronised, mated in time'. In 'The Shakespearian Aviary', an appendix to *The Shakespearian Tempest* (1932) Knight went further, exploring the significance of bird imagery over a wide range of the poems and the plays, with special reference to *The Phoenix* and *Antony*. The phoenix was shown as a favourite Shakespearian symbol of aspiration, love and immortality, 'upwinging beyond the world of appearance and multiplicity' and transcending antinomies in a mystic paradox. Nor, Knight implied, was this a mere Platonic commonplace; it belonged to a personal vision in which truth and beauty were seen as mortal categories; their death it was that created 'a third unknown immortality' celebrated in what Knight summed up as 'this bird song of tragic joy'. After these piercing insights the opinions of Muir and O'Loughlin were less profound, but they added to the appreciation both scholarship and common sense. The Phoenix in Golding's Ovid, the Eagle, Turtle and Swan of Royden's elegy on Sidney in *The Phoenix Nest*, with a 'Dialogue' in the same book, were shown to be likely influences. Shakespeare's poem was nevertheless an expression of personal experience; if commissioned for an occasion, so too was *Lycidas*, where Milton wrote of his own conflicts. Repeating von Mauntz's approach, Muir and O'Loughlin interpreted this underlying experience as the final break with Southampton, linked with the commencement of the tragic period. The transcendent love hymned in *The Phoenix and The Turtle* inspired Shakespeare's faith through the years leading on to *Antony and Cleopatra*, *King Lear*, *Cymbeline* and *The Tempest*.

The poem's historical occasion had still not lost its interest for some scholars. Bernard H. Newdigate, in an article and letters to *The Times Literary Supplement* (1936) and in his edition of *Jonson's Poems* (1936), described a manuscript version of Jonson's ode in *Loves Martyr*. It was inscribed with the initials of Lucy Countess of Bedford, whose only son died in 1601, the year of Chester's collection. If Lucy was Shakespeare's 'phoenix' as well as Jonson's, and the verses of both men were at first addressed to her, then the third stanza of Shakespeare's 'threnos' would have a literal significance. Newdigate's claim was contested in the same place by R. W. Short (1937), and in the same year a little comic relief from the Continent was administered by Georges A. Bonnard (*English Studies* 1937). To Bonnard the same lines of the 'threnos' seemed a good 'Elizabethan' joke at Sir John Salusbury's expense. 'Infirmity' and 'married chastity' were, of course, digs at poor Salusbury's matrimonial inadequacies. Putney's analogous reactions to *Venus and Adonis* were soon to be well received; but *The Phoenix and The Turtle* was set in another trajectory, and these humorous surmises failed to amuse.

In recent years new tendencies have begun to emerge, showing less concern with the poem as personal expression and more with its bearing on theories of philosophy and poetics. Cleanth Brooks in *The Well Wrought Urn* (1947) chose it as an illustration of 'the language of paradox', in company with Donne's *The Canonization*. As such it expressed those 'metaphysical' qualities which Brooks elevated into a general poetic principle. For J. V. Cunningham, 'metaphysical' retained its philosophical meaning: in *E.L.H.* (1952) he discussed the use in this poem of 'exact, technical, scholastic language' to define the union in love. 'Essence' properly signified the divine substance; 'distincts', 'division', 'number', 'property', all had theological connotations. Since the application of such terms to human experience of love was ruled out by scholastic teaching and 'not sanctioned...by the facts of nature', the union of the Phoenix and the Turtle must stand as a paradigm of the Trinity. Yet Valentine's description of Sylvia as 'my essence' in the romantic context of *Two Gentlemen of Verona* (one of Cunningham's illustrations) surely indicates that Shakespeare could, and did, 'locate the infinite Idea in the finite beloved'. A. Alvarez, on the other hand, in a sensitive though over-elaborated essay for *Interpretations* (edited John Wain, 1955), saw the theology as subservient to the human situation. The poem amounted to an affirmation 'that the highest mysteries of Love demand their own metaphysic, religion and logic'. As for the use of cumulative, unremitting paradox, this differed radically from Donne's looser analogical conceits, proving Shakespeare 'the more honest logician and not at all the Metaphysical poet'. C. S. Lewis (1954) also noted[3] that the poem was not in the 'technical' sense metaphysical; yet it was 'truly' metaphysical, and avoided mere romance sentiment by making Reason herself exalt Love over Reason. Walter J. Ong (*Sewanee Review*, 1955) took metaphor, 'the twinned vision', rather than the language of paradox as his province. Metaphor was man's best instrument for the apprehension of truth; and *The Phoenix and The Turtle*, as a 'metaphor of metaphor', expressed the duality yet unity of such 'abstractions' as love and death, mind and body, Christ and the Church. Turning from the sublime to the subliminal, Ronald Bates (*Shakespeare Quarterly*, 1955) claimed to have identified 'the bird of loudest lay' and 'the shrieking harbinger' by a review of ornithological image-clusters along the lines pioneered by A. E. Armstrong. The third stanza of the 'threnos' was not, as Bonnard had supposed, a deliberate joke, but a ludicrous 'intrusion' resulting from Shakespeare's 'almost unbalanced' repugnance at this time to the thought of sexual relationships. M. C. Bradbrook's rejoinder (*Shakespeare Quarterly*, 1955) expressed some forthright Johnsonian reactions. Had Shakespeare wanted to name his birds, he could have done so. 'Married chastity' and 'infirmity' had spiritual meanings for the Elizabethans. 'The power to refrain from specific associations', Miss Bradbrook commented, 'is not out of place in the reading of poetry': a remark to be written in gold on the portals of English Departments.

Two longer studies have appeared in the last decade. In *The Mutual Flame* (1955) Knight returned to *The Phoenix and The Turtle* as the second subject of his book. The poem was approached through a lengthy consideration of the other offerings in *Loves Martyr*. It was also taken, with the Sonnets, as expressing the 'bisexual' nature of Shakespeare's genius. Much attention was given to some undeserving verse, with dubious symbolical significances read into the heterogeneous collection, while Shakespeare's poem was arrived at only in a rather brief chapter. Here Knight's analogies with sonnets of Michelangelo were enlightening indications of a common sensibility; but as a whole this study adds little to the earlier, inspired appreciations. Less ambitious, perhaps, but more satisfying, is Heinrich Straumann's monograph *Phönix und Taube* (Zürich, 1953). Writing with much lucidity, Straumann reviewed the major critical trends bearing on this poem: the search for a personal allegory; the various symbolical interpretations; and the formal approach relating it to literary convention. All these might well be synthetized by assuming the presence of various levels of meaning. The poem could be read in three ways: as an occasional work honouring two actual and well-known persons; as a literary composition seeking means of expression through established forms; and as an imaginative creation voicing Shakespeare's innermost convictions on the values of beauty and truth, their tragic vulnerability, and their immortalization through love. Such was Shakespeare's main preoccupation in the sonnets, and in his plays after 1601, when he turned to the writing of tragedy and near-tragedy; the poem might thus be taken to mark a turning-point in his development. Much of this makes excellent sense in its blend of scholarship and criticism. Nevertheless, Straumann's conception of a turn towards a tragic view of life, associated with the loss of Southampton as friend (which endorses the opinions of Muir and O'Loughlin), may be thought open to question. What *The Phoenix and The Turtle* suggests with its locating of ideal values in the phenomenal world, its sense of cosmic antinomy, and its faith beyond reason in the transcending power of human love, is implicit in the sonnets, in the early love-tragedy *Romeo and Juliet*, and, for this reviewer, in the narrative poems. Not so much the note of tragedy, but the undertones of triumph, may indicate the true significance of this poem for Shakespeare's development. Above all else, it is 'a brave poem'.

SOURCES

Few outstanding discoveries have been established in this century, but there has been much sifting over of established facts and some interesting new points have been made. The main outline of the Venus and Adonis story was patently derived from *Metamorphoses* x; but did

Shakespeare turn to Ovid's original or Golding's translation? Dürnhofer's arguments in *Shakespeare's 'Venus and Adonis'* (Halle, 1890) that the Latin was his only source were disposed of by Hazelton Spencer in *Modern Language Notes* (1929): clearly Golding's book was either on Shakespeare's desk or not far away. The treatment of Adonis as a reluctant youth was explained by a conflation of his story with that of Hermaphroditus and, perhaps, Narcissus. Very recently this has been challenged by D. C. Allen (1960), who suggests that Ovid's digression on Hippomenes in the section of the Adonis story Shakespeare omitted may have called to mind the tragic myth of Hippolytus. H. T. Price (1945) saw the influence of Bion's elegy on the later part of the poem, and pointed out that the boar's 'love' for Adonis came from a 1588 translation of Theocritus' thirty-first idyll. Other details in the episode of the boar, according to D. T. Starnes (*Papers of the Modern Language Association*, 1945) came from Book 7 of the Golden Ass of Apuleius, with its account of the baying hounds, the boar's break-through, and the woman's frenzy at the slaying of her lover. Apuleius himself was indebted to Ovid's description of the Calydonian boar, which Anders in *Shakespeare's Books* (1904) proposed, and J. A. K. Thomson in *Shakespeare and the Classics* (1952) accepted, as a likely source. Lee (1905) listed a number of Renaissance versions of the Adonis story in Latin, Italian and French (though oddly omitting Ronsard). His claim to have discovered new sources was easily refuted, but the importance of these works as analogues has at last been touched on by D. C. Allen (1960). It would seem that at least the literary orientation of the poems is by no means an exhausted topic.

For *Lucrece*, discussion has mainly turned on the relative importance of Livy's History, Ovid's *Fasti* and Chaucer's *Legend of Good Women*, all recognized as probable sources since the eighteenth century. Ewig's survey in *Anglia* (1899) led him to conclude that Livy was the major influence. He was supported by Bush (1932), who pointed out, however, that some phrases in the poem and the 'Argument' were taken from Painter's English rendering in *The Pallace of Pleasure*. The 'Argument', moreover, suggested that Bandello's tale of Lucrece, or Belleforest's version of it, had influenced Shakespeare. Lee (1905) had first mentioned Bandello in this connection, and Marschall (*Anglia*, 1929) produced a complicated theory on his influence alternating with Livy's in successive stages of composition. A stimulating shock was administered by James M. Tolbert (*Texas Studies in English*, 1950) who believed that the 'Argument' had nothing to do with Shakespeare's poem. It was a mere publisher's afterthought, the work of some hack. If Tolbert's claims receive general acceptance, source-studies of *Lucrece* will undergo a welcome simplification. On the other hand, Shakespeare's intelligent use of the *Fasti*, as yet untranslated in English, has been demonstrated by Thomson (1952) and, with many specific examples, by Percy Simpson in *Studies in Elizabethan Drama* (1955) and J. Dover Wilson (*Shakespeare Survey*, 1957).

No precise 'source' can be claimed for a poem of the order of *The Phoenix and The Turtle*, and the discussion of 'influences' has tended to elaborate on earlier suggestions. Fairchild's (1904) analogies with Chaucer's *Parlement of Foules* and with a number of emblem-books have been repeated down the years without much strengthening of his case, which Muir and O'Loughlin (1937) rightly questioned. Classical influences were very widely diffused and broad resemblances are insubstantial evidence. Von Mauntz in *Shakespeares Gedichte* (1894) had pointed out the similarity of the invocation to Ovid's parrot elegy in *Amores* II. vi; Baldwin (1950) reaffirmed its relevance, and added Lactantius' *De Phoenice*. Lee, however, had noted in his *Life of Shakespeare* (1898; expanded 1916) that the poem might be a 'fanciful adaptation' of Matthew Roydon's elegy on Sidney in *The Phoenix Nest*, itself derived ultimately from Latin 'sources'. Muir and O'Loughlin (1937) took up Lee's suggestion and showed interesting resemblances to Roydon's verses, as well as to his 'Dialogue between Constancie and Inconstancie' in the same book. Affinities to the 'neither two nor one' theme in Drayton, in Donne and in much verse of the period had been perceived as far back as Malone.

TEXT

Venus and Adonis, with some of the early quartos, provided material for A. C. Partridge (*Shakespeare Survey*, 1954) in a detailed study of Shakespeare's orthography and punctuation. Spellings, elisions and the use of apostrophes were investigated, and deductions drawn on Shakespeare's practice in the early fifteen-nineties. Insufficient attention, however, was given to compositorial usage and print-shop practices, and Partridge's findings need to be supplemented.

NOTES

1. The literary high tide of this attitude may be seen in Joyce's *Ulysses*, where Stephen Dedalus expounds Shakespeare to his admiring fellow-intellectuals: 'The greyeyed goddess who bends over the boy Adonis, stooping to conquer, as prologue to the swelling act, is a boldfaced Stratford wench who tumbles in a cornfield a lover younger than herself.' Perhaps Stephen had been attending Dowden's lectures.

2. An impression conveyed by Rollins's excerpts (pp. 573–4). I have not been able to consult Downing's own article.

3. Alvarez explains (p. 9, footnote) that his essay was read as a paper some two years before he had read C. S. Lewis's book.

SONGS, TIME, AND THE REJECTION OF FALSTAFF

BY

PETER J. SENG

I

Any inquiry into the functions of the songs in Shakespeare's plays should be based on some consideration of what songs and music meant to Shakespeare and his contemporaries. Three points need to be kept in mind. First of all, Renaissance Englishmen knew a great deal more about music—especially its technical and social aspects—than do most people today. That Shakespeare's England was 'a nest of singing birds' has been pointed out by scholars with the wearisome regularity that only such a crystalline phrase can acquire. The famous metaphor is intended not only to connote the deep interest that music held for Elizabethan Englishmen, but also their strong impulse to lyric poetry at a time when those arts were not so separated as they are today. The songs in Shakespeare's England ranged from the madrigals, canzonets, and airs of the upper classes to the carols, cozier's catches, and street-songs of the lower orders of society. The astonishing volume of poetry produced in that era was swelled not only by courtly sonnets but also by broadside ballads. Consequently it seems fair to extend the famous metaphor a little by saying that while those singing birds included among them many nightingales and larks, they also included a goodly number of choughs, rooks, and daws.

A second point, also something of a truism, is that Shakespeare and his contemporaries thought about music in some ways that are considerably different from the ways it is thought about at the present time. For them music had real powers: it could exert a civilizing influence on rude men, turning 'savage eyes...to a modest gaze'. They felt that music could induce sleep, charm away madness, and cure all manner of physical and spiritual ills; it could abet right thinking and right doing and, if it were music of the right sort, could put man into harmonywith the world around him and with the sweet music of the spheres. They believed, finally, that the kind of music a man sang or enjoyed might well be a valid index of his inner psychological being.

A third point, less well-known perhaps, needs only to be mentioned to become obvious. Because of the habit of music in all ranks of Shakespeare's society, the performances of songs in his plays must have seemed far more natural and organic to the spectators in his audiences than renditions of song in the modern theatre seem to us who are, by and large, a non-singing people. We accept songs in a musical comedy today as a theatrical convention, whereas an actor on Shakespeare's stage who broke into song was very likely regarded as doing exactly what was to be expected under the circumstances. An Elizabethan lover could and was expected to serenade his lady; old cronies together in a tavern were expected to troll catches over their pots of ale. Even the 'spinsters and the knitters in the sun, And the free maids that weave their thread with bones' were accustomed to lighten their labours with song. Songs in Shakespeare's plays could be as natural and 'realistic' as the action or the dialogue.

31

All of these points are relevant to the songs—fragments of song, really—that occur in *The Second Part of King Henry the Fourth*. The snatches of ballads, carols, and drinking songs in that play reflect the lower spectrum of musical life in Shakespeare's England; they arise organically out of their dramatic situations and are realistic in terms of actual life; but those bits of song chiefly function in the play as ironic commentaries on the characters, episodes, and themes in 2 *Henry IV*.

In structure that play consists of a serious and a comic plot. The serious plot has to do with the King's attempts to put down the various rebellions against his rule; the comic plot is concerned with the intrigues of Falstaff and his companions. Between these two plots moves Prince Hal who, like a hero in an allegory, must on the one hand disengage himself from 'that reverend vice, that grey iniquity' Falstaff, and on the other 'redeem the time' and establish himself as a qualified and legitimate heir to the throne. Into this double plot, as I see it, are woven three themes or *leitmotifs* having to do with Justice, Disease, and Time. The serious plot makes a number of comments on the theme of Justice: it keeps in remembrance Henry's usurpation of the throne, his feelings of guilt over Richard's death; it details a new, a Machiavellian, kind of justice in John of Lancaster's treacherous offer of amnesty to the rebels, and a warmer, more human justice in Hal's reconciliation with the Lord Chief Justice of England. This same theme in the comic plot is woven into Falstaff's encounters with the Lord Chief Justice, with the abuses to which Falstaff puts the King's power of impressment, and into all his dealings with those suffragan Justices, Shallow and Silence. What Falstaff must learn is that the laws of England are *not* at his commandment, and that he is to have no voice of influence toward disorder and injustice in the court of Henry V.

The theme of Disease is carried over into 2 *Henry IV* from *Richard II*. As the dying John of Gaunt had pointed out in the earlier play, England was already ill and so was her king; and throughout both parts of *Henry IV* political intrigue and rebellion in England are referred to as a disease afflicting the country, a sickness that can only be cured by the letting of blood. This theme is further echoed in the fact that in Part Two the King becomes fatally ill and his old opponent Northumberland 'lies crafty-sick' (Induction, ll. 36–7). In the comic plot it is Falstaff who is diseased; he is literally and figuratively the infected member who must be cut away before order and health can be restored to Hal's moral universe.

The third motif woven into both plots has to do with Time, particularly time past put into sharp contrast with time present. This contrast provides an *ambiance* for both parts of *Henry IV*, but it presses most strongly on the second part. In the serious plot the past is represented by the frequent references to events and persons in *Richard II*, and by the pervasive sense of revolutionary sweep that is experienced in taking the three plays in order. First there is the melancholy Richard whose forlorn cry marks him as the last of England's medieval kings:

> Not all the water in the rough rude sea
> Can wash the balm off from an anointed king;
> The breath of worldly men cannot depose
> The deputy elected by the Lord. (III, ii, 54–7)

Then there is 'that vile politician, Bolingbroke', who knew better, and who by shrewd policy, including a fundamentally insincere promise of penance in the Holy Land, manages to establish his own dynasty on the throne. Finally, there is the newly crowned Henry V who rejects

Falstaff, reunites himself with his brothers, takes the Chief Justice as a second father, and turns his eyes toward France. Henry IV's transitional role was to thrust a medieval and chivalric England firmly into the past, and to establish on the throne a patriotic, nationalistic, and Renaissance English king. On the comic level of the play an 'Old England' has passed away as well: Nell Quickly and Doll Tearsheet are haled off by the beadles, Eastcheap roguery is no longer to be countenanced, and Falstaff, Shallow, and Silence reminisce in a Gloucestershire orchard about events that never were and a past that cannot be recaptured.

II

It is here, perhaps, well to deal with first matters first; and what has occupied more critics for more time than anything else in *2 Henry IV* has been the rejection of Falstaff at the end of the play. Some critics, indeed, have been so concerned with this problem that they have neglected other responsible moral issues with which the play is concerned: it has sometimes seemed as if they would give up virtuous standards before they would forgo cakes and ale. Whatever the reason, there has been an evident sentimental strain in Falstaffian criticism ever since Morgann's *Essay on the Dramatic Character of Sir John Falstaff* in 1777. Long before Morgann it was possible for Rowe to describe Falstaff as 'a lewd old Fellow…a Thief, Lying, Cowardly, Vainglorious, and in short every way Vicious'.[1] In 1765 Samuel Johnson pointed out that Falstaff 'has never uttered one sentiment of generosity, and with all his powers of exciting mirth, has nothing in him that can be esteemed'.[2] Both are severe critics by modern standards, yet coming before Morgann they were allowed their say. But since Morgann's *Essay* most critics have chiefly been concerned with exonerating their hero from every least breath of censure while crying up Hal as a censorious prig who blasts the old knight with a frigid, 'I know thee not, old man'. Among the few important modern critics who have *not* gone along with Morgann's sentimental estimate of Falstaff's character are J. Dover Wilson and E. E. Stoll;[3] but sixteen closely printed pages in the New Variorum Edition of the play[4] record the attempts of a majority of critics to justify Falstaff in one way or another.

There is no pleasure in opposing such an array of defenders nor in electing one's self a devil's advocate to calumniate the old knight's character; but those commentators who seek to canonize Sir John seem to be ignoring much evidence that tells against his alleged geniality and virtue. The most important piece of evidence seems to be Shakespeare's own dramatic intention.

In the highly amusing scene at the Boar's Head tavern in *1 Henry IV*, the playwright himself appears to raise the important dramatic problem he had to face in the *Henry IV* plays: What is to be done with Sir John Falstaff? In a burlesque dialogue Prince Hal imitates his father, the King, while Falstaff, playing the Prince, pleads his own cause:

That he is old, the more the pity, his white hairs do witness it; but that he is, saving your reverence, a whoremaster, that I utterly deny. If sack and sugar be a fault, God help the wicked! if to be old and merry be a sin, then many an old host that I know is damned: if to be fat be to be hated, then Pharaoh's lean kine are to be loved. No, my good lord; banish Peto, banish Bardolph, banish Poins: but for sweet Jack Falstaff, kind Jack Falstaff, true Jack Falstaff…banish not him thy Harry's company… banish plump Jack, and banish all the world. (II, iv, 514–27)

It is precisely at this moment that the sheriff and his officers arrive to arrest the Gadshill robbers. In the confusion that attends upon their arrival we are apt to miss Hal's words, 'I do, I will'. Whether Hal speaks them in *propria persona* or not, these words may be taken to indicate that Shakespeare's mind was made up.[5] Yet how was he to banish plump Jack and not banish all the world?

He found his solution to this problem, I believe, in the deliberate degradation of the character of Falstaff in *2 Henry IV*. There is a striking difference between the characters of the knight in the two plays. In *1 Henry IV* Falstaff is a capon-and-sack knight, and such villainy as he possesses is always softened and humanized by his ebullient good humour—laughter, in this instance, covering a multitude of sins. In *2 Henry IV* Falstaff is still the buffoon, but the high comedy that once attended his every entrance has now taken a bitter turn. He is indeed the cause 'that wit is in other men'; as of old he inspires their wittiest sallies, but now he has also become the butt of their coarsest jokes. It is no longer merely his corpulence and preposterous impudence that provokes laughter; it is his diseases. The change in his character and the change in the tone of humour is signalled from Falstaff's very first entrance on the stage:

Enter FALSTAFF, *with his page, bearing his sword and buckler.*

Fal. Sirrah, you giant, what says the doctor to my water?

Page. He said, sir, the water itself was a good healthy water; but, for the party that owed it, he might have moe diseases than he knew for. (I, ii, 1–6)

Thus begins the bitterer comedy of the sequel.

At the end of this scene a cruel light is thrown on the doctor's jest: Falstaff's visits to the stews have evidently made him a victim of their diseases. As the old knight says in a brief soliloquy:

A pox of this gout! or, a gout of this pox! for the one or the other plays the rogue with my great toe. 'Tis no matter if I do halt; I have the wars for my colour, and my pension shall seem the more reasonable. A good wit will make use of anything: I will turn diseases to commodity. (ll. 272–8)

Falstaff's first entrance in the play is clearly echoed at his entrance in II, iv. He has been partying at the Boar's Head with Mistress Quickly and with that 'pagan' of the old sect Doll Tearsheet. Supper is over as the scene begins, and the ladies, Doll somewhat indisposed, enter first. After a moment Falstaff follows them on to the stage singing the opening lines of an old broadside ballad. 'When Arthur first in court'— he sings; then he interrupts his song to mutter an order to a servant, 'Empty the jordan'. Then he resumes his song again, 'And was a worthy king,' only to break off his song once more as he turns to the women and addresses one of them, 'How now, Doll?' An appropriate gloss on the whole passage is one critic's naturalistic comment in Latin: *Raro mingit castus*.[6]

Shakespeare's audience, undoubtedly knowing the ballad, would have appreciated the ironies of this song. The lines Falstaff sings come from 'The Noble Acts newly found, of *Arthur* of the Table Round. To the tune of flying Fame.' According to Hales and Furnivall, Thomas Deloney was probably the author of the ballad, and the ballad itself is 'nothing more than a rhymed version of certain chapters in Malory's "Most Ancient and Famous history of the Renowned Prince Arthur"'.[7] Rollins has suggested that this ballad may have been the one entered in the Stationers' Registers in 1565/6 as 'a pleasaunte history of an adventurus knyghte of kynges arthurs Couurte', and has definitely identified with it the ballad entered by Edward Aldee, 8 June 1603, 'The noble Actes nowe newly found of Arthure of the round table'.[8]

There is little or no question about the popularity of this ballad in Shakespeare's day and hence its familiarity to his audiences. It was frequently quoted in the drama of the time, imitated, many times reprinted, and parodied even as late as 1656 in a pre-Restoration song-book. The name of the ballad even became, finally, the title to the tune to which it was sung, replacing the old tune-name, 'Flying Fame'.[9] It is possible, indeed, that this ballad helped to make its tune popular. Surviving copies of this broadside are to be found in the Pepys, Wood, Lord Crawford, Roxburghe, and Bagford ballad collections; there is a fragmentary version of it in the Percy Folio MS., and a reprinted version in Deloney's *Garland of Good-Will*, 1631.[10] The tune for the ballad has been transcribed by Chappell.[11]

The general character of the song Falstaff begins to sing is sufficiently indicated by its first few stanzas:[12]

> When *Arthur* first in Court began,
>   and was approoued King:
> By force of Armes great Victories won,
>   and conquest home did bring:
>
> Then into *Brittaine* straight he came,
>   where fiftie good and able
> Knights then repaired vnto him
>   which were of the Round-table.
>
> And many Justes and Turnaments,
>   before him there were brest:
> Wherein both Knights did then excell,
>   and far surmount the rest:
>
> But one Sir *Lancelot du Lake*,
>   who was approoued well:
> He in his sight and deeds of Armes
>   all other did excell.

Even with only so much of the ballad in mind we can discern Shakespeare's purpose in putting this song on Falstaff's lips. As a jolting broadside ballad it is a good index to the old knight's taste in verse and music; beyond this, the substance of the song is wholly inappropriate to Sir John, for it celebrates the antique world of romance and chivalry, a world of knights and ladies far more honourable than Falstaff and his dinner companions. Falstaff, in whom desire has outlived the performance, as Poins says, (II, iv, 283-4) is no Lancelot; nor, if one further ironic reverberation of this song may be permitted, is the politician-king Bolingbroke a King Arthur. The kind of chivalry the song is about is a kind that died in England with John of Gaunt, Richard, and Hotspur.

Not only is the substance of the song totally inappropriate to Falstaff, but it is also set in shocking contrast to the interpolated order to the servant: 'Empty the jordan.' The command echoes Falstaff's earlier concern with his 'diseases'. Lest the audience should miss the connection, Shakespeare has the knight allude to his infection a few lines further on:[13]

You make fat rascals, Mistress Doll.

Doll. I make them! gluttony and diseases make them; I make them not.

Fal. If the cook help to make the gluttony, you help to make the diseases, Doll: we catch of you, Doll, we catch of you; grant that, my poor virtue, grant that.

Doll. Yea, joy, our chains and our jewels.

Fal. 'Your brooches, pearls, and ouches:' for to serve bravely is to come halting off, you know: to come off the breach with his pike bent bravely, and to surgery bravely; to venture upon the charged chambers bravely,—

Doll. Hang yourself, you muddy conger, hang yourself!   (ll. 45–57)

In fact when Falstaff says of Doll 'she's in hell already and burns poor souls' (ll. 365–6) he may be making the ungentlemanly suggestion that she is the source of his affliction.

If all of this seems like a cruel conclusion to what was once so much high comedy, that is only because we are more sentimental about Falstaff than Shakespeare and his contemporaries were, and because our taste in humour is less broad than theirs. In *2 Henry IV* an old epoch had to make way for a new; Shakespeare had to banish Jack Falstaff, so he degraded him first and thereby avoided banishing the whole world. Finally, it should be noted that Falstaff is not the only person in the Boar's Head set who is degraded and banished; he is merely the first. In *Henry V* Bardolph and Nym are hanged for thievery, Pistol deserts the army to become a bawd, Nell Quickly dies of 'malady of France', and Doll Tearsheet becomes 'a lazar kite of Cressid's kind'.

III

Even as he had degraded the character of Falstaff in *2 Henry IV*, Shakespeare also made him a victim of Time. He degraded the knight to make the rejection palatable; he subjected him to Time to make it inevitable. The *leitmotif* of time irrecoverably past is sounded with Falstaff's first appearance in the play. With his accustomed impudence he pleads youth as an extenuation of his follies:

You that are old consider not the capacities of us that are young; you do measure the heat of our livers with the bitterness of your galls: and we that are in the vaward of our youth, I must confess, are wags too.   (I, ii, 195–200)

But the true facts are revealed in the Chief Justice's reproof which sounds like a literary 'Character of an Old Man':

Do you set down your name in the scroll of youth, that are written down old with all the characters of age? Have you not a moist eye? a dry hand? a yellow cheek? a white beard? a decreasing leg? an increasing belly? is not your voice broken? your wind short? your chin double? your wit single? and every part about you blasted with antiquity?   (ll. 201–8)

And to this portrait can be added Sir John's salient vice—a vice of old men—avarice. He has practised upon Mistress Quickly 'both in purse and in person' and perhaps upon Doll Tearsheet, too.[14] He has used the King's power of impressment to line his own pockets, and his call on Shallow enables him to swindle that Justice of a thousand pounds.

It is the Gloucestershire episodes of the play that give the fullest colour and development to the

Time motif in *2 Henry IV*. Time past is summed up in the reminiscences of Falstaff, Shallow, and Silence about days in the dim past when Jack Falstaff was a boy and a page to Thomas Mowbray, and John of Gaunt laid wagers on the skill in archery of one of Silence's friends.[15] They talk, too, about wild days and wilder nights at Clement's Inn. 'We have heard the chimes at midnight', says Falstaff; but then a little later, 'Lord, how subject we old men are to this vice of lying!' (III, ii, 229, 325–6). They not only live in the past but they delude themselves about it. Then in a final Gloucestershire scene which exactly parallels the after-dinner scene in Eastcheap, the three old men sit in Shallow's orchard after supper and delude themselves about the present as well. Thinking Falstaff is a person of influence at Court, Shallow curries favour with him; hearing of the King's death, Falstaff brags of his importance:

Master Robert Shallow, choose what office thou wilt in the land, 'tis thine. Pistol, I will double-charge thee with dignities.... Master Shallow, my Lord Shallow,—be what thou wilt; I am fortune's steward. ...Let us take any man's horses; the laws of England are at my commandment.   (v, iii, 129–44)

The scene is punctuated with six little snatches of song by Silence, songs prompted by the post-prandial conversations of Shallow and Falstaff. These songs serve to underline the ironic disparity between past and present, youth and age, and between the expectations of Falstaff and his companions and the fulfilment that awaits those expectations on a street in London.

Silence's first two songs are Shrovetide carols, once used to celebrate the three days of feasting and revelry that preceded the onset of Lent. Silence, too, has evidently heard 'the chimes at midnight', and probably many a carol as well in the long years of his life. 'I have been merry twice and once ere now (v, iii, 42)', he tells Falstaff. Senile and drunken at the board he probably feels that any party is a feast, and any feast a time for Shrovetide carols. 'We shall', he sings,

> Do nothing but eat, and make good cheer,
> And praise God for the merry year;
> When flesh is cheap and females dear,
> And lusty lads roam here and there
> So merrily,
> And ever among so merrily.

With Shallow's hospitable admonition to his guests, 'Be merry, be merry', Silence breaks into song again:

> Be merry, be merry, my wife has all;
> For women are shrews, both short and tall:
> 'Tis merry in hall when beards wag all,
> And welcome merry Shrove-tide.
> Be merry, be merry.

The songs are more appropriate than he knows. They celebrate a present feasting and revelry before a long lean Lent which is to come when King Henry V rejects Falstaff and his friends. The first song, hailing the glut of meat in the Lenten markets and regretting the scarcity of (suddenly Lenten-penitential) females, is probably further intended to remind an audience of Shallow's earlier boasts about his youthful amours in days long past:

I was once of Clement's Inn, where, I think they will talk of mad Shallow yet.

Sil. You were called 'lusty Shallow' then, cousin....

37

Shal. I was called any thing; and I would have done any thing indeed too, and roundly too. There was I, and little John Doit of Staffordshire, and black George Barnes, and Francis Pickbone, and Will Squele, a Cotswold man; you had not four such swinge-bucklers in all the inns o'court again: and I may say to you, we knew where the bona-robas were and had the best of them all at commandment.

(III, ii, 15–26)

The second song is a little more advanced in time; it eschews female company for a recreational night away from shrewish wives, a night of drinking with other greybeards. Neither the original tunes nor the sources of these fragmentary carols are known.

All the bona robas of earlier days are toasted in two of Silence's next three songs. The servant Davy has only to offer 'A cup of wine, sir?' and the old man starts to sing again:

> A cup of wine that's brisk and fine,
> And drink unto the leman mine;
> And a merry heart lives long-a.

Falstaff pledges a health to Silence who immediately responds:

> Fill the cup, and let come;
> I'll pledge you a mile to the bottom

And again:

> Do me right,
> And dub me knight:
> Samingo.

Behind the first and third songs may lie a drinking custom of young gallants in Shakespeare's time. The custom was first pointed out by Malone and then by Douce.[16] Illustrating the first song Douce cited Thomas Young's *Englands Bane: or, The Description of Drunkenesse* (1617), sigs. B3–B3ᵛ:

Their father the Diuell will suffer no dissentions amongst them, vntill they have executed his wil in the deepest degree of drinking, and made their sacrifice vnto him, & most commonly that is done vpon their knees being bare. The prophanenes whereof is most lamentable and destestable, being duely considered by a Christian, to thinke that that member of the body which is appointed for the seruice of God, is too often abused with the adoration of a Harlot, or a base Drunkard, as I my selfe haue seen (and to my griefe of conscience) may now say haue in presence, yea and amongst others been an actor in the businesse, when vpon our knees, after healthes to many priuate Punkes, a Health haue beene drunke to all the Whoores in the world.

Young's account, to be sure, is tinged with Puritanical horror at such boisterous doings; but it is supported by Malone's note on the third song:

It was the custom of the good fellows of Shakespeare's days to drink a very large draught of wine, and sometimes a less palatable potation, on *their knees*, to the health of their mistress. He who performed this exploit was dubb'd a *knight* for the evening.

Malone does not give his source for his information about this custom, but he cites *A Yorkshire Tragedy* (1608), sigs. A3–A3ᵛ:

Sam. Why then follow me, Ile teach you the finest humor to be drunk in, I learnd it at London last week.

Am: I faith lets heare it, lets heare it.

Sam—The bravest humor, twold do a man good to bee drunck in't, they call it knighting in London, when they drink vpon their knees.

Am. Faith that's excellent.

[*Sam.*] Come follow me, Ile giue you all the degrees ont in order.

And there are numerous other allusions to the song and the custom in the drama of Shakespeare's time.[17] Neither the sources nor music for the first two songs is known, but the original words and melody of the third song have survived in a number of manuscript copies.[18] The functions of the three songs are clear. What might be appropriate songs to lusty young London gallants provide an incongruous background for the old men sitting about Shallow's orchard. In this scene, ironically, their meretricious remembrance of things past is put into sharp contrast with the realities of desire that has outlived the performance; and they drink, and revel, and make plans for a future that has already been made vain.

The songs in *2 Henry IV* end exactly as they had begun, with a fragment of a ballad that refers to the ancient days of the past.[19] In his typically ranting fashion Pistol rushes in to announce that Prince Hal has succeeded to the throne: 'I speak of Africa and golden joys'. To which Falstaff replies in kind:

> O base Assyrian knight, what is thy news?
> Let King Cophetua know the truth thereof.   (v, iii, 105–6)

The antique reference is enough to set Silence off again with a line which is probably from the ballad 'Robin Hood and the Pinder of Wakefield'. This song like the first one sung by Falstaff in the play evokes a world of the past, a world concerned with a kind of honour and *gentilesse* that the fat old knight and his cronies in Eastcheap and Gloucestershire are far from sharing.

Aside from the specific functions mentioned above, the songs in *2 Henry IV* serve other purposes as well. As sung by Falstaff and the drunken Silence they are in themselves comic. They establish an atmosphere of rowdiness, dissolute conduct, and irresponsibility which reaches its apogee in Falstaff's cry, 'The laws of England are at my commandment'. They heighten the comic climax of the play and aggravate the downfall of Falstaff when he is rejected by King Henry V. Finally they set the new order in sharp contrast to the old. All that remains of an old world at the end of *2 Henry IV* is an aged Sir John Falstaff and his withered old companions. The world of Richard, Hotspur, and of Falstaff's youth has passed away just as surely as has the romantic world of Arthur, Lancelot, and Robin Hood. In a sense it was not Hal who rejected Falstaff at all; it was Time.

NOTES

1. In his edition of 1709; quoted in *A New Variorum Edition of Shakespeare: The Second Part of Henry the Fourth*, ed. Matthias A. Shaaber (Philadelphia, 1940), p. 584.

2. The same.

3. See, especially, chapter 1 of Wilson's *The Fortunes of Falstaff* (Cambridge, 1944), and Stoll's 'Falstaff' in his *Shakespeare Studies* (New York, 1927).

4. Pp. 584–99.

5. Harold C. Goddard, *The Meaning of Shakespeare* (Chicago, 1951), pp. 206–7, calls attention to the fact that this play episode is in a sense a 'rehearsal' of the banishment to come.

6. Henry Halford Vaughan, *New Readings and New Renderings of Shakespeare's Tragedies* (2 vols. 1878–81), I, 494.

7. *Bishop Percy's Folio Manuscript. Ballads and Romances* (3 vols. 1867–8), I, 84.

8. 'An Analytical Index to the Ballad-Entries (1557–1709) in the Registers of the Company of Stationers of London', *Studies in Philology*, XXI (1924), nos. 2107, 1951, and 2915.

9. Quotations, imitations, and parodies are to be found in Marston's *The Malcontent* (1604), sig. D1ᵛ, Beaumont and Fletcher's *The Little French Lawyer* (1647) (*Works*, ed. Waller and Glover, 1906, III, 399), Heywood's *The Rape of Lucrece* (1608), sig. C1ᵛ, Richard Johnson's *The Golden Garland of Princely Delight* (1620), sig. B3, *Choyce Drollery: Songs & Sonnets* (1656), p. 70, and in *The Golden Garland of Princely Delight* [1690], sig. B4. In his unpublished Harvard doctoral dissertation, 'English Broadside Ballad Tunes (1550–1700)' [1936], I, 17, Roy Lamson Jr. pointed out that the tune ranks as no. 17 in a list of the twenty-eight most frequently used broadside ballad tunes.

10. Since Deloney died in 1600 this ballad, if written by him, antedates the posthumous *Garland* (1631) by a considerable number of years. Copy for the *Garland* version of the ballad was undoubtedly a much earlier broadside issue.

11. *Popular Music of the Olden Time* (2 vols. 1855), I, 199, 272. Two distinct melodies went by the name 'Flying Fame', and Chappell transcribes both.

12. These opening stanzas are from a broadside copy, c. 1620–30, in the Houghton Library, Harvard, a copy described in *The Harvard Library Bulletin*, X (1956), 130–4.

13. The whole passage is a highly articulated *double entendre*. Literally it refers to the pikeman who charges in battle against the breaches and heavy guns, is wounded, and put into the hands of surgeons for treatment. The underlying meaning refers to sexual encounter and the need to undergo treatment for venereal infection. For specific interpretation see the notes, pp. 168–70, of the *Variorum Edition*, and Eric Partridge, *Shakespeare's Bawdy* (1955). As repellent as it may seem to Falstaff's modern friends to find their hero diseased in this noxious way, the fact seems clear from his own words: 'A man can no more separate age and covetousness than'a can part young limbs and lechery: but the gout galls the one, and the pox pinches the other: *and so both degrees prevent my curses*' (I, ii, 256–60). It would be gratifying to perform a general asepsis on the old knight's moral character. *De mortuis nil nisi bonum.* But it is impossible to give a clean bill of health to a man who continually infects himself.

14. See II, i, 25–41, 124–8, and II, iv, 36 ff.

15. The most poignant and realistic scenes in the play deal with such reminiscences. See III, ii and v, iii.

16. Malone in his edition of the play, 1790, and Douce in *Illustrations of Shakespeare and of Ancient Manners* (1839), p. 293.

17. See Jonson's *Epicoene* (1609) (*Works*, ed. Herford and Simpson (1937), V, 226), Lodge's and Greene's *A Looking Glasse for London and England* (1594) (*Plays and Poems*, ed. Collins (1905), I, 189), Chapman's *All Fools* (1605) (*Plays and Poems*, ed. Parrott (1914), II, 156), Massinger's *The Great Duke of Florence* (1627) (ed. Stockholm (1933), p. 59), Randoph's *The Drinking Academy* (edited from manuscript by Tannenbaum and Rollins (1930), p. 8), Marston's *Antonio and Mellida* (1602), sig. H4, and Nashe's *Summer's Last Will and Testament* (1600), ed. McKerrow (1958), III, 264.

18. Frederick W. Sternfeld, 'Lasso's Music for Shakespeare's "Samingo"', *Shakespeare Quarterly*, IX (1958), 106–16, includes a transcription of the treble setting of Lasso's music for the song, and an account of other instances of the music. See, also, John P. Cutts, 'The Original Music of a Song in *2 Henry IV*', *Shakespeare Quarterly*, VII, (1956), 385–92.

19. The source is probably 'Robin Hood and the Jolly Pinder of Wakefield', broadside copies of which are preserved in the Bagford, Pepys, Crawford, Roxburghe, and Wood ballad collections. Falstaff also refers to this ballad in *The Merry Wives of Windsor*, I, i, 177. Curiously enough in the Pepys copy this ballad is printed together with the ballad from which Falstaff's own fragment of song earlier in the play is derived.

SHAKESPEARE'S SONNETS AND THE ELIZABETHAN SONNETEERS

BY

JOAN GRUNDY

In a sonnet addressed to Spenser, Keats remarks,

> The flower must drink the nature of the soil,
> Before it can put forth its blossoming.

This describes very well Shakespeare's relationship to his fellow-sonneteers. However different the blossom he produced, their work, their example, provided the soil from which it sprang. The relationship is a complex one, and I wish to examine only one aspect of it here, namely Shakespeare's attitude to the accepted 'poetic' of the sonnet-sequence, in the hope that this may throw light upon the way in which the tradition has been adapted to suit an individual talent.

Convention is so much the ruling power in the Renaissance sonnet-sequence that even the principles and assumptions upon which the sonneteer claims to be writing are themselves a part of the convention. Thus the 'poetic' which I am about to outline is in its context what we might call the governing conceit, consistent and true only within its own largely artificial limits. The sonneteer for the most part wears a double mask—as poet, no less than as lover. One would not wish to take his critical statements out of their context and add them to Gregory Smith's collection of Elizabethan critical essays. Within their context, however, in the special world, the charmed if not always charming circle which we enter whenever we open a collection of Elizabethan sonnets, they are valid. And occasionally, when the poet is using the convention without being confined within it, they acquire a validity beyond it, and conceit becomes statement.

Fundamental to the sonnet-writer's poetic is the idea of the poem as a speaking picture. It is used with varying degrees of awareness and emphasis, sometimes being set at the very start of the sequence, as in Sidney's

> Loving in truth, and fain in verse my love to show,
> That She, dear She, might take some pleasure of my pain,
> Pleasure might cause her read, reading might make her know,
> Knowledge might pity win, and pity grace obtain,
> I sought fit words to paint the blackest face of woe;

at other times being introduced later with apparent casualness so that it perhaps appears as no more than one image among many: for example, in Spenser's *Amoretti* it appears in sonnet XVII, in Griffin's *Fidessa* in sonnet XIX. But whatever emphasis the poet gives to the idea in the form of the conceit or its actual placing or development, it appears to be always present in his mind as the shaping and directing idea of the poem as a whole. The picture may be of the beloved's

41

beauty or of the lover's sufferings, but usually combines both: thus Barnes, using the common variant of the picture in the mirror, writes

> Mistress! Behold in this true speaking Glass,
> Thy Beauties graces!...
> But, in this Mirror, equally compare
> Thy matchless beauty, with mine endless grief.
>
> (*Parthenophil and Parthenophe*, I, 1–2, 9–10)

and Daniel puts the position clearly:

> Then take this picture which I heere present thee,
> Limned with a Pensill not all vnworthy;
> Heere see the giftes that God and nature lent thee,
> Heere read thy selfe, and what I suffred for thee.   (*Delia*, XXXIIII, 5–8)

'Heere see...', 'Heere read...': each implies, and is eloquent of the other: the vivid picture of her beauty testifies to the extent of his pain; the picture of his pain bespeaks the greatness of her beauty; or, as Henry Constable puts it,

> payne in verse
> Loue doth in payne, beautie in loue appeare.   (*Sonnets*, III, iii, 6)

Pain, love, and beauty, each expressive of the other, are thus the subject of the sonneteer's portrait-art. As we have already noticed, a common variation of this basic idea is that of the poem, not as a painted picture, but as a mirror. The two images are so close as to be often fused: thus Griffin asserts,

> My Pain paints out my love in doleful Verse.
> (The lively Glass wherein she may behold it!),   (*Fidessa*, XIX, 1–2)

and even Sidney answers his own question,

> How can words ease, which are
> The glasses of thy daily-vexing care?

with the thought,

> Oft cruel fights well pictured-forth do please.
>
> (*Astrophel and Stella*, XXXIV, 2–4)

Whichever image is used, the emphasis is on expressiveness, on the fullness and truthfulness of the representation. Sometimes it is suggested that the poet's face or heart provides a more effective reflection of the lady's beauty than the mirror she holds in her hand: this is well known from Spenser's

> Leaue lady in your glasse of christall clene,   (*Amoretti*, XLV, 1)

or Daniel's

> O why dooth *Delia* credite so her glasse.   (XXIX, 1)

Face, heart, and poem receive and give back the lady's beauty, sometimes directly, sometimes indirectly, and, with a neat duality worthy of Dorian Gray, self-portraiture and the portraying of the beloved are seen as at once separate and the same. The sonneteer's self-consciousness is as an artist: he creates, and is constantly asserting that he creates. If the poem is a mirror, it is one which he likes to look both at and *into*, and before which he never tires of parading. However humble as a lover, he is usually proud and even boastful as an artist: Delia's picture is 'limned with a Pensill not all vnworthy', and it is 'with a feeling skill' that Sidney 'paints his hell'. The only exception to this self-confidence is likely to be when the lover claims that the subject is beyond the power of art to express, as in Spenser's assertion that her 'glorious pourtraict' 'cannot expressed be by any art'—

> A greater craftesmans hand thereto doth neede,
> that can express the life of things indeed—   (XVII, 13–14)

or as in Chapman's,

> Her virtues then above my verse must raise her,
> For words want art, and Art wants words to praise her.
>   (*A Coronet for his Mistress Philosophy*, VIII, 13–14)

As Hallett Smith has pointed out in his *Elizabethan Poetry* in relation to Sidney, the sonnet-writer is usually aware of addressing two audiences, his beloved, and the general public, and at times plays off one against the other. Most sonneteers indeed present us with a triangular relationship, with 'the world' playing an indispensable role of spectator, usually admiring, but capable on occasion of criticism and envy too, as for instance in *Amoretti*, LXXXV,

> The world that cannot deeme of worthy things,
> When I doe praise her, say I doe but flatter.

Daniel especially keeps 'the world' in view: 'had she not beene faire and thus vnkinde', 'the world had neuer knowne' of his sorrows; as it is, the world may mark and judge:

> Let this suffice, the world yet may see;
> The fault is hers, though mine the hurt must bee.   (XV, 13–14)

And his poems abound in such statements. For Daniel, as for Spenser and others, this world audience comprises future, and even occasionally past, as well as present generations. It is here that the idea, particularly characteristic of *Delia*, of the poem as a 'monument' comes in: monument, mirror, and picture are closely linked, since it is the picture in the mirror that will preserve the beauty of the beloved for future generations to see. Implicit in all such claims upon the world's attention is the idea that the beloved is the nonpareil for beauty and, usually, for cruelty also: this in its turn makes the lover the unique exemplar of suffering, so that altogether it is not surprising that the spectacle should provide material for 'the worlds wonder' (a common phrase in sonnet-literature).

This poetic of the sonnet-form is not, of course, an English creation. The ideas are for the most part commonplaces of sonneteering wherever it is practised, even by Petrarch himself. But the Elizabethan sonneteers exemplify it so fully that it is reasonable to suppose that Shakespeare's acquaintance with it came principally through them. His kinship with them in this respect, his willingness to be one of them by accepting their basic assumptions, needs little demonstration. His poem is a love-poem, and its central purpose is, according to his oft-repeated statements, to blazon the beloved's beauty, for future generations even more than for present ones. Thus it too aims to be a speaking picture, of that lasting kind which serves as a monument:

So long as men can breathe, or eyes can see,
So long lives this and this gives life to thee (xviii, 13–14)

Your monument shall be my gentle verse,
Which eyes not yet created shall o'er-read. (lxxxi, 9–10)

That the beloved is regarded as the nonpareil, 'the very archetypal pattern and substance' of beauty and truth, to quote J. W. Lever,[1] cannot be adequately illustrated by a few lines: the idea is the base and fabric, the very life-blood, of these poems. All these ideas, except that past generations, not future ones, are in question, are brought together in sonnet cvi, with its concluding emphasis on wonder:

For we, which now behold these present days,
Have eyes to wonder, but lack tongues to praise.

The reader needs little reminder of such celebrated passages.

This, however, is only a beginning. Shakespeare, in his usual comprehensive way, shares a common platform with other sonneteers. But he does not stay there. He develops and expands some elements and rejects others, so that we are led to conclude, in this as in so many respects, 'This is, and is not, a Petrarchan sonnet-sequence'. Thus he makes little use of the idea of the poem as a mirror. His awareness of it is clear from sonnet ciii, which may be compared with the sonnets of Spenser and Daniel quoted earlier:

Look in your glass, and there appears a face
That over-goes my blunt invention quite. (6–7)

He recognizes too its close association with the 'eternalizing' theme; at least, his use of the image in a different context suggests this:

Thou art thy mother's glass, and she in thee
Calls back the lovely April of her prime. (iii, 9–10)

His otherwise complete neglect of it is probably to be connected with his attitude to the closely-related idea of the poem as a painted picture. Even this idea, although it seems implicit in his claims concerning his poetry's immortalizing powers, is never explicitly accepted, except in sonnet xvi, where it is subordinated to the idea that the young man should perpetuate himself through generation:

And you must live, drawn by your own sweet skill,

and in sonnet ci, which questions the validity of such activity. The reason why Shakespeare does not commit himself explicitly to the idea seems to be that he cherishes a higher ambition: he has what we might call a Pygmalion complex and hopes that somehow the image he creates may be real. Thus there is constant emphasis upon the *life* that will be preserved in his verses, for which the lines already quoted from sonnet xviii may serve as one example among many. The idea of poetry conferring a 'life beyond life' through fame is, of course, familiar enough, although actually (in Elizabethan sonnet-literature as a whole) the theme is not so popular as may be supposed from the frequency with which we meet it in Shakespeare and Daniel. Nor is it normally used with the urgency, the desired near-literalness of the word 'life', that it has in Shakespeare. Thus while Daniel chiefly implies that his verse will be a *record* of the past, and will confer the kind of immortality that comes through fame, Shakespeare seems to be reaching out after something more truly vital; his desire, however impossible of achievement, is by recreating his loved one within the medium of language to stay the flux of time. Daniel is talking of the permanent recording of the past, Shakespeare mainly of its arresting. Daniel, for instance, emphasises the perpetuating of Delia's *name* (in the sense of fame)—in sonnets XXXV, XXXIX, XLVI, XLVII, XLVIII—whereas Shakespeare talks about preserving the young man's life, truth, self, being, but never, in this context, merely his name.² The conventional notion of the portrait is thus always dissolving in his verse into something less rigid and definable, yet at the same time it provides a point of departure, or area of reference, for these transcendencies. The poem is to be a picture, but not a *mere* picture.

The increased emphasis on the *life* to be conferred by his portrait replaces, in Shakespeare's verse, the normal sonneteer's emphasis upon his own '*feeling* skill': the identification of beauty, love, and pain is not made. Shakespeare does write about his own sufferings, but un-self-consciously and without self-pity. His love is, literally, not self-regarding; he has therefore no interest in displaying or surveying it in his verse, and no grounds for equating self-portraiture with the portraying of the beloved. This introduces a fundamental change: the sonnet-sequence in Shakespeare's hands loses its affinity with the love-complaint. Here are no 'tears of fancie', no 'blackest face of woe'. The contrast with Daniel's *Delia* is particularly striking, in view of their many affinities. Daniel leaves us in no doubt concerning the character of his poem: these are 'fatal anthems, lamentable songs', 'wailing verse', the product of an 'afflicted Muse'. Indeed, his description of his verse as 'A wailing deskant on the sweetest ground', played by the Muse upon his heart-strings (XLVII), aptly summarizes the triangular relationship under discussion. Shakespeare, on the other hand, speaks of himself in sonnet XXX as possessing 'an eye, unused to flow', and, as far as this sequence is concerned, this is true.

Something of the same self-effacement is seen in his attitude to that fashionable judge and arbitrator in the sonneteer's drama, 'the world'. J. W. Lever has observed that 'the world' supplies the role almost of a fourth personage in Shakespeare's sequence; we ourselves have already noted its appearance in the work of his fellow-poets. At times he does write of it as the interested spectator of his personal drama, but on two occasions at least he produces a significant variation on the common theme of the world, unenchanted and, in the poet's eyes, coldly envious and censorious, condemning his excessive praise of his beloved as flattery. In each case, Shakespeare turns the idea against himself. Thus in sonnet LXXI he warns his beloved,

> But let your love even with my life decay,
> Lest the wise world should look into your moan
> And mock you with me after I am gone.   (12–14)

And in sonnet CXLVIII, on the dark lady, he asks,

> If that be fair whereon my false eyes dote,
> What means the world to say it is not so?   (5–6)

where, ironically, the world is right. But, generally speaking, he shows a notable lack of interest in what the world thinks of himself, or of his sonnets. There is nothing akin to Daniel's

> Beholde the message of my iust complayning,
> That shewes the world how much my griefe imported,   (*Delia*, L, 3–4)

or even to Lodge's

> Show to the world, though poor and scant my skill is,
> How sweet thoughts be, that are but thoughts of Phillis.
>
> (*Phillis*, I, 13–14)

It is, rather, he himself who looks on, and views the world in its relationship to his beloved. The latter is 'the world's fresh ornament' (I, 9). Sometimes he is in direct relationship with the world, and of equal stature with it:

> Ah! if thou issueless shalt hap to die,
> The world will wail thee, like a makeless wife;
> The world will be thy widow, and still weep
> That thou no form of thee hast left behind,   (IX, 3–6)

sometimes the world shrinks to nothingness in comparison with him:

> For nothing this wide universe I call,
> Save thou, my rose, in it thou art my all.   (CIX, 13–14)

Such statements bring 'the world' into the sonnet-drama, not as spectator, but as participator. It would perhaps be going too far to suggest that Shakespeare was aware of all this; but he has, it would appear, in such instances subtly transformed a familiar and fairly rigid feature of the sonnet convention, and given it new depth and vibrancy.

Finally, there is that fairly large group of sonnets to be considered, in which Shakespeare reflects on his own practice and compares it with that of others. Similar discussions occur in only one other Elizabethan sequence—*Astrophel and Stella*. Shakespeare and Sidney alone among Elizabethan sonneteers[3] question the aims and methods, in other words the values, of the Petrarchan convention. Among continental writers, as Sidney probably knew, anti-Petrarchanism was one of the recognized and legitimate stances; its adoption did not entail any expulsion from the tribe, or any desire for expulsion. The question we are faced with in both Sidney's case and Shakespeare's is: How far do they really *mean* what they say? Are we still within the enclosed circle of convention, where no lies are told because nothing is affirmed, or have we broken away from it? Is Shakespeare, as Richard B. Young has suggested Sidney is doing in 'You that do search for every purling spring' (xv), raising the critical problem of sincerity for merely rhetorical purposes?[4] We seem in examining such sonnets to be on a circular journey, wondering where finally to halt; whether Art or Nature should have the last word. And it may be that there is a kind of naïve sophistication in immediately supposing it to be Art. The problem in Shakespeare's case and Sidney's is not, however, identical, since if we take, as we must, the poet's general practice into consideration, we are more likely to concede Shakespeare's claims to have avoided the faults he censures than we are Sidney's. True, he does more than warble his native woodnotes wild, but he has not that *exhibitionism* of style which is a normal characteristic of the Petrarchan poet, good or bad. At the same time, his critical comments do often recall

Sidney's, both in content and expression, and it seems likely that there was some conscious imitation or reminiscence here. Sonnet XXI and the celebrated sonnet CXXX ('My Mistress eyes...') have much in common with sonnets III and VI of *Astrophel and Stella*. There is the same scornful enumeration of the hyperboles of the fashionable sonneteer, and the same assertion of the writer's own simplicity and the sufficiency of his subject. But Shakespeare's argument is more straightforward than Sidney's. He is merely asserting that the beauty of his beloved will stand comparison with the best, though not with sun and stars and so on; Sidney under a show of modesty is claiming superior powers of expression for himself:

> For me, in sooth, no Muse but one I know,
> Phrases and problems from my reach do grow,
> And strange things cost too dear for my poor sprites.
> How then? even thus—in Stella's face I read
> What Love and Beauty be, then all my deed
> But copying is, what in her Nature writes. (III, 9–14)

These lines, however, may also be compared with a passage in Shakespeare's eighty-fourth sonnet:

> Lean penury within that pen doth dwell
> That to his subject lends not some small glory;
> But he that writes of you, if he can tell
> That you are you, so dignifies his story,
> Let him but copy what in you is writ,
> Not making worse what nature made so clear,
> And such a counterpart shall fame his wit,
> Making his style admired every where. (LXXXIV, 5–12)

This is Shakespeare at his most Sidneyan: the central image, that of copying Nature's writing, is the same, and the conclusion, that this will make the writer famous for his style, is actually more typical of Sidney than it is of Shakespeare. (See, for example, *Astrophel and Stella*, sonnets XV and XC.) Even here, however, there is an essential difference in attitude. The implication in Sidney's sonnet that the poet has become a new and more successful kind of plagiarist—Nature's ape, not Pindar's —is missing in Shakespeare's. Instead, the point Shakespeare is making is that it is impossible for him to enhance his subject; he will do enough if he can but reproduce it. In other words, the centre of interest in Sidney's sonnet, for Sidney, is his own achievement; in Shakespeare's, it is his subject, and the key words are 'if he can tell / That you are you'. And this difference in emphasis, in orientation of interest, is typical. Sidney's strictures upon other sonneteers are really secondary to his main theme in his 'critical sonnets' (I, III, XV, XXVIII, for example), which is not a condemnation of eloquence, but an expression of his joy at having found a shorter way to it, having found its very source in fact, in Stella. Shakespeare too acknowledges that his beloved gives his pen 'both skill and argument' (sonnet C; Sidney, in sonnet XV, has the phrase 'love and skill'), but he is generally more attentive to the latter than the former. Sidney's Muse, unlike Shakespeare's, is never 'tongue-tied' (except in the situation described in the opening sonnet, when he 'took wrong ways'). It is exuberant and confident, airily overlooking (for the most part—sonnet L is an exception) the 'intolerable wrestle with words and meanings' that is involved even in copying Nature, as indeed Sidney himself over-looks it in the *Apology*. Shakespeare, on the other hand, is so conscious of the inadequacy of words that at one point he reaches the conclusion that it

> shall be most my glory, being dumb. (LXXXIII, 10)

Of course, Shakespeare does write; Sidney does wrestle with words. But the attitudes they take up are characteristic and significant. Sidney begs 'no subject to use eloquence' (XXVIII); he does not need to, since he has one, so to speak, at his finger-tips ('And Love doth hold my hand and makes me write', XC). Shakespeare, on the other hand, begs no eloquence for his subject, since it requires none.

This leads us back to the consideration of Shakespeare's quarrel with his fellow-sonneteers, in particular his 'rival poets'. Shakespeare's criticisms are more drastic than Sidney's, which, as we saw, are at one level scarcely criticisms at all, their main purpose being to praise Stella and at the same time to commend his own verse. For Shakespeare his own 'true plain words' and 'what strained touches rhetoric can lend' his rivals' verse are at genuine and open war. How close his expression comes to Sidney's is shown by the comparable lines in Sidney's fifteenth sonnet,

> those far-fet helps be such
> As do bewray a want of inward touch. (XV, 9–10)

Yet essentially his position is close to that of Wordsworth in the preface to the *Lyrical Ballads*—much closer than Sidney's is. He refuses to 'interweave any foreign splendour of his own' with the beauty of his beloved, knowing that this is more likely to impair than to enhance it:

> I never saw that you did painting need
> And therefore to your fair no painting set. (LXXXIII, 1–2)

This is the error into which his rivals have fallen:

> And their gross painting might be better used
> Where cheeks need blood; in thee it is abused. (LXXXII, 13–14)

In the sonnets in which he treats this theme (LXXII–LXXXV, CI, CIII, and, to some extent, XXI, XXXII, and LXXIX), Shakespeare shows an obsessive anxiety, quite lacking in Sidney, lest the colours of rhetoric should falsify the picture of his beloved. He is not merely being superior about his fellow-sonneteers: he is expressing his own artistic dilemma. This seems concentrated for him in the idea of 'praise'. This is the problem he faces: how to present the beloved directly, without praising, or how to praise without seeming to flatter. Sidney certainly had raised the question, but only incidentally:

> What may words say, or what may words not say,
> Where Truth itself must speak like Flattery? (XXXV, 1–2)

He had concluded:

> Not thou by praise, but praise in thee is rais'd.
> It is a praise to praise, when thou art prais'd. (*ibid.* 13–14)

Shakespeare does not find the answer so easily. In sonnet XXI he seems to equate praise with hyperbole and therefore with flattery, concluding

> I will not praise that purpose not to sell.

Yet in sonnet LX he places his hopes on it:

> And yet to times in hope my verse shall stand,
> Praising thy worth, despite his cruel hand. (13–14)

In sonnet LXXXII his concern is that this worth is 'a limit past my praise'; in CIII he asserts rather the futility of such praising:

> The argument all bare is of more worth
> Than when it hath my added praise beside!

In LXXXIV he shows himself suspicious of praise of the wrong kind; the poem begins

> Who is it that says most? which can say more
> Than this rich praise, that you alone are you?

and ends

> You to your beauteous blessings add a curse,
> Being fond on praise, which makes your praises worse.

There is praise and praise: that fact explains much, not only in Shakespeare's criticism of his fellow-sonneteers, but also in his whole relationship to them, and the personal adjustments he makes to the convention.

It is no new discovery that the love that Shakespeare expresses in his sonnets is of a peculiarly selfless kind: the point has often been made. What I hope has emerged from the foregoing comparison is that this fact governs his attitude to the conventional sonneteering 'poetic' in every aspect of it, and equally determines the use to which he puts it. There are, of course, sonnets in which he is merely playing the fashionable game—sonnets XLIII–XLVI, for instance, which employ the fashionable themes of sleeplessness, absence, and the war between eye and heart—in which he does exhibit the ordinary sonneteer's self-concentration, as he does also, to ironic effect, in many of those concerning the dark lady. But in the core of the sequence—the sonnets concerning the young man—he both re-examined the sonneteer's 'poetic', and gave it, through his practice, a philosophical and critical depth that it had not possessed before. In this, as in so much else, he turned the dreams and fancies of his predecessors into truths, for truth, not fancy, was his subject.

NOTES

1. *The Elizabethan Love-Sonnet* (1956), p. 184.
2. In sonnet CVIII, he has the line 'Even as when first I hallow'd thy fair name', but this is clearly a deliberate echo of the Lord's Prayer, taking up the phrase 'like prayers divine' in line 5.
3. Drayton occasionally shows something of the same critical spirit, but not often, and he may be directly imitating Sidney.
4. Richard B. Young, *English Petrarke: a Study of Sidney's Astrophel and Stella* (Yale, 1958), p. 6.

LOVE'S CONFINED DOOM

BY

M. M. MAHOOD

I

The present trend of criticism is bringing Shakespeare's poems and his plays together. A dramatic element is recognized in short poems of many kinds—Shakespeare's sonnets, Keats's odes, the lyrics of Yeats. Like plays they attempt to give through some fiction (the truest poetry is the most feigning) form, and so meaning, to experiences whose real-life occasions are now lost to us and are, in any case, none of our business. A sonnet cannot help in the interpretation of a play, nor can the play throw any light on the sonnet's meaning, if the two works are thought of as belonging to different grades of imitation; if the sonnet, for example, is a snippet of biography or a poetic exercise. But if the two kinds of poetry are regarded, despite their differences in magnitude, as products of the same imaginative process, then our reading of the one can illumine our understanding of the other. In particular, these cross-references can lead us to a fuller understanding of the main theme of the sonnets: the complex and profoundly disturbed relationship of the poet with the friend to whom most of the sequence is addressed.[1]

Sonnet XXXIII provides an example of the elucidation that such cross-references can afford:

> Full many a glorious morning have I seen
> Flatter the mountain-tops with sovereign eye,
> Kissing with golden face the meadows green,
> Gilding pale streams with heavenly alchemy;
> Anon permit the basest clouds to ride
> With ugly rack on his celestial face,
> And from the forlorn world his visage hide,
> Stealing unseen to west with this disgrace:
> Even so my sun one early morn did shine
> With all-triumphant splendour on my brow;
> But out, alack! he was but one hour mine;
> The region cloud hath mask'd him from me now.
> Yet him for this my love no whit disdaineth;
> Suns of the world may stain, when heaven's sun staineth.

It is not at all easy, in reading this, to grasp what the friend has done—if the clouds represent some blot on his reputation with the world at large, or the relationship of poet and friend has been clouded by the friend's unkindness. Is the clouding involuntary or deliberate? The grammatical structure of the second quatrain leaves us in doubt whether the sun hides his visage, stealing away in shame, or whether, untouched himself, he simply permits the clouds to hide it. 'Celestial' implies that the friend, like the sun, belongs to the immutable order of heavenly bodies who are not themselves affected in any way by the rack of clouds passing below them in the sublunary world's insubstantial pageant. Yet if the friend merely allows his glory to be eclipsed and is himself in no way blemished it is hard to see what Shakespeare intended by 'disgrace', since the word whenever used by him (with the possible exception of 'And then grace us in the disgrace of death' in *Love's Labour's Lost*, where it can mean 'disfigurement') has a derogatory meaning. 'Stain' also is a teasingly imprecise word. It can mean to darken, or even to eclipse or to be eclipsed (as in *Antony and Cleopatra*, III, iv, 27), though a much commoner meaning is to blemish or to become blemished.

If we turn to the plays for parallels in thought, diction or imagery which may throw light on Shakespeare's intention in sonnet XXXIII, we are immediately struck by two passages which bear a close resemblance to the second quatrain of the sonnet. When Richard II appears on the walls of Flint Castle, Hotspur exclaims

> See, see, King Richard doth himself appear,
> As doth the blushing discontented sun
> From out the fiery portal of the east,
> When he perceives the envious clouds are bent
> To dim his glory and to stain the track
> Of his bright passage to the occident.

To which the Duke of York adds

> Yet looks he like a king: behold, his eye,
> As bright as is the eagle's, lightens forth
> Controlling majesty: alack, alack, for woe,
> That any harm should stain so fair a show !   (III, iii, 62–71)

The verbal resemblances between this and sonnet XXXIII are close, but no closer than others to be found in a passage of *Henry IV, Part I*. Hal, parting from his Eastcheap companions, lets the audience into the secret of his relationship with them:

> Yet herein will I imitate the sun,
> Who doth permit the base contagious clouds
> To smother up his beauty from the world,
> That, when he please again to be himself,
> Being wanted, he may be more wonder'd at,
> By breaking through the foul and ugly mists
> Of vapours that did seem to strangle him.   (I, ii, 220–6)

In the first passage the sun image is used of a weak man who, for all his show of controlling majesty, is controlled by his subjects; in the second, of a strong man who conceals his true nature for reasons of policy. This contrast heightens rather than solves the contradictions of sonnet XXXIII. But fortunately the plays also offer a number of parallels with the sonnet's magnificent opening quatrain which may take us a little further in understanding the poem.

The first of these is in *Henry VIII*, when Wolsey, disgraced by the King ('That sun, I pray, may never set!'), laments that

> No sun shall ever usher forth mine honours,
> Or gild again the noble troops that waited
> Upon my smiles. (III, ii, 410–12)

The context is one of betrayal; however hard Wolsey seeks, like the poet in sonnet after sonnet (for example, XXXV, which is closely connected with XXXIII and in which 'Thy adverse party is thy advocate') to justify the King, every audience is perturbed by Henry's treachery. The use of 'gild' is significant. Shakespeare nearly always employs the word in a derogatory sense to suggest the brilliance that masks corruption: 'England shall double gild his treble guilt'; 'men are but gilded loam'; 'the gilded puddle'; 'gilded tombs do worms infold'. Goneril is 'this gilded serpent'. Even a seemingly neutral use of the word turns out to be ambiguous. When Antony sends a jewel to Cleopatra after his parting with her, the queen greets the messenger with the words

> coming from him, that great medicine hath
> With his tinct gilded thee. (I, v, 36–7)

Gold is cordial. Antony is life-giving, 'sovereign' like the sun. Yet at this moment he is bound for Rome and marriage with Octavia. A mainspring of the play's action is Cleopatra's uncertainty as to whether Antony is dust a little gilt or gilt o'er-dusted. This is exactly the uncertainty in which the poet of the sonnets stands in relation to his friend.

'Alchemy', like 'gild', was not a word which necessarily implied deception to the sixteenth-century reader. But it too is used by Shakespeare in contexts of betrayal. As J. W. Lever has shown[2] there is a meaningful resemblance between the opening of sonnet XXXIII and the lines in *King John* in which the King, having treacherously abandoned the cause of Constance and her son Arthur by agreeing to the French match, declares of the marriage day

> To solemnize this day the glorious sun
> Stays in his course and plays the alchemist,
> Turning with splendour of his precious eye
> The meagre cloddy earth to glittering gold. (III, i, 77–80)

Even more interesting is the way the word is used in *Julius Caesar*:

> O, he sits high in all the people's hearts:
> And that which would appear offence in us,
> His countenance, like richest alchemy,
> Will change to virtue and to worthiness. (I, iii, 157–60)

Although Cassius gives warm assent to this 'right well conceited' description of Brutus, the play itself leaves us in lasting doubt over the effect of such alchemy. Does it in fact turn the assassination into a golden deed, or does it only gild over the conspirators' guilt? Public virtue, Shakespeare hints here and elsewhere in the plays, never cancels out private wrong, and the noblest Roman of them all is branded with the lasting reproach of *Et tu, Brute*.

To Coleridge the opening of sonnet XXXIII represented one mark of the poetic imagination at

its best: its ability to transfer a human and intellectual life to images of nature.³ Just as Venus'
sense of loss at Adonis' departure is precisely matched by the experience of watching a shooting
star vanish in the night sky, so Shakespeare finds in the treacherous overclouding of a bright
summer's day the exact image for his disappointment in his friend's deliberate coldness. This
disappointment is not the almost impersonal regret felt by Hotspur and York at Richard's
weaknesses; it is the personal pain that Henry V could give his old companion, Falstaff. So much
is suggested by the beginning of sonnet XXXIV—'Why didst thou promise such a beauteous day',
where the hurt is scarcely healed by the tears the friend sheds. 'And they are rich and ransom all
ill deeds' may well be spoken with deep irony to the man who thinks his patronage can pay for
his unkindness. For in italicizing the word 'Flatter' in his quotation, Coleridge unerringly
indicated the tone of sonnet XXXIII and the succeeding sonnet. Flattery forebodes treachery.
What Shakespeare dreads in his friend is not the folly of youth—that he is almost eager to
condone—but the cold strength of maturity.

II

If Thorpe's arrangement of the sonnets has any significance, sonnet XXXIII represents the first
cloud across the friendship, and the poet never subsequently speaks with the simple trust that we
find, say, in sonnet XXIX. When Shakespeare later made use of the image of the rising lark which
supplies the unforgettable sestet of that sonnet, he gives it a bitter setting; it becomes the incidental music to Cloten's attempt to corrupt Posthumus' wife. And when, within the sonnet
sequence itself, Shakespeare returns in sonnet XCI to the theme of love's riches as compensation
for the world's neglect—'And having thee, of all men's pride I boast'—the final, misgiving
couplet quite alters the sonnet's effect:

> Wretched in this alone, that thou mayst take
> All this away and me most wretched make.

Another sonnet concerned with the friendship's value is the forty-eighth, which contrasts the
care the poet has taken to stow away his material wealth on leaving for a journey with the way
his most precious possession of all, the friend himself, is left 'the prey to every vulgar thief':

> Thee have I not lock'd up in any chest,
> Save where thou art not, though I feel thou art,
> Within the gentle closure of my breast,
> From whence at pleasure thou mayst come and part.

The lingering monosyllabic line 'Save where thou art not...' is heavy with mistrust. Such a
mistrust is experienced by the Helena of *A Midsummer Night's Dream*, whose affection has been
so freely and foolishly given and who still cannot quite believe, when all the mistakes of a midsummer night are over, that Demetrius is hers:

> And I have found Demetrius like a jewel,
> Mine own, and not mine own.   (IV, i, 195–6)

The motif of a treasure in a casket which occurs several times in the sonnets is of course an
integral part of *The Merchant of Venice*. Here the critics draw our attention to one particularly

close parallel. Bassanio, making his choice of the leaden casket, moralizes over the way the world is still deceived with ornament:

> So are those crisped snaky golden locks
> Which make such wanton gambols with the wind,
> Upon supposed fairness, often known
> To be the dowry of a second head,
> The skull that bred them in the sepulchre. (III, ii, 92–6)

Sonnets LXVII and LXVIII also protest at the deceptions of the time, which are held to accord ill with the friend's 'truth'. His beauty is his own as beauty was in the days

> Before the golden tresses of the dead,
> The right of sepulchres, were shorn away,
> To live a second life on second head;
> Ere beauty's dead fleece made another gay.

The poet's intention seems to be that both Bassanio and the friend should stand for truth in a naughty world. Sonnet LXVII in fact strengthens this connection by saying that nowadays Nature is bankrupt—'Beggar'd of blood to blush through lively veins'; and Bassanio's wealth, he tells Portia, all flows in his veins. But though he is frank enough to tell her this when he first comes wooing he does not then tell her what he later confesses, that he is 'worse than nothing' and that he is in fact indebted to Antonio for coming like a day in April 'To show how costly summer was at hand'. It is unfashionable at present to regard Bassanio as a fortune-hunter, yet in this same scene Gratiano puts the facts of the matter honestly enough when he says 'We are the Jasons, we have won the fleece'. If generations of critics have been perplexed by the discrepancies between Shakespeare's apparent intentions in portraying Bassanio and the character who emerges from the play, the reason may be that Shakespeare's presentation of the character is related to a real-life discrepancy between what he wishes his friend to be and what he fears he is. So in the sonnets, with their many verbal parallels to *The Merchant of Venice*: Shakespeare strains in sonnet LXVII and sonnet LXVIII to dissociate his friend from the corruption of the times and in sonnet LXIX blames those times for adding to his friend's fair flower 'the rank smell of weeds'; yet the collection as a whole shows him to be haunted by the fear that his friend is all the time a lily that festers.

Such a re-reading of *The Merchant of Venice* in the light of the sonnets helps us towards an answer to the question with which the play opens: why is the Merchant himself so sad? Already in the first scene Antonio hints at the true source of his sadness:

> My ventures are not in one bottom trusted,
> Nor to one place; nor is my whole estate
> Upon the fortune of this present year:
> Therefore my merchandise makes me not sad. (I, i, 42–5)

Discriminatory stress here falls on *bottom, place, merchandise*; Antonio has not entrusted all his wealth to one ship, but he has entrusted all his affection to one man and is obsessed by thoughts of the hazards he runs in this venture. In the story, as Shakespeare shapes it out of the casket tale and the tale of the cruel bond, Bassanio is faithful to Antonio, whose fears are therefore ground-less. But they are none the less real to the audience. Antonio begins as he ends, the odd man out, awakening in the audience a sympathy which is extraneous to the play's general effect and so quite different from any emotions which Shylock may arouse. In Antonio's readiness to stake all for his friend, his parting from him, his letter, his willing resignation, we find the dramatic expression of that 'fear of trust' at which Shakespeare hints also in Bassanio's speech on orna-ment, and which runs through so many sonnets to find, perhaps, its most eloquent expression in sonnet xc:

> Ah, do not, when my heart hath 'scaped this sorrow,
> Come in the rearward of a conquer'd woe;
> Give not a windy night a rainy morrow,
> To linger out a purposed overthrow.
> If thou wilt leave me, do not leave me last,
> When other petty griefs have done their spite,
> But in the onset come; so shall I taste
> At first the very worst of fortune's might.

The same fear of trust may be the case of a similar disproportion in another of Shakespeare's middle comedies, *Twelfth Night*. The Antonio of that play feels for Sebastian a devotion which belongs to an altogether different order of experience from the Duke's infatuation with Olivia or Olivia's mourning for her dead brother. Viola's silent passion comes within reach of it, and for this reason she is deeply moved by Antonio's reproaches to her for not yielding his purse (a situation handled with cheerful heartlessness in *The Comedy of Errors*). Bewildered as she is by this meaningless demand, she can recognize his anguish of disillusion, an anguish oddly misplaced in Illyria:

> Let me speak a little. This youth that you see here
> I snatch'd one half out of the jaws of death,
> Relieved him with such sanctity of love,
> And to his image, which methought did promise
> Most venerable worth, did I devotion...
> But O how vile an idol proves this god!
> Thou hast, Sebastian, done good feature shame.
> In nature there's no blemish but the mind;
> None can be call'd deform'd but the unkind:
> Virtue is beauty, but the beauteous evil
> Are empty trunks o'erflourish'd by the devil. (III, iv, 393–404)

Two persistent themes of the doubting sonnets—the youth's beauty, promising 'most venerable worth' and the poet's worshipping devotion—are to be found here, and Antonio's speech of further reproach in the last act adds another: the contrast between the speaker's spendthrift affection and the friend's careful calculations of the risks involved:

> His life I gave him and did thereto add
> My love, *without retention or restraint,*
> All his in dedication; for his sake
> Did I expose myself, pure for his love,

Into the danger of this adverse town;
Drew to defend him when he was beset:
Where being apprehended, his false cunning,
Not meaning to partake with me in danger,
Taught him to face me out of his acquaintance,
And grew a twenty years removed thing.   (v, i, 83–92)

This relationship of Antonio to Sebastian stands up like a great inselberg of eroded experience in the green landscape of comedy. And in a history play of the same period, *Henry V*, surprising prominence is given to the theme of trust betrayed, in Henry's eloquent reproaches to the traitor Scroop. The loosely episodic construction of the play is not injured by the stress Shakespeare lays on an incident which is briefly treated by the chroniclers. But this emphasis once again suggests that Shakespeare was haunted by the fear that his self-possessed friend would one day repudiate him:

O, how hast thou with jealousy infected
The sweetness of affiance! Show men dutiful?...
Free from gross passion or of mirth or anger,
Constant in spirit, not swerving with the blood,
Garnish'd and deck'd in modest complement,
Not working with the eye without the ear,
And but in purged judgement trusting neither?
Such and so finely bolted didst thou seem:
And thus thy fall hath left a kind of blot,
To mark the full-fraught man and best indued
With some suspicion. I will weep for thee;
For this revolt of thine, methinks, is like
Another fall of man.   (ii, ii, 126–42)

Among the sonnets, sonnets xc–xciv, a sequence of mounting mistrust which most of the rearrangers leave undisturbed, and which culminates in the much-discussed 'They that have power', come very close in theme and tone to Henry's speech. Sonnet xciii speaks, with all the bitterness of *Twelfth Night's* Antonio, of the youth's deceptive beauty, and like Henry V the poet here associates outer fairness and inner corruption with original sin; so calamitous and yet so inescapable does the friend's betrayal appear to him:

But heaven in thy creation did decree
That in thy face sweet love should ever dwell;
Whate'er thy thoughts or thy heart's workings be,
Thy looks should nothing thence but sweetness tell.
    How like Eve's apple doth thy beauty grow,
    If thy sweet virtue answer not thy show!

III

The sonnets we have hitherto discussed are among the least conventional in the sequence. In many of the more conventional ones, however, it is noticeable that Shakespeare is making use of the convention to relieve or to escape from his intolerable doubts of his friend's loyalty. Thus one of the oldest themes which the sonnet absorbed from medieval love poetry, the poet's abject self-abasement before the god-like nature of the friend or mistress, eases the poet's dread of betrayal by supplying a justification for it. Such a rationalization of fear is found, alongside the melancholy which the fear induces, in Shakespeare's depiction of Antonio in *The Merchant of Venice*. His words at the trial—

> I am a tainted wether of the flock,
> Meetest for death: the weakest kind of fruit
> Drops earliest to the ground; and so let me: (IV, i, 114–16)

are as movingly unconvincing as is sonnet LXXXVIII:

> With mine own weakness being best acquainted,
> Upon thy part I can set down a story
> Of faults conceal'd, wherein I am attainted,
> That thou in losing me shalt win much glory.

Glory of this kind is won by Hal at the end of the second part of *Henry IV* when he repudiates Falstaff; and there are several sonnets in which the relationship between the young, handsome and conspicuous friend seems closely to parallel that of the Prince of Wales and his reprobate old companion. Of these sonnet XLIX comes nearest to the culminating scene of *Henry IV, Part II*:

> Against that time, if ever that time come,
> When I shall see thee frown on my defects,
> When as thy love hath cast his utmost sum,
> Call'd to that audit by advised respects;
> Against that time when thou shalt strangely pass
> And scarcely greet me with that sun, thine eye,
> When love, converted from the thing it was,
> Shall reasons find of settled gravity,
> Against that time do I ensconce me here
> Within the knowledge of mine own desert,
> And this my hand against myself uprear,
> To guard the lawful reasons on thy part:
>   To leave poor me thou hast the strength of laws,
>   Since why to love I can allege no cause.

At the end of the play, love is converted from the thing it was when Hal, succeeding to the throne, declares 'I have turned away my former self' and takes as his new counsellor the strength of laws in the person of the Lord Chief Justice. If we take, from the back of the gallery or the back of history, a long view of the Hal–Falstaff relationship, the rejection is justified. But the sonnet gives us a sombre close-up of the matter from the viewpoint of the rejected companion, in which cold prudence shows itself in the 'advis'd respects' (a phrase already used of majesty in *King John*) and in the profit-and-loss calculations with which the friend casts his utmost sum. The reasons of settled gravity serve, to borrow a telling phrase from sonnet LXXXIX, 'to set a form upon desired change'. Gravity belongs to the court and in particular to the Lord Chief Justice who tells Falstaff 'There is not a white hair on your face but should have his effect of gravity'. 'What doth gravity out of his bed at midnight?' Falstaff asks when a nobleman of the court comes to summon Hal to a reckoning with his father; and gravity is dismissed by levity while the scene of reckoning is played out as an Eastcheap farce. But in the charade, Falstaff is soon turned out of the role of Hal's father; and the royal resolution—'I do, I will' with which Hal encounters Falstaff's plea not to banish honest Jack is put into effect when the new-crowned Henry V passes 'strangely'. The Lord Chief Justice follows, to waken Falstaff rudely from his long dream in which he, and not the Lord Chief Justice, will replace Hal's father—

> Thus have I had thee, as a dream doth flatter,
> In sleep a king, but waking no such matter. (*Sonnet* LXXXVII)

In the play as well as the poems, Shakespeare seeks to exorcize the haunting fear of betrayal by showing such betrayal to be justified in the light of prudence, a cardinal virtue, and of policy, the wisdom of governors. But the reproach of disloyalty remains, breaking out in the sonnets through ambiguous words and phrases, and perplexing for centuries the audiences of *Henry IV*.

Readers who are distressed by the self-abasing tone of such sonnets may turn with relief to those that make use of a contrary convention and promise the friend immortal life in the poet's verse. Yet many of these 'eternizing' sonnets are not so much the expression of confidence as of fear, the same persistent fear of the friend's treachery. In anticipation of that betrayal, the poet tries to perpetuate his friend in his verse as he now is and while he is still the poet's friend. He seeks 'To make him seem long hence as he shows now' (sonnet CI). But what he seems and shows may be quite other than what he actually is, and some of these sonnets are as profoundly ironic as the Duke's words to Angelo in the last act of *Measure for Measure*, when the deputy still appears 'unmoved, cold, and to temptation slow':

> O, your desert speaks loud; and I should wrong it,
> To lock it in the wards of covert bosom,
> When it deserves, with characters of brass,
> A forted residence 'gainst the tooth of time
> And razure of oblivion. (v, i, 9–13)

Because the characters of brass may ultimately speak of the friend as someone very different from the man the poet knows, the poet insists on his power to perpetuate him in his verse, not as a paragon of all the virtues—in fact we are told very little about the young man, as all Shakespeare's biographers have cause to complain—but simply as the poet's friend—

> But you shall shine more bright in these contents
> Than unswept stone besmear'd with sluttish time. (*Sonnet* LV)

Sluttish time not only neglects the gilded monuments but actually besmears them; the poet is fighting to preserve his friend against 'all-oblivious *enmity*' and beyond that, it may be conjectured from the same sonnet's ambiguous final couplet, from the ultimate truth of his nature which the poet dreads to see discovered:

> So, till the judgement that yourself arise,
> You live in this, and dwell in lovers' eyes.

So too in the greatest 'eternizing' sonnet, the Ovidian sonnet LX, Time appears as the enemy not only of the youth's beauty but of his virtue too. Time feeds on the rarities of Nature's truth, and the eclipses which fight here against the glory of maturity can be, as they are in sonnet XXXIII, the darkened reputation which comes even in a man's lifetime from 'envious and calumniating time'.

The ravages of Time are the subject of sonnet LXIV—'When I have seen by Time's fell hand...'. But here there is no promise of an immortality in verse to offset the melancholy close:

> Ruin hath taught me thus to ruminate,
> That Time will come and take my love away.
> This thought is as a death, which cannot choose
> But weep to have that which it fears to lose.

Commentators on this sonnet are much struck by the resemblance between its second quatrain and the speech of King Henry in *Henry IV, Part II* beginning 'O God! that one might read the book of fate'. Both passages picture the sea's encroachment upon the land and the land's upon the sea. It is worth following Henry's speech in the play a little further, to see what application he makes of the image:

> O, if this were seen,
> The happiest youth, viewing his progress through,
> What perils past, what crosses to ensue,
> Would shut the book, and sit him down and die.
> 'Tis not ten years gone
> Since Richard and Northumberland, great friends,
> Did feast together, and in two years after
> Were they at wars it is but eight years since
> This Percy was the man nearest my soul,
> Who like a brother toil'd in my affairs
> And laid his life and love under my foot. (III, i, 53–63)

Time will also come and take Shakespeare's love away—by death perhaps, although in the natural course of things the poet would die the earlier; the *Henry IV* passage shows rather that Time may take him away as it took Northumberland from Richard and has taken Hotspur from Henry. Here again then destructive time is equated, as Derek Traversi has said, with the 'necessary flaw at the heart of passion'.[4]

So the millioned accidents of time creep in, the poet says in sonnet CXV, between men's vows and 'Divert strong minds to the course of altering things'. In this last sonnet, however, the vicissitudes of time are made to serve a new turn of thought by explaining how it has been possible for the poet's love to increase. This sonnet therefore belongs with those that make use of a third conventional idea of love poetry and of the sonnet in particular, the constancy of the poet's love. Whatever the friend may do, the poet's affection will last for ever and a day. There is thus a natural transition from this sonnet to the boast of sonnet CXVI that love is not love 'Which alters when it alteration finds'. Sonnets CVII and CXXIV also belong to this group, and when, after all that has been written about these two difficult poems, one rereads them in their place in the sequence it is hard to see how the 'love' they celebrate could ever have been taken to mean the friend himself and not Shakespeare's affection for the friend. The 'confin'd doom' of CVII can surely only mean the limits which cynical onlookers have set to Shakespeare's friendship, limits suggested perhaps by a knowledge of the friend's true nature. But in defiance of these prophecies, the poet claims his love is not 'the child of state'—

> It fears not policy, that heretic,
> Which works on leases of short-number'd hours.

The friend's love may well be diverted from its true allegiance by policy; he has already revealed himself as a calculating young man, and the time may come when he will cast his utmost sum and, knowing his estimate, will reject the poet. But in contrast the poet's love stands 'hugely politic'; it embraces the whole state of existence and to him it is inconceivable that he could ever 'leave for nothing all this sum of good'—

> For nothing this wide universe I call,
> Save thou, my rose; in it thou art my all.

Sonnet CIX, from which these lines are quoted, presents the poet 'like one that travels' bringing 'water for my stain'. Verbally it closely parallels the passage in *Henry IV*, *Part II* from which T. W. Baldwin begins his study of the relationship between the poems and the plays:[5]

Falstaff. But to stand stained with travel, and sweating with desire to see him; thinking of nothing else, putting all affairs else in oblivion, as if there were nothing else to be done but to see him.

Pistol. 'Tis 'semper idem', for 'obsque hoc nihil est:' 'tis all in every part.   (v, v, 25–31)

In this of course Falstaff's devotion is anything but disinterested, and I have already suggested that it is one of Shakespeare's ways of evading the fear of trust to present Falstaff as a character who deserves the dismissal he gets. But Falstaff does not alter where he alteration finds. He believes that he will be sent for soon at night and when that last hope is gone, Falstaff himself has nothing left to live for: 'The king hath killed his heart.'

IV

In suggesting that the deep fear of love's confined doom and the various ways of coming to terms with that fear—by accepting the justice of the doom, by stressing poetry's power to escape devouring time and by protesting the poet's own unchanging loyalty—are the motive forces of most of the sonnets between XXXIII and CXXIV, and an important element in several of Shakespeare's middle plays, I have run the risk, especially where the plays are concerned, of appearing to be a biographical speculator. But while I am convinced the fear of trust is a factor to be reckoned with in our reading of the poems and plays, I would not suggest following this clue out of the text and into Shakespeare's life. We know too little about the labyrinthine processes by which experience is transformed into the work of art. The warning of a Victorian editor of the sonnets, Robert Bell, is apposite: 'the particle of actual life out of which verse is wrought may be, and almost always is, wholly incommensurate to the emotion depicted, and remote from the forms into which it is ultimately shaped'.[6] Some trifle light as air may have rendered Shakespeare the man jealous of a friend's affection and so created the tormented 'I' of the sonnets as well as the two Antonios and certain aspects of Falstaff.

If the recognition of the 'fear of trust' as a strong element in the sonnets and middle plays throws no clear light on Shakespeare's biography, it might be expected to help in the critical evaluation of these works. But here we meet a long standing difference of opinion between those critics—they are mostly practising poets like Yeats, Auden and Empson—who hold that poetry should be the clear expression of mixed feelings and those others, and they include some of the best commentators on the sonnets, who feel that ambiguities of tone and verbal meanings constitute a defect because they indicate the poet has insufficiently realized his experience in a poetic form. For these critics the lack of moral explicitness in, say, *The Merchant of Venice* and *Henry IV* will always be a blemish on these plays, and they are likely to prefer *Integer vitae* to 'They that have power', or the perfect control of 'When in disgrace with fortune...' to the sounding imprecision of 'Not mine own fears...'. If I here stop short of an evaluative conclusion to these few observations on the Sonnets and middle plays, it is not because I feel such evaluations can be dismissed as a matter of taste, but because they need a definition of critical principles that lies outside the scope of the present essay. And even when we are furnished with such principles we are likely to find that in critical evaluation, as in biographical inquiry and other activities of scholarship, we may come to the pericardium, but not the heart of truth.

NOTES

1. See especially J. W. Lever, *The Elizabethan Love Sonnet* (1956). The many studies of parallels between plays and sonnets are summarized in Hyder Rollins's Variorum edition (1944), II, pp. 63–9. To the works there cited should now be added T. W. Baldwin, *The Literary Genetics of Shakespeare's Poems and Sonnets* (1950).

2. *Op. cit.* pp. 221–2.

3. *Biographia Literaria*, ed. J. Shawcross, II, pp. 17–18.

4. *Approach to Shakespeare* (1946), p. 46.

5. *Op. cit.* p. 157. Actually use is not made, in Baldwin's study, of the striking resemblance between these passages, which is discussed by J. W. Lever, *op. cit.* p. 238, nor of the resemblance between sonnet XLIX and *Henry IV*.

6. Quoted by Hyder Rollins, *op. cit.* II, 139.

BEASTS AND GODS:
GREENE'S *GROATS-WORTH OF WITTE*
AND THE SOCIAL PURPOSE OF
VENUS AND ADONIS

BY

MURIEL C. BRADBROOK

I. THE PLAYER'S CHALLENGE

Precisely because it is of a different kind, there has been very little attempt to see *Venus and Adonis* as the work of one whose nature was already subdued, like the dyer's hand, to the popular stage-writings of his day. In this, Shakespeare has succeeded in what was surely his initial intention, to make a second reputation for himself. To appear in print was to make a dignified bid for Fame; the author at once achieved recognition and respectful notice, even among those who despised, or affected to despise, the work of the common stages. In a few years, the students of St John's College, Cambridge, in the person of Judicio would commend William Shakespeare the poet—'Who loues not *Adons* loue or *Lucrece* rape?'—while they gave a pulverizing defence of William Shakespeare the playwright to Kempe:

Few of the vniversity pen plaies well, they smell too much of that writer *Ouid*, and that writer *Metamorphoses*, and talke too much of *Proserpina & Iuppiter*. Why heres our fellow *Shakespeare* put them all downe, I and Ben Ionson too.[1]

This elegant poem, redolent of Ovid, joins Marlowe and Shakespeare; for like *Hero and Leander*, it is witty and challenges abstinence on behalf of the flesh. Both poets had also been joined for rebuke, though each for very different reasons, in a work which appeared a few months before *Venus and Adonis*. Shakespeare's first venture into print, while not a direct reply to Greene's *Groats-worth of Witte*, may be regarded as a response provoked by this piece of vilification. Because I would see Greene's attack as more sustained and even more insulting than it is usually thought, I would suggest it produced a degree of irritation that writing alone could cure.

Shakespeare's intention is signified by the dedication to the Earl of Southampton, and by the motto. He was dissociating himself from baseness:

Vilia miratur vulgus...

is more characteristic of Ben Jonson (who translated it 'Kneel hinds to trash') than of the tolerant Shakespeare; it betrays the spirit in which the work was published. *Venus and Adonis* furnishes a literary equivalent of the application to Herald's College for a coat of arms:

mihi flavus Apollo
Pocula Castalia plena ministret acqua.

The gulf that lay between popular playwriting and courtly poetry may be measured in that scene of *Histriomastix*, where the artisan players presented Troilus boasting to Cressid:

> Thy knight his valiant elboe weares,
> That When he shakes his furious Speare,
> The foe in shivering fearefull sort,
> May lay him downe in death to snort.　　　　　　　(II, i)

They were dismissed in disgrace and an Italian lord observed:

> I blush in your behalfes at this base trash;
> In honour of our Italy we sport,
> As if a Synod of the holly Gods,
> Came to tryumph within our Theaters.　　　　　　　(II, i)

If both Shakespeare's poem and Greene's pamphlet are read, not in terms of their classical background but as pictorial imagery, they seem to me to provide a coherent pattern—a disparagement, or rhetorical invective, against the common player; and a counter-challenge of nobility, by a common player. Greene in scorn affixes the beast's mask upon his enemy: Shakespeare counters this by evoking a goddess, and celebrating the triumphs of the senses and the flesh in divine, human and animal forms.

2. The Antics and the Upstart Crow

It may be well here to recall a few dates:

3 September 1592: Death of Robert Greene.
20 September 1592: Registration of Greene's *Groats-worth of Witte*.
8 December 1592: Registration of Henry Chettle's *Kind-Harts Dreame*, containing an apology for printing the *Groats-worth of Witte*.
18 April 1593: Registration of Shakespeare's *Venus and Adonis*.

To which might be added the conclusion of T. W. Baldwin, based on an examination of the literary sources, that *Venus and Adonis* was written 'most likely just a few weeks or at most months before' registration, and the fact that it was announced in the letter of dedication as Shakespeare's first work in print.[2]

In a passage which ever since the eighteenth century has caused much throwing about of brains, Greene had addressed three gentlemen-playwrights (Marlowe, Nashe, Peele):

Base minded men all three of you, if by my miserie you be not warnd: for vnto none of you (like mee) sought those burres to cleaue: those Puppets (I meane) that spake from our mouths, those Anticks garnisht in our colours. Is it not strange, that I, to whom they all haue beene beholding: is it not like that you, to whome they all haue beene beholding, shall (were yee in that case as I am now) bee both at once of them forsaken? Yes trust them not: for there is an vpstart Crow, beautified with our feathers, that with his *Tygers hart wrapt in a Players hyde*, supposes he is as well able to bombast out a blanke verse as the best of you: and beeing an absolute *Iohannes fac totum*, is in his owne conceit the onely Shake-scene in a countrey.[3]

Greene puts Shakespeare among the lowest and most scurrilous type of actor, the antic or mome; these grotesque characters with animal heads and bombast figures came into Court revels with mops and mows, for dumb shows of detraction and scorn. In the first unbridled Christmas festivities of Elizabeth's reign, cardinals, bishops and abbots appeared at court in the likeness of crows, asses, and wolves; in 1564 Cambridge students pursued the Queen to Hinchingbrooke with a dumb show presenting the imprisoned Catholic prelates—Bonner eating a lamb, and a dog with the Host in his mouth—a dumb show from which the Queen rose and swept out, taking the torchbearers and leaving the players in darkness and disgrace.[4] Such antics were no longer in favour at Court; but they were seen in country merriments and in the afterpieces of the common stages. The players had brought their enemy Gosson on the stage in some such monstrous form. 'We will have, if this fadge not, an antique' (*Love's Labour's Lost*, v, i, 154–5) suggests that even village players rated the form below a show.

In 1570 first appeared *A Marvellous History entitled, Beware the Cat*, a 'Christmas Tale' attributed to William Baldwin. He describes how he had been at Court with Edward Ferrars, King Edward VI's Lord of Misrule, and some others; they lay abed together discussing the play of *Æsop's Crow* which the King's players had been learning, and which Baldwin discommended, saying:

it was not Commicall to make either speechlesse things to speake: or brutish things to commen resonably. And although in a tale it be sufferable...yet it was vncomely (said I) and without example of any authour to bring them in liuely personages to speake, doo, reason, and allege authorites out of authours (ed. 1584, A4^{r-v}).

This introduction to a queer ribald collection of witch stories about Irish cats—by turns horrific and bawdy, and like the shows at Court, with a strong anti-Papal bias—implies that a play of *Æsop's Crow* first gave speaking parts to antics. It might have been remembered, and thus might have given point to Greene's earlier rebuke to the actors:

why *Roscius*, art thou proud with *Esops* Crow, being pranct with the glorie of others feathers? of thy selfe thou canst say nothing, and if the Cobler hath taught thee to say, *Aue Caesar*, disdain not thy tutor, because thou pratest in a Kings chamber: what sentence thou vtterest on the stage, flowes from the censure of our wittes.[5]

Whether Greene's upstart Crow be, in the literary sense, Æsop's Crow, or as Dover Wilson would have it, Horace's Crow,[6] he is primarily neither, but an Antic taught to speak by poets and unnaturally spurning his teachers. Garnished in the 'colours' of Greene's rhetoric, as in the colours of brilliant playing suits, if his plumes were pulled, he would appear a mere Crow of the old kind. Yet there is one of these Crows who has not only learnt to speak verses but to write them; with him, the beast form is an inward one, for like all players, he is treacherous and cruel; by concealing his predatory nature within, he is transformed from Crow to Tiger. As an antic took to speech so a player has now taken to writing; Shakespeare, like the original Crow, violates decorum.

The kind of player Greene suggests is one who had begun as a tattered, gaudily dressed stroller, with the slipperiness, the capacity for betrayal, of all wandering tribes—gipsies, fiddlers, minstrels, tinkers. The disparagement laid on him is akin to that of the mock-blazon devised for the Duttons when they claimed the academic title of Comedians:

Three nettles resplendent, three owles, three swallowes,
Three mynstrellmen pendent on three payre of gallowes,
Further sufficiently placed in them
A knaves head, for a difference from alle honest men.
The wreathe is a chayne of chaungeable red,
To shew they ar vayne and fickle of head;
The creste is a lastrylle whose feathers ar blew,
In signe that these fydlers will never be trew....[7]

Greene's bespattering is of this kind, with bestial comparison, and social denigration. Its theatrical, not its literary echo, is cruellest. Three years before the appearance of Greene's *Groats-worth of Witte*, Martin Marprelate had been brought on the common stages to be lanced and wormed in the form of an ape; and when the shows were banned, Lyly lamented:

He shall not bee brought in as whilom he was, and yet verie well, with a cocks combe, an apes face, a wolfs bellie, cats clawes, &c.[8]

Several years after, at the end of *Poetaster*, Jonson showed Tucca gagged and vizarded, Fannius fitted with fool's coxcomb and cap, and in the epilogue proclaimed:

Blush, folly, blush: here's none that feares
The wagging of an asses eares,
Although a wooluish case he weares.
Detraction is but basenesse varlet;
And apes are apes, though cloth'd in scarlet.   (v, iii, 626–30)

There were plenty of hybrids as extraordinary as the crow with a tiger's heart. Greene was not writing for scholars; the context evoked a direct visual memory for his readers. Stage pieces would naturally spring to mind, though a Latin phrase might follow for the few.

3. THE STRUCTURE OF GREENE'S 'GROATS-WORTH OF WITTE'

This passage on Shakespeare, the highest point of Greene's invective, is not detachable from the rest of the pamphlet, in which the poet tells his life-story as the tale of the prodigal Roberto, born in a rich mercantile city [Norwich], disinherited by his father, cheating his brother, and cheated later by a drab. As Roberto sits lamenting under a hedge, he is accosted with smooth and consoling words:

But if you vouchsafe such simple comforte as my abilitie may yeeld, assure your selfe, that I wil indeuour to doe the best, that either may procure you profite, or bring you pleasure: the rather, for that I suppose you are a scholler, and pittie it is men of learning should liue in lacke.   (p. 33)

The stranger, so civil in his demeanour, turns out to be a player:

A player, quoth *Roberto*, I tooke you rather for a Gentleman of great liuing, for if by outward habit men should be censured, I tell you, you would bee taken for a substantiall man. So am I where I dwell (quoth the player) reputed able at my proper cost to build a Windmill. What though the world once went hard with me, when I was faine to carry my playing Fardle a footebacke; *Tempora mutantur*,

I know you know the meaning of it better than I, but I thus conster it, its otherwise now; for my very share in playing apparell will not be sold for two hundred pounds. Truly (said *Roberto*) tis straunge, that you should so prosper in that vayne practise, for that it seemes to mee your voice is nothing gratious.

(pp. 33–4)

This player with the ungracious voice goes on to say he is famous for acting Delphrigus and the King of the Fairies, that he has thundered in the Twelve Labours of Hercules, and played three scenes of the Devil in *The Highway to Heaven*. Moreover, he is author as well as player—a 'countrey Author' 'passing at a Morrall' who wrote *The Dialogue of Dives*; finally, for seven years he was absolute interpreter of the puppets. His repertoire was on the level of the Antic, though more respectable.

> But now my Almanacke is out of date:
> > *The people make no estimation,*
> > *Of Morrals teaching education.*
> Was not this prettie for a plaine rime extempore? if ye will ye shall haue more. (p. 34)

This caricature of an untrained player-poet, who is none the less wealthy, and can speak in-gratiatingly, must not be taken for an individual likeness. For, apart from anything else, some of it is stock stuff, borrowed from Nashe's preface to Greene's own *Menaphon*:

Sundry other sweete gentlemen I know, that haue vaunted their pennes in priuate deuices, and tricked vp a company of taffata fooles with their feathers, whose beauty if our Poets had not peecte with the supply of their periwigs, they might haue antickt it vntill this time vp and downe the Countrey with the King of *Fairies*, and dined euery day at the pease porredge ordinary with *Delphrigus*. But *Tolossa* hath forgot that it was sometime sacked, and beggars that euer they carried their fardels on footback....[9]

Nevertheless, there was one especially noted player-poet when Greene was writing; one who according to a later tradition had been a schoolmaster in the country, and therefore might well have been supposed to begin with morals teaching education; this is the player-poet alluded to by name later as a so-called Comedian who is fit only to antic it up and down the country. The player with the ungracious voice might have been recognizable to contemporaries; for it is worth noting that Chettle begins his apology with a tribute to Shakespeare's acting ability ('excellent in the quality he professes'). The kind of play in which this player began is the kind which in Shakespeare's 'lost years', before the arrival of the University Wits, must have provided the repertory of all common players.

Greene used the popular method of detraction, taking a pre-existing formula, and working in an ascription or two which would fit a particular person—a method of denigration by suggestion, still practised, for example, in the speeches of learned counsel or of politicians who know their art. Seaside photographers of the past invited sitters to pose with their heads stuck through a cardboard cut-out, so that they appear to be taking part in a comic donkey race or rowing on a choppy sea. So, in this kind of caricature, the personal touch and the public property are conjoined; the individual is dressed in an ass's head or a calf's skin and the joke depends on contrast between the human and the dummy parts. Clowns who sought voluntary ridicule at an Elizabethan fair would compete at the sport of grinning through a horse-collar; here ready-made detraction was clapped on a selected victim.[10]

In the *Groats-worth of Witte*, Greene makes two contrasting uses of beast-fables, literary equivalent of the antic show of scorn. The cheating courtesan gives Roberto a 'caveat by the way, which shall be figured in a fable' of the Fox and the Badger, directed against the red-haired fox who was also the red-haired Greene. The whole work ends with a 'conceited fable of that old Comedian Æsop' told by Greene; in this farcical afterpiece to his tragic story, the improvident Poet appears as the Grasshopper, while the provident Ant represents the Player, who refuses succour in time of need:

> Packe hence (quoth he) thou idle lazie worme,
> My house doth harbor no vnthriftie mates:
> Thou scorndst to toile, & now thou feelst the storme,
> And starust for food while I am fed with cates.
> Vse no intreats, I will relentlesse rest,
> For toyling labour hates an idle guest. (pp. 48–9)

Here is the 'forsaking' and cruelty of which Greene has already complained—and in his letter to his wife, he reveals he was like to have died in the streets.

It is when, in the course of the narrative, Roberto's time for repentance comes that the narration turns into confession, and Greene speaks for the first time in his own person:

Heere (Gentlemen) breake I off *Robertoes* speach; whose life in most parts agreeing with mine, found one selfe punishment as I haue doone. Heereafter suppose me the saide *Roberto*, and I will goe on with that hee promised.... (p. 39)

Having thrown off the vizard, Greene gives his precepts, and appeals to the gentlemen playwrights; in exactly parallel manner, having presented the unnamed player-poet in the narrative, he then attacks a similar figure, but directly and by name, in the confession. Some link may be supposed between the two. The construction of this pamphlet is not haphazard as it at first appears.

4. CHETTLE'S REPLY TO GREENE

In the epistle to the 'Gentlemen readers' prefixed to *Kind-Harts Dreame*, Chettle makes handsome apology to Shakespeare as player, as citizen and as poet:

my selfe haue seene his demeanor no lesse ciuill than he exelent in the qualitie he professes: Besides, diuers of worship haue reported, his vprightnes of dealing, which argues his honesty, and his facetious grace in writting, that approoues his Art.[11]

Shakespeare is cleared from the imputation of being an antic, or a dishonest skipjack player, and though he has not published, he is allowed by report facetious grace in Art. But against this must be set a tribute to Greene in the body of the work, where his ghost appears to protest against the cruel imputations that are being put about after his death:

the fifth, a man of indifferent yeares, of face amible, of body well proportioned, his attire after the habite of a schollerlike Gentleman, onely his haire was somewhat long, whome I supposed to be Robert Greene, maister of Artes; of whome (howe euer some suppose themselues iniured) I haue learned to speake, considering he is dead, *nill nisi necessarium*. He was of singuler pleasaunce the verye supporter, and to no mans disgrace bee this intended, *the only Comedian of a vulgar writer in this country* [my italics]. (p. 13)

Kind-Harts Dreame is a reply to the general case against players, a humble plea for the liberty of honest, if lowly, wanderers. The pamphlet consists of five newsletters from five apparitions (including Greene, and Richard Tarlton the clown, who defends harmless pastime) seeking to deliver a 'bill invective against abuses now reigning' to be borne by Piers Penniless' Post to the infernal regions. The fiddler, the juggler, the simple-hearted narrator come from London fairgrounds. There is little chance that William Cuckow or Kind-Hart the toothdrawer could be taken for anyone but themselves; that is perhaps the purpose of the very full description they are given.[12]

That Greene's name is often attached to scurrilous pamphlets and that he appears so often coupled with Tarlton,[13] whose jests were exceptionally bawdy, may appear surprising to anyone who remembers the inoffensiveness of his romance and the delicacy of much of his work: though it should be recalled that Chettle said he had expunged from the *Groats-worth of Witte* a certain accusation against Marlowe, which to publish 'was intollerable'.

The whole chain of scurrilous invective and lachrymose repentance put out under Greene's name shows his sales-value for printers; in the *Groats-worth of Witte*, from the first appearance of the player with falsely 'civil demeanour' to the afterpiece of the Ant and the Grasshopper, Shakespeare might not unjustly consider himself to be bearing the brunt of a widely-read invective. That the attack cut deep may be easily supposed. Years later, even Polonius remembered that 'beautified' was a vile word. After extracting an apology from Chettle, Shakespeare went on to safeguard his reputation with a work whose elegance and modishness was recognized within the walls of Greene's own college and university. His 'facetious grace in writing' was publicly shown by a work of learning (Art). Its unabashed celebration of the delights of the flesh gave an answer more convincing than a directly aimed reply to the terror-stricken repentance of the poor wretch who, by his own confession, had been guilty of all the faithlessness and promise-breaking with which he charged the players.

5. 'VENUS AND ADONIS'

Venus and Adonis, sumptuous and splendidly assured, was designed not to answer Greene, but to obliterate the impression he had tried to make. In this it seems to have succeeded. Yet, because Shakespeare was a player, there remain a few traces in the poem of the very different Venus he had known upon the common stages—the Venus of the first actor-playwright, Robert Wilson, a contemporary of Tarlton. It is a vindication of the goddess, no less than of the player.

Love appears as a character in each of Wilson's three plays, as well as in some others which Shakespeare may have known.[14] On the stage she is more often condemned than praised, especially by Wilson, who marries her to Dissimulation, and sets her to woo Contempt. The language of scorn employed by Adonis is mild compared with that of Contempt, who first seduces Venus from Mars and then leaves her to lament:

> So flies the murderer from the mangled lims,
> Left limles on the ground by his fell hand.
> So runnes the Tyger from the bloodles pray,
> Which when his fell stomacke is of hunger stancht,
> Thou murdrer, Tyger, glutted with my faire,
> Leaust me forsaken, map of griefe and care.[15]

There may be a faint echo in the final prophecy of Shakespeare's mourning Venus; a more curious similarity is that Contempt, like Adonis, is described as being most incongruously smaller than Venus; if Shakespeare's Venus can tuck Adonis under her arm, Wilson's Contempt is described as a sort of false Eros, a 'little Goosecap God', a 'little little seeing God'. Greene himself had written a lyric in which Adonis seems almost confused with Eros:

> In *Cypres* sat fayre *Venus* by a Fount,
> Wanton *Adonis* toying on her knee,
> She kist the wag, her darling of accompt,
> The Boie gan blush, which when his louer see,
>   She smild and told him loue might challenge debt,
>   And he was yoong and might be wanton yet.[16]

The climax of Wilson's *The Cobler's Prophecy* is the denunciation of Venus by other gods and her degradation from heavenly rank, since she is known to be but 'Venus alias Lust'; and so is given only 'the detested name of Lust or Strumpet Venus'.

Shakespeare's goddess is admonished by Adonis:

> 'Call it not love, for Love to heaven is fled,
> Since sweating Lust on earth usurp'd his name...
> Love comforteth like sunshine after rain,
> But Lust's effect is tempest after sun:
> Love's gentle spring doth always fresh remain,
> Lust's winter comes ere summer half be done;
>   Love surfeits not, Lust like a glutton dies;
>   Love is all truth, Lust full of forged lies.   (793–804)

The same attitude prevailed on the private stage, for in Court plays Venus was in conflict with Diana's nymph, Elizabeth. The comedies of Lyly gave Shakespeare a model, especially for the one which was shortly to follow *Venus and Adonis*, in the winter of 1593–4, *Love's Labour's Lost*.[17] This was eventually published 'as it was presented before her Highness this last Christmas', the first of Shakespeare's plays to achieve this honour. In his poem, Shakespeare also addressed himself to the courtly group, Lyly's select audience. Socially Greene and Lyly were poles apart, and to turn from the one to the other was to step from tavern to Presence Chamber.

Many of Lyly's plays, especially *Midas* and *Campaspe*, are like Ovidian Romance in dramatic form, yet they lack its vivid sensuous expansiveness. Lyly's was an artificial world; his 'natural' objects were a collection of rarities brought together by simile. The Venus of Lyly may, like

Shakespeare's, fall in love with a fair boy (*Sapho and Phao*), but she remains a voice only, a speaking part undefined by sympathy, in a series of rhetorical statements:

O Cupid, thy flames with Psyches were but sparks, and my desires with Adonis but dreames, in respecte of these vnacquainted tormentes...(IV, ii, 14–16).

In *Gallathea*, Venus loses Cupid to Diana, and in *Sapho and Phao* to Sapho; in *The Woman in the Moon*, she is shown at her worst, inspiring the heroine with nymphomaniac fury. Venus in Lyly always represents lust; the cool impersonality of his style, no less than the need to consider his royal patroness, would not admit the true goddess. Cupid is a more important figure than Venus for Lyly; desire not passion presides. The fragile elegance of his dialogue combined with an underlying stratum of conventional morality, in spite of its airy mockery and sophistication. Elizabeth, in the person of Sapho, triumphed over Venus:

Venus, be not chollerick, Cupid is mine, he hath giuen me his Arrowes, and I will giue him a new bowe to shoote in. You are not worthy to be the Ladye of loue, that yeelde so often to the impressions of loue. Immodest Venus, that to satisfie the vnbrideled thoughtes of thy hearte, transgressest so far from the staye of thine honour!...Shall I not rule the fansies of men, and leade Venus in chaines like a captiue? (v, ii, 57–67)

Except by Adonis, Shakespeare's goddess is never condemned in the moralizing manner of Wilson or Lyly. The poem is finely balanced between accepted animalism and a strange pathos. Although at the end she flies away to Patmos, in the poem itself Venus displays all the helpless weakness as well as the beauty of the flesh. She sweats, pants, weeps, swoons—or pretends to swoon[18]—runs like a country lass with no power to save her lover from the boar, though by an instinct of prophecy she foretells his death and the inevitable woes of all who love. She frantically compares herself with the boar; her wooing is paralleled with the hunt. The little hunted hare, the snail who 'shrinks backward in his shelly cave with pain' and the wounded hounds embody more poignant forms of pain and fear than Venus herself. Proud horse and raging boar provide splendid cartoons of lustihood and fury. As he transformed the squalid Venus of the stage, so Shakespeare transformed the grotesque animal forms of his detractor into genuine instinctive creatures, conceived in full naturalistic detail. *Venus and Adonis* is a great work of release, an assertion of natural energies. The artificial beasts of the mime, like the artificial world of Lyly, have been exorcized and left behind; instead, the true animal world—including the human animal—appears, so palpable and so warmly evoked that Shakespeare's contemporaries were quite swept away. Many a Gull besides Gullio was beautified with Shakespeare's feathers:

Marry I thinke I shall entertaine those verses which run like these:
Euen as the sunn with purple-coloured face
Had tane his laste leaue on the weeping morne, etc
O sweet Mr Shakespeare, Ile haue his picture in my study at courte.[19]

Venus and Adonis is at once a claim to social dignity for its author, a justification of the natural and instinctive beauty of the animal world against sour moralists and scurrilous invective, a raising of the animal mask to sentient level, the emancipation of the flesh. Since, however, he did not continue this kind of poetry after the *Rape of Lucrece*, it may be that without the stimulus of Greene's attack Shakespeare would not have been moved to write Ovidian Romance, or, if he wrote, to insist at once upon the dignity of print, with all that this implied of a bid for Fame.

Of Shakespeare it might be said,

> Cet animal est très mechant,
> Quand on l'attaque, il se défend

—not with the common style of disclaimer but with positive demonstration of new and dazzling capacities. In *Venus and Adonis*, a lofty form and classic authority is invoked to display the continuity of animal, human and divine passion; the 'vulgar' are rejected only in their narrow prejudice, for the natural at all levels is celebrated.

The player has shown his capacity to move in a world of gorgeous paganism, to write upon a noble model, and to deal with love in aristocratic boldness and freedom. The dedication to Southampton, with its modest apology for 'these unpolished lines' is at once disarming and 'gentle', the tone courtly but unaffected. This could not be calculated; it is the natural consequence of that civility of demeanour which Chettle had so admired.[20]

NOTES

1. *Second Part of the Return from Parnassus* (ed. J. B. Leishman, 1949), I, ii, 301–3 and IV, iii, 1766–70.

2. T. W. Baldwin, *On the Literary Genetics of Shakespeare's Poems and Sonnets* (Urbana, 1950), pp. 45–8.

3. *Greene's Groats-worth of Witte* (ed. G. B. Harrison, Bodley Head Quartos, 1923), pp. 45–6.

4. E. K. Chambers, *The Elizabethan Stage*, I, 128 describes the Hinchingbrooke affair; p. 155, the mumming in Coronation year, which happened on Twelfth Night. For late examples of similar shows, see Sheila Williams, 'The Pope-Burning Processions of 1679, 1680, and 1681', *Journal of the Warburg and Courtauld Institutes*, XXI (1958), 104–18.

5. *Francesco's Fortunes* (1590), B4ᵛ–C1ʳ. See Chambers, *op. cit.* IV, 236. *Francesco's Fortunes*, a version of Greene's life-story preceding his *Groats-worth of Witte*, contains further abuse of the players. Ferrars actually presented masks of cats and bagpipes before Edward VI in 1553 (A. Feuillerat, *Documents Relating to the Revels* (Bang's Materialien, no. 44, Louvain, 1914), p. 145).

6. J. Dover Wilson, 'Malone and the Upstart Crow', *Shakespeare Survey* IV (1951), 56–68 returns to Malone's view that Greene accused Shakespeare of plagiarism. I would still incline to that set out in Peter Alexander's *Shakespeare's Henry VI and Richard III* (1929), for reasons which the present article will indicate.

7. Chambers, *op. cit.* II, 98–9. The Duttons were nicknamed 'Chameleons' because they changed their livery and allegiance so often. Cf. *The Defence of Coneycatching* where Greene is accused of saying 'as they were comedians to act, so the actions of their lives were chameleon-like: that they were uncertain time-pleasers, men that measured honesty by profit, and that regarded these authors not by desert but by necessity of time' (Chambers, *op. cit.* III, 325. This refers to actors in general).

8. *Pappe with an Hatchet*. See Chambers, *op. cit.* IV, 229–33 for this and other examples of the stage attack on Martin Marprelate.

9. Chambers, *op. cit.* IV, 236. Such borrowing is constant; for example, in his *Farewell to Folly*, Greene borrows the description of a morris dancer, in burlesque style, from Laneham's Letter on the Princely Pleasures of Kenilworth.

10. C. R. Baskervill, in *The Elizabethan Jig* (Chicago, 1929), p. 67, quotes a 'box' rhyme into which any names could be fitted that the reciter desired:

> 'If I had as fair a face
> As John Williams his daughter Elizabeth has
> Then would I wear a tawdry lace,
> As Goodman Bolt's daughter Mary does:

> And if I had as much money in my purse
> As Cadman's daughter Margaret has,
> Then would I have a bastard less
> Than Butler's maid Helen has.'

Ready-made rhymes may have been used by Clowns in their 'extempore' after-pieces. This one was heard in Oxfordshire in 1584.

11. Ed. G. B. Harrison (Bodley Head Quartos, 1923), p. 6.

12. Such care was not misplaced. Nashe in writing to his printer to deny his authorship of 'a scald trivial, lying pamphlet, cald *Greens Groats-worth of Wit*' says of the very knight of the Post whom Chettle uses in *Kind-Harts Dreame*: 'In one place of my Booke, *Pierce Penilesse* saith but to the Knight of the Post, *I pray how might I call you*, & they say I meant one *Howe*, a Knaue of that trade, that I neuer heard of before' (*Works of Thomas Nashe* (ed. R. B. McKerrow, 1904-10), I, 154).

13. *Tarlton's Newes out of Purgatory*, supposedly published by Robin Goodfellow, and *The Cobbler of Canterbury*, with an invective against *Tarlton's Newes*, both collections of fabliaux, appeared in 1590. *Greene's Vision* (1592) denounces *The Cobbler*, which had been attributed to Greene. *Greene's Newes from Heaven and Hell* (1593) presents both Tarlton and Greene, who ends as 'the maddest goblin that euer walked in the moonshine' (was Robin Good-fellow a nickname for him perhaps?).

14. *Three Ladies of London* (1582?), *The Pleasant and Stately Moral of Three Lords and Three Ladies of London* (1590), and *The Cobler's Prophecy* (before 1594). Wilson was a member of Leicester's Men and afterwards of the Queen's Men. *The Rare Triumphs of Love and Fortune* was played before the Queen by Derby's Men at Windsor, 30 December 1582; published 1589. Love appears also, with Death and Fortune, in the Induction to *Solyman and Perseda* (anonymous, company unknown, published 1592).

15. *The Cobler's Prophecy* (Malone Society Reprint), 1540-5. Armado compares his own wooing to the roaring of the Nemean lion! (*Love's Labour's Lost*, IV, i, 87-92).

16. From *Perimides the Blacke-Smith* (1588). See T. W. Baldwin, *op. cit.* p. 88.

17. I do not know whether it has been noted how completely Trachinus' speech in praise of the court against academics (*Sapho and Phao*, I, ii, 6-25) agrees with the arguments of Berowne in *Love's Labour's Lost*. For the latest account of topical references in this play, see Walter Oakeshott, *The Queen and the Poet* (1960).

18. Wilson's Venus also pretends to swoon when rebuked by Mars, in order to win her lover to penitence.

19. *First Part of the Return from Parnassus* (ed. J. B. Leishman, 1949), III, i, 1028-33.

20. Cf. Herbert Howarth, 'Shakespeare's Gentleness', *Shakespeare Survey* 14 (1961), 90-7; the view of the social purpose of *Venus and Adonis* is similar to that expressed here.

FROM SHAKESPEARE'S VENUS TO CLEOPATRA'S CUPIDS

BY

ADRIEN BONJOUR

The famous vision of Cleopatra's barge, which stuck so vividly in Enobarbus's mind, centres on the image of the Queen that beggars all description—a paragon of majesty and loveliness, a figure so magic in beauty that it out-Venuses Venus:

> O'er-picturing that Venus where we see
> The fancy outwork nature. (II, ii, 205–6)

Now it looks as if in the following picture Shakespeare's fancy had indeed outworked nature with delicately sophisticated craftsmanship:

> on each side her
> Stood pretty dimpled boys, like smiling Cupids,
> With divers-colour'd fans, whose wind did seem
> To glow the delicate cheeks which they did cool,
> And what they undid did. (II, ii, 206–10)

However apposite it seems to compare the plump and chubby boys, who are fanning the Queen, with Cupids, it looks at first sight as if the far-fetched image of the wind, kindling the coral cheeks that it is meant to cool, were in fact some stray conceit culled from the stock of Shakespeare's early work—a strange survival of the young poet's tendency to revel in the quaintest of finely chiselled euphuisms. Such a spontaneous impression, I suggest, is at one and the same time both justified and sorely short of the actual significance of what happens to be vastly more than a pure conceit.

It is justified in so far as the apparently euphuistic image has its ultimate source in one of the most typical among the swarm of honey-tongued conceits that teem in Shakespeare's own sugared lines of *Venus and Adonis*. It falls short of the full significance of this delicate image inasmuch as it ignores the connotations which lurk behind it, connect it, filigree-like, to a set of other kindred images, and point (as soon as it is viewed within a wider context) to the very core of Cleopatra's complex nature.

Let us approach the problem warily by first intimating to what a surprising extent Shakespeare's phraseology and images anticipated in his salad days of *Venus and Adonis* the luscious mellow maturity of *Antony and Cleopatra*. One of the most penetrating insights into the very hub of Cleopatra's whirling microcosm flashes from another passage—the often quoted, but never worn out, lines about Egypt's ever new and for ever young appeal:

> Age cannot wither her, nor custom stale
> Her infinite *variety*: other women *cloy*
> The *appetites* they *feed*: but she *makes hungry*
> Where most she *satisfies*. (II, ii, 240–3)

73

Now at the very beginning of *Venus and Adonis*, it will be recalled, the goddess of love, 'like a bold-fac'd suitor' woos the young huntsman with eloquently lustful language. She urges him to alight from his horse and, enticingly promising her 'tender boy' to unveil a thousand honey secrets, invites him to sit down

> where never serpent hisses,
> And being set, I'll smother thee with kisses:
> And yet not *cloy* thy lips with loathed *satiety*,
> But rather *famish* them amid their plenty,
> Making them red and pale with fresh *variety*. (17–21)

Italics, indeed, are hardly needed to indicate that not only the whole trend of the later passage, but most of its significant words, are already there, and more than in germ, in the earlier extract. The main difference is this: what Venus merely promises, and vainly tries to accomplish, Cleopatra richly fulfills. That Venus's promise is but an idle lure, the rest of the poem amply testifies. For Venus's passion is equated with Lust and keenly contrasted by Adonis with Love. The one soon withers while the other keeps its bloom:

> Love's gentle spring doth always fresh remain,
> Lust's winter comes ere summer half be done;
> Love surfeits not, Lust like a glutton dies. (801–3)

But the self-same entities which are so sharply sundered and opposed in *Venus and Adonis* are resolved in *Antony and Cleopatra* into a *tertium quid*: a smooth excellence—a sovereign capacity of combining as it were the advantages of both antinomies. This new creation, by the way, is curiously akin to Keats's dream of a happy love and supreme felicity. Where's the maid, he sighed, whose lip mature is ever new? Yea, *où sont les neiges d'antan*? Alas, gone is Cleopatra with her gentlewomen, like the Nereides; vanished is the rare Egyptian, and no such maid is ever met beneath the visiting moon. Full well the poet knew that everything is spoilt by use: the laurels all are cut, and Autumn's red-lipped fruitage, too, cloys with tasting. Hence Keats's longing for a love that would not wither—hence his dream of a more happy love,

> For ever panting, and for ever young;
> All breathing human passion far above,
> That leaves the heart high-sorrowful and cloy'd.

It would seem that Shakespeare had long anticipated such a vision and, with his Cleopatra, whom age could not wither nor custom make stale, had embodied beforehand Keats's dream of getting it both ways. But he would not have dreamt of reconciling the incompatible had he not first experienced, like Keats, how quickly at a touch sweet pleasure melteth.[1] And precisely, *Venus and Adonis* leads us back to the formative stage in which the opposites, far from being fused, are still poles apart. Now the formative stage is likewise to be sought there in the case of Cleopatra's apparition, o'er-picturing Venus—and this of course takes us back to our pretty dimpled cherubs and their fans.

The little cluster of associations which lies at the basis of our apparent conceit revolves round the ambivalent image of the wind which may serve two opposite ends: a current of air may cool, but it may also kindle. And consequently the wind often involves in Shakespeare's mind kindred images of *heat* and *fire*, and *glowing coals*, linked in their turn to a burning love or passion (often with an undertone of lust); whereas wind may turn into *vent*, or *breath*, and hence ultimately lead to *pants* suggestive of passionate love, or love-making. Now many of the elements forming that neat little spiral of clustered images can be seen again and again in a looser stage, scattered throughout *Venus and Adonis*, yet clearly submitted already to the ever increasing force of mutual attraction. The two opposite functions suggested by *wind* may be found, separately expressed, in two distinct and contrasting images.

The shadow has now left the place where Venus and her 'tender boy' had lain down, in the midday heat, and Adonis cries out:

> The sun doth burn my face; I must remove.

But Venus, loath to let him go, tells him:

> I'll sigh celestial *breath*, whose gentle *wind*
> Shall *cool the heat* of this descending sun. (189–90)

Further down, after the lively steed-and-mare intermezzo, Adonis is left a while alone. But Venus soon approaches:

> He sees her coming, and begins to *glow*,
> Even as a dying *coal* revives with *wind*. (337–8)

These opposite effects produced by the same agency necessarily involve a latent possibility of ambiguity. And such ambiguity underlies the very first image used in *Antony and Cleopatra* with reference to the lovers: Antony's heart, indeed

> reneges all temper,
> And is become the *bellows* and the *fan*
> To *cool* a gipsy's *lust*. (I, i, 8–10)

Here again we may point to a parallel passage in *Venus and Adonis* where amorous desire is likened to a glowing coal that must be cooled. Towards the beginning of the poem, Venus, in her passion, is already described as 'red and hot as coals of glowing fire'. And now, referring to the surge of what she euphemistically calls 'sweet desire', she urges:

> Affection is a *coal* that must be *cool'd*;
> Else, suffer'd, it will set the heart on *fire*. (387–8)

In *Antony and Cleopatra* the image is of course much more condensed: the glowing coal has been dropped—though a faint reminiscence of it may well linger in the connotations of the word 'bellows'—and the fire of love is understood. Part of the full image is thus implicit; but there it is none the less, for it is crystal clear that in order to be cooled the gipsy's lust had to be kindled first, and obviously by the same agent who now alone can quench what he had set on fire! In spite of the treasures of ingenuity that some critics have lavished to cajole us into assimilating the bellows to the fan, it seems much more natural to concede that the bellows inevitably suggest the glowing of a coal and, juxtaposed as they are with a fan, conjure up again in a bold ellipsis the image of the antithetical virtues of the Shakespearian wind. Our set of recurrent imagery in *Venus and Adonis* thus helps us to a right understanding of that much discussed image.

In fact, it was Venus's tragedy that poor Adonis should have been so manifestly efficient (however involuntarily) in kindling the coal of her devouring passion, yet so utterly unwilling and unable to cool it again. And hence the wondrous war of white and damask so constantly committed in her nicely-gauded cheeks: what a sight it was

> To note the fighting conflict of her hue,
> How white and red each other did destroy!
> But now her cheek was pale, and by and by
> It flash'd forth fire, as lightning from the sky. (345–8)

I am not sure whether the conventional image of such constantly warring hues did not play its modest part—though perhaps at several removes—in the genesis of our apparent conceit. For it must be acknowledged that the 'conceit' necessarily implies, at bottom, the notion of a similar interplay of colours in Cleopatra's delicate cheeks.

But Cleopatra's, on the whole, was a much happier lot than that of poor famished Venus, since her man of men—whose heart she was about to purse up on the river Cydnus—certainly had in abundance what coy young Adonis so patently lacked, and there was little danger that her passion, once kindled, should not be deliciously refreshed and cooled. However this may be, it looks as if Shakespeare's mind, when conceiving of this highly refined little *tableau de genre* in *Antony and Cleopatra*, had unconsciously summoned up to the silent sessions of his thoughts remembrance of his own Venus of yore. And it so happened that these reminiscences of early laid images were brooded anew; and bred, like your serpent of Egypt, by the operation...not of your sun, but of a genius grown mature, they ultimately hatched into a Super-Venus. More than an Ovidian metamorphosis, this meant a new creation. But the links, however tenuous, between the conventional conceits of *Venus and Adonis* and some flashes of the imagery that inform *Antony and Cleopatra* are none the less unmistakable and instructive.

Even in matters minor but as various as a delicate touch descriptive of a smile, or the poetical notion of art perfecting nature, or the reference to a mythological fable, not to mention the choice of just those elements which best impart the surge ethereal of love, the early poem more than foreshadows the later tragedy.

When Venus in her 'swelling passion' invites Adonis to be her deer, graze on her lips and feed at will on that alluring park of hers, within the circuit of her ivory arms—

> At this Adonis smiles as in disdain,
> That in each cheek appears a pretty dimple. (241–2)

If we remember that, on the one hand, those pretty dimples are said to be made by Love and the young man is called a 'tender boy' and 'rose-cheek'd Adonis', and that, on the other hand, Cleopatra is compared in our passage to Venus, and her attending pretty dimpled boys to smiling Cupids, the parallel becomes interesting.[2]

Moreover, the brilliant evocation of Cleopatra—the cynosure on Cydnus—as

> O'er-picturing that Venus where we see
> The *fancy outwork nature*, (II, ii, 206–7)

presents in a dense and arresting form the quintessence of what was already (and more laboriously) expressed in the lines about the perfection of the young hunter's courser:

> Look, when a *painter* would *surpass* the life,
> In *limning* out a well-proportion'd steed,
> His *art* with *nature's workm*anship at strife,
> As if the dead the living should *exceed.* (289–92)

When it came to express the power of love, few 'exempla' were as classical and suggestive as that of the god of war ensnared in Venus's toils and enslaved. Venus herself refers to it to illustrate her might and show Adonis how privileged he was to have, unask'd, what Mars himself begged for:

> I have been woo'd, as I entreat thee now,
> Even by the stern and direful god of war,
> Whose sinewy neck in battle ne'er did bow,
> Who conquers where he comes in every jar;
> Yet hath he been my captive and my slave. (97–101)

Again, this must have been remembered by Shakespeare when he wanted to convey how, in the eyes of his Roman friends, the greatest soldier of the world was turned into a woman's fool:

> those his goodly eyes,
> That o'er the files and musters of the war
> Have glowed like plated Mars, now bend, now turn,
> The office and devotion of their view
> Upon a tawny front: his captain's heart,
> Which in the scuffles of great fights hath burst
> The buckles on his breast, reneges all temper. (I, i, 2–8)

What Venus elaborates in three full stanzas is here condensed in half that space and with more powerful imagery.

That the mythological fable was in Shakespeare's mind is further proved by Mardian's subtly humorous repartee to Cleopatra. 'Indeed?' the Queen exclaims, rather surprised at hearing that Mardian, though a eunuch, has affections (passions). Whereupon Mardian replies:

> Not in deed, madam; for I can do nothing
> But what indeed is honest to be done:
> Yet have I fierce affections, and think
> What Venus did with Mars. (I, v, 15–18)

Notice that he does not say 'what Mars did with Venus'. Apart from making some lascivious innuendoes, Mardian, it is clear, insinuates that Venus was the active agent: in other words, what Venus did with Mars was to render him her slave. He thereby deftly hints at Cleopatra's own 'supremacy' over Antony.

Thus, the poetical equating of Antony with Mars and Cleopatra with Venus—a many-faceted motive, used with sovereign subtlety—most probably suggested itself when dormant reminiscences from the early poem were stirred to life by Shakespeare's creative vision of the peerless lovers.

Finally, Venus has a definition of love which certainly anticipates one of the most significant images prompted to Cleopatra by her immortal longings. The evocation of a tripping fairy and a dancing nymph leads Venus to express what may well be called the ethereal aspect of love:

> Love is a spirit all compact of fire,
> Not gross to sink, but light, and will aspire. (149–50)

This is suggestive of something immaterial, hence weightless and moving upward, contrasted to the downward drop of things material, gross and bound to sink. Now this fiery spirit is precisely the kind of love implicit in Cleopatra's magnificent phrase:

> I am fire and air; my other elements
> I give to baser life. (v, ii, 292–3)

Everything is there again, for each word, each connotation, suggests its opposite. But what is caught here is the very essence of the thing, expressed with pregnant simplicity—a sheer miracle of compression.

We suggested at the outset of our inquiry that the delicately sophisticated image of the pretty dimpled boys and their fans was vastly more than a mere conceit: for once it is read within a larger context, it leads us to the core of Cleopatra's complex and perplexing nature. For one thing it must be remembered that the description of the Venus-like Queen in her barge represents the only full-length portrait of Cleopatra in state throughout the whole play—and as such its function is manifold. Its immediate purpose, within the scene, is of course to intimate by the sheer magic of her appeal the full potency of the spell she has cast upon Antony. Made receptive, more than ever, to her prodigious power of attraction, we penetrate at once the truth, inexorable and stark, of Enobarbus's pronouncement—his ominous 'never'. With the finality of the Raven's 'nevermore', it tolls the knell of Antony's Roman day. Never indeed will Antony 'leave her utterly': she is his Eastern star, and in the East his pleasure lies.

But another important function of this retrospective apparition is to lend the significant statements that so forcibly complete and crown the portrait of the enchanting Queen a full perspective. The set piece conjures up, in a way, Cleopatra's aura—a bewitching mixture of feminine glamour and graceful majesty, a sensuous appeal so radiant that everything around becomes suffused with Love: 'the inanimate is felt as animate'[3] and the elements themselves grow amorous. The statements topping the set speech give us the gist of Cleopatra's inward nature. Taken together, they represent a brilliant epitome of Cleopatra's whole personality. For no feature perhaps is so specific of her unique individuality as what may be called her transmuting power. To her *cri-du-cœur*

> none our parts so poor,
> But was a race of heaven, (i, iii, 36–7)

the earliest appearance of the motive, Enobarbus now adds the sober confirmation:

> vilest things
> Become themselves in her. (ii, ii, 243–4)

This transmuting power it is that makes the holy priests bless her when she is riggish, that enables her to hop forty paces through the public street and, panting and breathless, breathe forth power.

Our apparent conceit, I suggest, is poetically linked with such striking and vivid images, since they convey her capacity of turning the lowest into the highest, of making of a fault a virtue, of transforming a thing into its very opposite. The wind did seem to glow the delicate cheeks that it was meant to cool: and thus what the divers-coloured fans undid they did. The paradox is but a subtle hint of a much deeper paradox which underlies the very nature of the enigmatic Queen.

If I felt my eye rolling in the fine Christian frenzy of certain critics, I might even be tempted to interpret the very act of Cleopatra's death as an ultimate reverberation of that great thematic opposition. By having this knot intrinsicate of life at once untied, Cleopatra, I would thus rhapsodize, deliberately undid that fleeting and terrestrial life of hers—giving up a world which had become too vile for her. But what she undid in this low earthly realm she apparently did in the heavenly sphere: leaving her other elements to baser life and turning into fire and air meant gaining a new and perennial life—in other words achieving immortality.

But my frenzy is merely human, and I think it safer to leave such airy fabrics spinning their own fiery wheels in the vast Icarian spaces of mythical criticism, and keep to a more homely loom. The charm with which Cleopatra yields herself to death and makes of an apparent weakness a sheer display of strength[4] matches in grandeur the apotheosis of her apparition upon the river Cydnus. And the picture of the pretty dimpled boys, those ministering Cupids, glowing with their fans the delicate cheeks of their Venus-like Queen in the very act of cooling them is perhaps a symbol, or at least a vivid reflection, of the great paradox of Cleopatra's nature. Who, be it remembered, was so textured that she made of her very defects perfection: transmuting thus an apparent negative into a real positive—nay, into the peak and summit of achievement.

NOTES

1. Though John Middleton Murry does not seem to mention it, there is a possibility that both *Venus and Adonis* and *Antony and Cleopatra* played a part in the genesis of this theme, as the keyword 'cloy' would suggest. For one thing the theme is first introduced in *Fancy*. And in the earliest version of the poem the keyword appears in evidence in a couplet which was later omitted:

'Every pleasure, every joy,
Not a mistress but doth cloy.'

Now in this early version there is a passage, likewise suppressed when the poem was published (see H. W. Garrod, *The Poetical Works of John Keats*, 2nd ed. (Oxford, 1958), pp. 266–7), in which we have a lively reference to Adonis:

Mistress fair!
'Thou shalt have that tressed hair
Adonis tangled all for spite,
And the mouth he would not kiss,
And the treasure he would miss....'

This passage again closes with a reappearance of our theme:

'Never fulsome, ever new,
There she steps! and tell me who
Has a Mistress so divine?
Be the palate ne'er so fine
She cannot sicken.'

I would be the last to deny that 'in those suppressed lines the intimate connection of Keats's poem as he originally wrote it with his love [for Fanny Brawne] is manifest' (*Keats and Shakespeare* (1926), p. 107). But I submit that the theme might well derive both from personal experiences and from literary reminiscences. If so, *Venus and Adonis* no doubt belongs to its literary genesis. As to Keats's admiration for *Antony and Cleopatra*, it is too well known to need further comments here.

2. It is worth pointing out, moreover, that there is only one other instance of dimpled smiles in the whole Shakespearian canon; and that this is found in a later play (*Timon of Athens*, IV, iii, 119).

3. L. C. Knights, *Some Shakespearean Themes* (1959), p. 145. There is, no doubt, a deliberately hyperbolic element not only in Cleopatra's 'infinite variety' but in the whole physical and psychological portrait of the Queen which lends the end of the scene a subtly rhapsodic aspect. See M. Charney, 'Shakespeare's Style in *Julius Caesar* and *Antony and Cleopatra*', *E.L.H.* XXVI (1959), 365.

4. 'The strength of Cleopatra has never appeared more clearly than in the charm with which she yields herself to death' (M. Van Doren, *Shakespeare* (1941), p. 281).

VENUS AND THE SECOND CHANCE

BY

J. W. LEVER

From Bion to Ronsard, from Ovid and Lucretius to Chaucer and Spenser, the poets of humanism have been charmed by Venus—and in more than the polite sense alone. She has revealed herself in many forms: as a shepherdess in Arcadia; a lovely lady in an allegorical garden; *alma Venus*, the all-creating mother; *Aphrodite Urania*, the queen of heaven. By some she has been portrayed as a cruel, a fickle, or a feckless tyrant; others have caught her smiling. Only Shakespeare, it would seem, viewed her as thoroughly absurd, a fat white woman whom nobody loved. Forty years old, fluttery and apprehensive, loquacious and perspiring: such is the impression which the heroine of his first poem has made upon several distinguished scholar-critics. Nor is Venus only ridiculous. She is also the personification of lust, that sullies all it touches; mistress of the dark horse from Plato's *Phaedrus*; a figure of evil eminence comparable with Milton's Satan. It is strange to think of Shakespeare, with the romantic comedies and the sonnets in praise of increase still to write, taking so hard a view, or views, of the love goddess. An alternative to be reckoned with is that these attitudes are rather the projections of a twentieth-century puritanism and its dissatisfaction with some Renaissance ways of interpreting love. After all, it is understandable that an age much concerned with obliterating the humanist image of man should feel profoundly out of sympathy with Shakespeare's approach. His poem is erotic, but not prurient; it is also philosophical, without an improving ideology. For modern readers the story should be carried to a more entertaining conclusion; or, from the other standpoint, should teach a lesson that sexuality does not pay. There should be no alarming intrusion of the boar; or, if boar there must be, let it punish Adonis for sins committed, not refused. At best, therefore, the poem (it is, after all, by Shakespeare) must be taken as a very funny story which somehow forgets the joke, or as a highly cautionary tale which, in showing the dangers of caution, does not point the moral at all well.

Those who regard *Venus and Adonis* as a great and truly Shakespearian poem should not ignore its comical aspects. There is certainly humour here, as there is, too, in Shakespeare's tragedies. There is also latent tragedy, a quality never quite absent from his comedies. But the poem is, in fact, not a comedy or a tragedy. It is not a drama. It is occupied with narrating a myth, and characteristically the aim is to maintain a certain detachment or 'distancing' of sympathetic response. Literary myths (religion and anthropology hardly concern us here) do not enter into the current of human life; they interpret life through a fictional paradigm, telling how nature became as we know it, how death or winter came into the world, how paradise happened to be lost. Hence the persons of literary myth are not wholly human personages, but rather less and rather more; creatures of impulse, and also natural or supernatural forces. For much the same reason, they are not moral abstractions. They precede or illuminate human morality, but they do not, unless transformed into allegorical figures, define or direct it. Our responses to Venus, therefore, as well as to Adonis and the non-human creatures that play their parts in the story, should proceed from the recognition that she and they are essentially mythical beings.

First and last, in her assumption of flesh and in her ascension back into the sky, Venus is a divinity. That nothing of the mystery might be lost, Shakespeare renounced the Arcadian trappings provided in Ovid or Ronsard, where the goddess in rustic attire enjoyed a leisurely pastoral honeymoon with Adonis, roaming the hills, hunting, making cheese or making love in a hut or a cave through numberless days. Suddenly and from nowhere she materializes 'like a bold fac'd suter', corporeal enough to pluck the 'tender boy' from his horse and push him to the ground. Yet at no point in the narration is she clearly visualized. Writers who seek pictorial analogies have forgotten that she is neither naked nor clothed, neither a Titian nude nor a tapestry shepherdess. Nor is Venus of any determinate age; her beauty as the spring doth yearly grow; as a divine being, she is of course beyond time. When Adonis fails to succumb at the first onset, she makes it plain that she is no mortal woman. Let him feel her hand with his: it will 'dissoule, or seeme to melt'. The primrose bank on which she lies is miraculously unstirred; its 'forcelesse flowers' support her like 'sturdy trees'. Two 'strengthles doues'— substituted for Ovid's more substantial swans—will draw her at her pleasure through the skies. Moreover, she can assume a variety of shapes by which immortals are known to human fancy.

> Bid me discourse, I will enchant thine ear,
> Or, like a fairy, trip upon the green,
> Or, like a nymph, with long dishevel'd hair,
> Dance on the sands, and yet no footing seen.

These words ring far-off bells for Titania and Ariel's 'sweet sprites'. They, and not Doll Tearsheet or Mistress Quickly, belong in the company of Venus.

But she is also Venus Genetrix, the cosmic force of *natura naturans*, epitomising the Lucretian and late-Renaissance vision of 'the whole realm of Nature in growth and fertility'.[1] In this aspect Venus makes her appeal first of all on the plane of reason, with a statement of her doctrine of increase.

> By law of nature thou art bound to breed,
> That thine may live when thou thy self art dead;
> And so, in spite of death thou dost survive,
> In that thy likeness still is left alive.

Here Shakespeare expressed one of his own profoundest convictions as a young writer, that breed was man's only chance in life. The doctrine was elaborated with extensive analogies in the earlier sonnets to the Friend; it was implicit or declared in the romantic comedies, and it appeared even in *Measure for Measure* as the primary datum on which all considerations turned:

> Your brother and his lover have embraced:
> As those that feed grow full, as blossoming time
> That from the seedness the bare fallow brings
> To teeming foison, even so her plenteous womb
> Expresseth his full tilth and husbandry.   (I, iv, 40–4)

Secondly, Venus urges her love at the vegetable level of mindless sentience, where human sexuality merges with all the vague, pleasurable sensations of landscape and fecundity. 'Ile be a parke, and thou shalt be my deare.' Her woman's body, as every lover knows, is also mountain and dale, hillock and brakes, grassland and springs, where the innocent male creature may pasture and take shelter. When these persuasions also fail to move the boy, animal nature in its most vigorous form is called up to supply a living object-lesson. The breeding jennet and the trampling courser belong indeed to Venus Genetrix; they are her splendid beasts and enact their spirited drama of courtship at her bidding. This was the theme of Lucretius's invocation at the beginning of *De Rerum Natura*, of the first chorus in Seneca's *Hippolytus*,[2] and of Spenser's great hymn in the Temple of Venus:

> The Lyons roare; the Tygres loudly bray;
> The raging Buls rebellow through the wood,
> And breaking forth dare tempt the deepest flood
> To come where thou doest draw them with desire.
> So all things else, that nourish vitall blood,
> Soone as with fury thou doest them inspire,
> In generation seeke to quench their inward fire. (*Faerie Queene*, IV, x, 46)

The horses' antics are presented with a touch of cool irony, rather as Berowne might view them; but they are hardly a parody of human courtship. Rather do they pattern off the thing itself—joyous, melancholy, gallant, absurd—the very madness of lovers for which only one cure exists. Exponents of *Shakespeare Moralisé* have equated the courser to Plato's vicious, mis-shapen horse of the allegory in *Phaedrus*; this is to slander the paragon of quadrupeds, who displays all the points of equine excellence and surpasses an actual beast as much as the ideal horse of a great painter, 'his Art with Natures workmanship at strife', surpasses any common specimen. None the less, the picture is incomplete. For perfection one thing more is needed: 'a proud rider on so proud a back'. 'Proud' and 'back' have their comprehensive Elizabethan connotations: a human lover, his reason directing but not harshly curbing his desires, would indeed be creation's lord. Unfortunately it is just this mature co-ordination that Adonis rejects; and his rejection gives rise to both the comic and the tragic ingredients of the poem.

The boy is not a very complex figure. As Venus sees him, he is the beauty of the universe in both realms of nature and spirit, 'The fields chief flower...Staire to all Nimphs, more louely then a man'; the very essence of those qualities again to be incarnate in the Friend of the Sonnets. But if the mythical Adonis surpasses actual mankind in beauty—just as his horse surpasses all common quadrupeds—he is at the same time the archetypal young human male in his wilfulness and conceit. Venus, queen of the skies and mistress of all nature, who has subdued Mars the God of war, is utterly baffled in her dealings with this coy adolescent. She estimates Adonis by her own non-human standards, calling his moist palm 'Earths soueraigne salue', taking his breath as 'heauenly moisture, aire of grace'. In kissing him she matches the assaults of her own birds of prey on the more timid species, though her sallies are, of course, as harmless as love itself. Yet Adonis is obdurate and unmoved. He blushes, pouts, lours and frets, with no thought for anything but his strayed horses. And meanwhile the goddess, who has taken on human form for his sake, suffers in the flesh from heat and desire. Exposed at once to the burning rays of a heavenly and an earthly 'sunne', the love-sick queen herself sweats, blushes and weeps like any mortal. It is a preposterous and not uncomical situation, though hardly the vaudeville farce that our own age, much concerned that the body should be deodorized, air-conditioned and hermetically capsuled, would wish to make it.

As for Adonis, once he finds his tongue he has several excuses to make. Only one kind of love appeals to him.

> 'I know not love', quoth he, 'nor will not know it,
> Unless it be a boar, and then I chase it.'

Besides, he is too young: if he should yield prematurely, he will very likely forfeit his manhood.

> The colt that's back'd and burden'd being young
> Loseth his pride and never waxeth strong.

This equine analogy may seem, for the boy's situation, oddly framed, but the question is not very important. Venus knows that if Adonis prefers the hard hunt to love, he is likely for ever to forfeit his 'pride', and his life into the bargain. Well might she have said, as Seneca's (or rather, Studley's) Phaedra said of Hippolytus:

> Alas be not so manly now, this manlinesse forbeare,
> And rather choose to live a man with womans sprite and feare,
> Then as no man with manly heart in darcknesse deepe to sit:
>
> (*Hippolytus V*; 'Tudor Translations', I, 180)[3]

For her part she resorts to feminine tactics, lets herself faint, pretends to be dead, and for a little while finds the boy assiduous, even affectionate. But soon enough Adonis recovers and casts about for further excuses, telling Venus that he is like the ungrown fry that fishermen reject, or like a green plum that, early plucked, is sour to the taste. On such matters Venus is presumably the better judge.

The follies of lovers, and the graver follies of those who refuse to love, make up the fabric of Shakespeare's comedies: Titania wasting her raptures upon a mortal; Lysander and Demetrius prating of reason in the enchanted woods; Silvius scorning Phebe; Bertram, another would-be hero, refusing Helena. In the comedies, tragic catastrophe is always potential, though happily averted. Tragedy is waiting for Adonis too, in the inseparable Shakespearian antinomies of beauty and destruction, love and death, creation and chaos. He is the field's first flower, and whatever is most beautiful is also most vulnerable. The instrument for his catastrophe is the Boar. Those who regard this poem as 'a diverting parody', 'a flawless trifle' and the like have not paused long to see what aspect of reality that brute embodies. Shakespeare's boar is by no means of the order of other wild creatures—lions, bears and wolves—mentioned by Ovid as possible hunting risks. In the presence of Adonis such beasts are tame and innocuous. Nor is Shakespeare's boar the agent of a jealous Mars, as in Ronsard, nor of 'Stygian gods', as Spenser implied.[4] He is himself alone, like the king who wore his crest; a mindless nemesis at the core of life. Venus warns Adonis of what the brute will do to him:

> Alas, he nought esteems that face of thine, . . .
> But having thee at vantage,—wondrous dread !—
> Would root these beauties as he roots the mead.

Like Time in the Sonnets, the Boar too 'feeds on the rarities of nature's truth', and in desperation Venus repeats her arguments for love and increase as man's only safeguard. But Adonis interrupts her 'idle ouer-handled theame' and counters with his own moral lecture. In the presence of Love descended from heaven, he avers that 'loue to heauen is fled'. He declaims against 'Lusts winter' to one whose beauty is that of eternal spring; against lust's gluttony to one who would famish his lips amid their plenty. All the commonplaces of the moralists are fetched out glibly, till at last he breaks off in embarrassment:

> More I could tell, but more I dare not say;
> The text is old, the orator too green.

In fact (so far as we are dealing with facts) the text was not old. Adonis is committing an anachronism, like Lear's Fool who speaks a prophecy of Merlin though living before Merlin's time. But his moralising has a proleptic relevance, for such lust as he denounces will indeed appear on earth, in the state of fallen sexuality induced by Venus's curse.

Adonis breaks from the embrace of Venus and runs off into the night. Having refused the little death, he will suffer the great one. The boy who knows not love, unless it be a boar, is about to find the love he is seeking.

Venus remains to lament him. She is now as helpless on earth as any mortal girl who has been rejected by her lover; pathetic, and perhaps a little foolish. Deliberately Shakespeare turns her passion to favour and to prettiness. Anticipating Ophelia, Venus 'sings extemporally a wofull dittie', while the caves insensibly echo her griefs. Undoubtedly, through some Renaissance rendering, and probably through Ronsard's, Shakespeare knew Bion's elegy; but unlike Bion or Ronsard, he had no vision of a sympathetic nature overcome by sorrow. For the pagan world the Adonis myth explained the cycle of the seasons: when the lover of Venus died, mountains and rivers, trees and flowers, joined in the mourning with Echo as their voice. But in *Venus and Adonis* nature is supremely indifferent. The echoes merely parrot any sound they hear; summer preserves its bright, meaningless smile.

> The flowers are sweet, their colours fresh and trim,
> But true-sweet beauty lived and died with him.

As in the 'threnos' of *The Phoenix and The Turtle*:

> Truth may seem, but cannot be;
> Beauty brag, but 'tis not she....

It is a world of seeming where Venus now wanders, clutched at by the boughs of trees, hearing the baying of the hounds and starting at her own thoughts as if an adder had reared itself up in her way. This had been the place 'where neuer serpent hisses'; now, that paradise is lost and death is everywhere. Vainly Venus 'exclaimes on death', vainly she flatters him, or deludes herself that Adonis cannot die:

> For he being dead, with him is beauty slain,
> And, beauty dead, black chaos comes again.

The moment comes when she sees his corpse, and learns the truth.

Finally, the goddess of love curses her own gift, making love 'fickle, false, and full of fraud', suspicious and perverse, 'cause of warre, and dire events', cause, too, of 'dissention twixt the sonne, and sire'. Cressida, Hermione, Helen and Phaedra will all suffer or cause suffering in the time to come. Her curse delivered and weary of the world, Venus yokes her doves and mounts back into the skies, making for her shrine at Paphos, where she 'Meanes to immure her selfe, and not be seen'. With her she takes the purple and white flower of Adonis, who had so desired to 'grow unto himselfe'. Metamorphosed into a part of inanimate nature, the boy at last belongs to her.

Here, properly speaking, ends Shakespeare's story of Venus and Adonis. Ronsard had cynically added a surprise coda, to the effect that Venus at once forgot her lover and solaced herself with the Phrygian shepherd Anchises. *Telles sont et seront les amitiez des femmes*, he concluded: women's loves were like the April flowers that last for only a day. As treated by Ronsard, the metamorphosis had become a simile, just as the mythological figures had become little other than human lovers in a pastoral setting. But a more idealistic poet might also endow human personages with a mythical aura so that actuality might be poetically sublimated. In Spenser's *Astrophel* the Adonis story served for an elegy in honour of Sir Philip Sidney. Like Adonis, Astrophel was 'a gentle shepheard borne in Arcady', 'the fairest flowre in field that ever grew', slain by a boar while hunting savage beasts on foreign soil. His Stella was as fair as Venus; but being a mortal mistress, she chose to follow her lover, proving 'that death their hearts cannot divide'. Pitying both, the gods changed them into a single flower with a star in the centre. Subjoined to *Astrophel* was a second elegy, 'The Dolefull Lay of Clorinda', a person who represented Sidney's sister. Clorinda took over Venus's complaint against Death, 'devourer of all worlds delight'; but, unlike Venus, she found Christian consolation in the immortality of the spirit:

> Ah no: it is not dead, ne can it die,
> But lives for aie, in blisfull Paradise:
> Where like a new-borne babe it soft doth lie,
> In bed of lillies wrapt in tender wise...

For Shakespeare's more representational art there was a wide disparity between the myth of a beautiful shepherd boy slain by a boar and the historical fact of a heroic soldier killed in battle. But the distance was gradually bridged in the personal medium of the sonnets. Through the time-sequence of the loosely associated groups the Friend, born to greatness, matures from a beautiful, Narcissus-like boy who refuses marriage to the conqueror of Time who, in sonnet LV, paces forth 'Gainst death and all-oblivious enmity'. The evolution is complex, realistic, and tells nothing but the truth. The Friend has, indeed, escaped the Boar in adolescence; instead he survives into corruption, a lily that festers, the living corroboration of Venus's statement that fair flowers ungathered rot and consume themselves. Both he and his lover the poet experience the effects of lust, 'the expense of spirit in a waste of shame', consequent upon Venus's curse. Both are stained by the world and wrinkled by time. But the Friend, who rejected immortality by breed, is at last immortalized through the marriage of true minds. Not Eros, progenitive love, but Agape, the creative love of the imagination, redeems him—and with him, the truth and beauty of nature—from Time and the Boar.

This hard-won prize of a second chance for life, this vision of antinomies transcended through a love still rooted in human nature and the phenomenal world, was the recompense and illumination of Shakespeare's later dramas. The early tragedies, like the narrative poems, lacked such ultimate conviction; in them paradise was lost, it would seem irretrievably. But in

Shakespeare's maturity he won through to the concept of tragic drama as a paradoxical triumph. It was thus that the Venus and Adonis myth received its full explication in the late love-tragedy, *Antony and Cleopatra*.

In this play Antony is Adonis allowed, like the Friend, to grow up; a great soldier, like Spenser's Astrophel, but on an even grander scale. Unlike the chaste, self-regarding boy, he willingly acts Mars to Cleopatra's Venus:

> Over my altars hath he hung his lance,
> His batter'd shield, his uncontrolled crest,
> And for my sake hath learn'd to sport, and dance,
> To toy, to wanton, dally, smile and jest,
>   Scorning his churlish drum and ensign red,
>   Making my arms his field, his tent my bed.   (*Venus and Adonis*, 103–8)

As for Cleopatra, though Venus in her eternal youth, her infinite variety, even her feminine wiles (her swoons and ardours, her pretence of death), though appearing as Venus in her barge, and wearing 'the habiliments of Isis' in the market-place, she is very much a mortal queen. Both lovers evince a tarnished splendour. In their natures reign 'All frailties that besiege all kinds of blood'; and the setting of their courtship is no Arcadia of innocent sexuality, but a corrupted empire torn by 'war and dire events', where the Boar rages in human form. Cleopatra's own Egypt is a fallen country infested with serpents; the snake is never far from her thoughts, until the time comes for her to die of its sting. In this lost paradise her wooing of Antony is comic and sensual, immoral and thoroughly reprehensible. Shakespeare's vision, however, miraculously transcends all this with its perspective of a paradise regained in the union of love and death. Through the fiery consummation of that union, the mortal lovers become immortals: in no world of nature, nor in a spiritual heaven, but in another, unknown country of the imagination.

> Where souls do couch on flowers, we'll hand in hand
> And with our sprightly port make the ghosts gaze.

It is a regal metamorphosis, very different from that of the flower of Adonis; different, too, from that of Clorinda's Astrophel, as a new-born babe in a bed of lilies, which may have suggested the couching souls. Antony and Cleopatra belong not with these in their repose, but as successful rivals to Dido and 'her' Aeneas, also united after death as Shakespeare, not Virgil, saw them.

This country of the imagination has no rightful place in either the Christian or the pagan universe. It is not Lucretian, nor is it Platonic. But it is not for that reason to be dismissed as a sentimental fantasy. Cleopatra's dream-projection of 'an Emperor Antony' is defended against Dolabella's sad scepticism in words that Shakespeare chose as carefully as any he wrote:

> nature wants stuff
> To vie strange forms with fancy; yet, to imagine
> An Antony, were nature's piece 'gainst fancy,
> Condemning shadows quite.   (v, ii, 97–100)

In fancy, the ruined Antony crests the world; shakes the orb like thunder; pours forth a bounty that has no winter in it. In fancy, Cleopatra the deposed queen of occupied Egypt becomes his empress. Yet these very paradoxes are truth in its supreme manifestation. 'The art itself is nature', overcoming nature's limitations through her masterpiece, the human spirit. In the last analysis, nature is no longer 'with her selfe at strife'. Chaos is an illusion; the Boar and Caesar are not fortune, but fortune's knaves. And Venus and Adonis, fallen and risen as Cleopatra and her Antony, live to triumph in the kingdom of the second chance.

NOTES

1. M. C. Bradbrook, *Shakespeare and Elizabethan Poetry* (1951), p. 51. This article owes much to the admirable chapter on the Ovidian Romance.

2. Don Cameron Allen, in his contribution 'On *Venus and Adonis*' in *Elizabethan and Jacobean Studies Presented to F. P. Wilson* (1959), pp. 106–7, is, to my knowledge, the first person who has suggested that the Hippolytus myth influenced Shakespeare's poem. That influence seems to have operated, in many more respects than Ovid's account would suggest, through Seneca's *Hippolytus*, most probably in Studley's translation.

3. A passage from Phaedra's lament not to be found in Seneca's original.

4. *Faerie Queene*, III, vi, 46. In III, i, 37, the boar's attack is attributed to 'the chance that dest'ny doth ordaine'.

SOME OBSERVATIONS ON *THE RAPE OF LUCRECE*

BY

D. C. ALLEN

Lucrece, the heroine of Shakespeare's second brief epic and the human opposite of his foolish and frustrated Venus, had long been for men, and hence for their wives, a gracious yet tragic example of married love. During most of the Middle Ages, she was placed on the short-list of wives and widows celebrated for their chastity and faith; sometimes she was bracketed with the patriotic Judith, whose established purity helped to disestablish a tyrant.[1] In Chaucer's *Legend of Good Women*, she takes her place in the assembly of the virtuous, but Chaucer was only presenting in English a directory of ladies already consecrated in decency by the master poets across the Channel. If we want to see her on parade, we have only to turn through the books of Eustache Deschamps:

> Car de Dydo ne d'Elaine,
> De Judith la souveraine,
> Ne d'Ester ne de Tysbee
> De Lucresse la Rommaine,
> Ne d'Ecuba la certaine,
> Sarre loial ne Medee
> Ne pourroit estre trouvee
> Dame de tant de biens plaine.[2]

This is an impressive procession even though one may have his doubts about the credentials of some of the marchers. But no matter what our reservations, Judith is here and so is Hecuba, the queen whose tragedy softens the despair of Shakespeare's Lucrece.

Deschamps concludes his poem by remarking that all these women are like 'stars shining beyond the mountain in the dawn'. They are aloof, unearthly ideals of femininity lost in the dark folds of history. Though men of the Renaissance knew from Livy that Lucrece had been dead for two thousand years, she seemed, thanks to their nostalgia for antiquity which shortened chronological distances, to be near at hand. 'There is no one so stupid', the Italian critic Sperone Speroni writes, 'who has not heard of her by hearsay or through his reading'.[3] Shakespeare underlines this statement when he tells us that Aaron, a Moor, and Olivia, a lady of Illyria, knew about her almost as much, perhaps, as he did himself. But Shakespeare's age was also one that trusted in monuments, that felt the presence of illustrious dead as it surveyed the marble aisles and floors of churches. If one doubted the testimony of the ancients, one had only to go to Viterbo to read the plaque erected to a noble wife by her sorrowing husband.

D.M.S.

COLLATINUS TARQUINIUS DULCISSIMAE CONIUNGI ET INCOMPARABILI LUCRETIAE PUDICITIAE DECORI, MULIERUM GLORIAE. VIXIT ANN. XXII. MEN. III. DI. VI. PROH DOLOR QUANTUM FUIT CARISSIMA.[4]

But there was another reason why men remembered Lucrece and why her tragedy attracted the attention of the young poet; she was not only a Roman heroine but also the centre of a Christian controversy.

A decade after Shakespeare's poem was in print, the Vice-Chancellor of Altdorf attended the production of a play about Lucrece at his university.[5] As he left the theatre he met some of the faculty arguing heatedly about the true nature of the lady's virtue. Her advocates quoted Ovid, Vergil, Florus, Valerius Maximus, and many other ancients in her cause; the serious negative was supplied with cartridge by St Augustine. Being a man of pompous moderation, the Vice-Chancellor spread oil on the flames by quoting, as he says, a Latin version of a Greek poem. The poem was actually first written in Latin by a Frenchman, and the Vice-Chancellor merely established his right to office with this blunder; but the poem, which presents the essential paradox, was widely known and I shall make do with a later English version:

> Were that unchast mate welcome to thy bed,
> *Lucrece*, thy lust was justly punished.
>   Why seek'st thou fame that di'dst deservedly?
> But if foule force defil'd thine honest bed,
> His onely rage should have bene punished:
>   Why diest thou for anothers villanie?
> Both wayes thy thirst of fame is too unjust,
> Dying, or for fond rage, or guiltie lust.[6]

The personal feeling of the Vice-Chancellor towards Lucrece was, I am happy to say, kinder than that of the poet, who simply echoed the saintly opinion of St Augustine.

To stern Tertullian and austere Jerome,[7] Lucrece was a splendid example of pagan domestic virtue, a woman whose actions might well be countenanced by Christian ladies possessed of the inner light. With the views of these mighty predecessors, St Augustine, who was inclined to condemn even the worthiest heathen when he was making a case against the spiritually unredeemed, heartily disagreed. In the *City of God* he attacks the conduct of Collatine's poor wife. 'This case is caught between both sides to such a degree that if suicide is extenuated, adultery is proved; if adultery is denied, the conviction is for suicide.' There is no way, he thinks, to resolve the problem. 'If she was adulterous, why is she praised? If she was chaste, why was she killed?' If she had been a Christian, she would have eschewed 'Roman pride in glory' and found another way 'to reveal her conscience to men'.[8]

For the sixteenth century the tragedy of Lucrece was a kind of casuistic problem, a matter of legal gamesmanship for canon lawyers.[9] From controversy of this nature the case got into the writings of the humanists, and we find Speroni remarking that Lucrece was of 'imperfect chastity' or she would have held fort against the assaults of Tarquin. A truly chaste woman, he assures us, would have died before surrender; but Lucrece abandoned her virtue just as a distressed ship jettisons its cargo. Her compliance with the desires of Tarquin was, in fact, an act midway between the forced and the voluntary.[10] With this view the French humanist, Henri Estienne, agrees: 'poore *Lucretia* did not judge aright of herselfe and her own estate'. Suicide is no revenge. 'Be it that her death were Vindicative, yet it were but a revenge of the injury done to the defiled body, and not of the wrong done to the undefiled mind, which is the seate of chastitie.'[11] The story of Lucrece was, I expect, made important for Shakespeare by this ancient yet current controversy; and without the benefit of this knowledge, we are nonplussed by the tenor of certain areas of his poem.

One may comprehend Shakespeare's consideration of the great argument by watching his Lucrece after the departure of Tarquin. She recites arias on Time, Night, and Occasion; then, looking at her sharp-nailed fingers, she blames them for not defending their 'loyal dame'. A few stanzas later (1149–76), the notion of suicide crosses her mind, and she recalls what Augustine has said, or, in a historical sense, is going to say: '"To kill myself," quoth she, "alack, what were it, But with my body my poor soul's pollution?"' The moral dilemma is made almost emblematic when Lucrece—almost her own symbol—lies dead in 'rigols' of pure and corrupt blood (1737–50); the Christian rather than the Roman lesson is to be read in this stylized *cul-de-lampe*. The living nature of the questions about Lucrece's action is also italicized when Brutus, who fails to speak the lines of the historians, says to the hysterical husband:

> Is it revenge to give thyself a blow
> For his foul act by whom thy fair wife bleeds?
> Such childish humour from weak minds proceeds:
> Thy wretched wife mistook the matter so,
> To slay herself, that should have slain her foe. (1823–7)

We must, I think, face the fact that Shakespeare read the story of Lucrece in its Christian context. There was no question in his mind about its tragic import, but he felt that it must be glossed in terms of Christian options. Lucrece should have defended herself to the death, or, having been forced, lived free of blame with a guiltless conscience. Her action was rare and wonderful, but a little beyond forgiveness.

Shakespeare's recognition of the double understanding of the Lucrece story explains, I think, the symbolic mileposts that guide us through this poem as they lead us through Spenser's *Faerie Queen*. His successors cling to the literal, and as a result Heywood's *The Rape of Lucrece* is simply a jolly exercise in dramatic bad taste, whereas Middleton's (?) *The Ghost of Lucrece*, while clinging to Shakespeare's text and superficially appearing to recognize the problem, fails to understand the ultimate lesson of Shakespeare's poem. If one looks across the Channel to the play on the legend by Nicolas Filleul, to the anonymous *Tragedie sur la Mort de Lucresse*,[12] to Chevreau's *La Lucresse Romaine Tragedie*, or to Du Ryer's *Lucrece Tragedie*, one discovers that only the last play takes notice of the question, tacking it on in an annotating speech of two dozen lines[13] that is a limping intruder in the neo-classic scene. But if Shakespeare's poem cannot be interpreted in terms of its English successors, it can only be partially understood when read under the light of its predecessor *Venus and Adonis*.

The conventional statements about the relation of these two poems need not be rehearsed; it is almost enough to say that they are no more in opposition with each other than are 'L'Allegro' and 'Il Penseroso' with which they are sometimes compared. Milton's poems, I think, represent a progressive course of thinking about the preparation of the poet-prophet; Shakespeare's poems are a similar sequence of discourses on the nature of human love. The poems are continuations rather than contradictions. In *Venus and Adonis* love, though veiled by courtly compliment, is discussed mainly on the basis of animal heat and placed outside the limits of a proper definition of the reasonable life. The animal theme returns in *Lucrece*, but in this second poem (a rougher Venus taking one part) the opposition comes from a different aspect of love: the devotion of a wife to her fleshly honour. The problem, as in subsequent plays, has something to do with *honour*, but it is also concerned with a total estimate of chastity on a higher level.

In *Venus and Adonis* the animal metaphors that point towards the ultimate theme depend to a degree on the hunter and the hunted; the same type of metaphor controls the first third of *The Rape of Lucrece*, but here the hunt is less equal than in the other poem. Tarquin is not a proper hunter pitted against an equal quarry. He enters in the night when only owls and wolves are heard because he is the 'night owle' that will catch the sleeping dove. In due course, he is compared to a serpent, a 'grim Lion', a 'faulcon towring', a 'Cockeatrice', a 'rough beast', a 'night waking Cat', a vulture, and a wolf. After his crime is done, he changes into a 'full-fed Hound, or gorged Hawke', and then slips away like a 'theevish dog'. Lucrece is naturally an innocent thing of nature: a 'white Hind', a mouse, a doe, a lamb, but more commonly a dove, a 'new-kild bird', a lesser fowl crouching under the shadow of the hawk's wings. She continues conscious of her metaphoric identity and eventually compares herself with the birds and with her mythological similar, Philomele. In the end, a 'pale swan', she sings before she dies.

These comparisons are plain enough and certainly to be expected, but whereas in *Venus and Adonis* there are several real animals—a stallion, a jennet, a hare, and a boar—in the cast of characters, *Lucrece* has only one. As Tarquin creeps to the bed of Lucrece bearing the 'lightless fire', 'Night-wandering weasels fright him, yet he still pursues his fear'. We know from the annotations on this passage that 'especially among the British' it is inauspicious to meet a weasel,[14] but the British were not alone in this superstition which was widely enough held in the sixteenth century to produce the axiom: 'Quidquid agis, mustela tibi si occurrat, omitte: Signa malae haec sortis bestia prava gerit.' But the weasel was more than a warning; it was a sign 'of evil to those whose houses they infest'.[15] The literal weasel not only warns Tarquin, but foretells the evil that awaits Lucrece. But the literal weasel is more than a weasel. The poet who was going to make us see the spider Iago without saying 'spider' can make us see who the weasel, well-known as a bird-nester, is; and we can annotate the concealed metaphor with a stanza from one of the great Renaissance Latin poets.

> Tu fera passeribus pestis sturnisque fuisti,
>   Quos trahere e nidis ars tibi summa fuit.
> Teque suis visae pullis timuere columbae,
>   Et magnis avibus parvulae terror eras.[16]

But Tarquin, who is evil on the animal level, sins against his creed when he attains human shape. Long before he commits his rape, he denounces himself: 'O shame to knighthood, and to shining Armes.' He is a warrior in arms but not in love, because he carries over the violence of battle to the tents of Love. The animal metaphors which bring Shakespeare's two poems momently together change when Tarquin crosses the threshold of Lucrece's bed-chamber; and, as befits a poem laid against a background of war and siege, love and battle make the terms of the analogues. 'Love', says the quiet poet George Herbert, 'is a man of war', and Shakespeare knew this trope only too well. He may have learned it from the *Aeneid* (XI, 736–7), or from the Latin elegiac poets;[17] but his probable master was Ovid, who gave him in the *Fasti* the basic material of his poem, and whose great pattern poem, 'Militat omnis amans et habet sua castra Cupido', is in the first of the *Amores*. From this book of the heart we learn that lovers and soldiers are the same except that the comrades of 'Frater Amor' are never demobbed.[18] The wars that they fight under the erotic banners are, however, seldom bitter and never violent.

From the texts of the Roman poets the troubadours,[19] the goliards,[20] the stilnovists,[21] and the only begetters[22] of Renaissance French and Italian poetry took their lessons. As a consequence of this long tradition, Shakespeare cannot avoid these comparisons when he writes about soldiers and their women. Tarquin says that 'Affection is my captain' and follows the metaphor through three stanzas as he follows the passageway to Lucrece's chamber. His lusts obey their 'Captain', too; and as he stands beside the sleeping young woman, his pulsing veins are 'like straggling slaves for pillage fighting'. But these figures are all ironic when applied to Tarquin. He is not a soldier of love fencing with his dear enemy or sharing her field-bed as an amorous companion; even when the metaphors turn to those of siege and assault, they are improperly in his company and exhibit him for what he is.

The theme of love as a siege comes also from Ovid's comparison between the soldier battering at the walls of an armed camp and the excluded lover weeping outside his beloved's locked door: 'Ille graves urbes, hic durae limen amicae Obsidet: hic portas frangit, at ille fores.' In the age of chivalry, when the taking of fortified places was a high military science, the metaphor of the capture of love's castle is fairly common. 'Que ja castels frevols qu'es assatzatz,' writes the troubadour Ponz de Capduelh, 'Ab gran poder.'[23] Raimon de Toulouse, an expert in both the arts of love and war, says that castles and towers are of no avail when love attacks. 'Ja castels ni tors No us cugetz que s'tenha, Plus gran forsa 'l venha.'[24] *Le Roman de la Rose*[25] ends with a great siege in which the beloved is rescued; and 'Le Hault Siege d'Amours' of Jean Molinet[26] plays on the theme of the amorous but gentle war. It is, of course, in this classical-medieval tradition that ardent Tarquin gallops from the siege of Ardea to the ravishing of Lucrece, but there is no indication that he has read its literature rightly.

Romeo driven back from Rosaline's walls can only commend her for not staying 'the siege of loving terms, Nor bide th'encounter of assailing eyes'. The 'false lord' Tarquin runs furiously like an enraged captain at the breaching of a wall; and, as Shakespeare sees him charge, 'Honour and beauty, in the owner's arms Are weakly fortress'd from a world of harms'. Lucrece's husband is likewise unaware that 'This siege...hath engirt his marriage'. The unknightly ravisher—his heart beating like a drum—lets his hands 'scale' the 'round turrets' of the lady's breasts, and by this action informs her that she 'is dreadfully beset'.

> His hand, that yet remains upon her breast,—
> Rude ram, to batter such an ivory wall!—
> May feel her heart—poor citizen!—distress'd,
> Wounding itself to death, rise up and fall,
> Beating her bulk, that his hand shakes withal.
> This moves in him more rage and lesser pity,
> To make the breach and enter this sweet city.   (463–9)

In keeping with the traditional tropes, Tarquin sounds 'a parley', and the pale face of Lucrece appearing over the turret of her white sheets seems a flag of surrender. 'Under that colour I am come to scale Thy never-conquer'd fort'. Lucrece, like a damsel of the romances, defends herself with words, but the situation is once again ironic. She is no coy and half-persuaded girl refuting the kindly arguments of her decent lover. She cannot prevail, and the fortress of her chastity is overcome not by favour but through force and duress. But though the castle of her virtue falls to an exterior force, the walls of Tarquin's soul are also demolished by interior revolt. 'Her subjects with foul insurrection Have batter'd down her consecrated wall.' One of the central paradoxes of *Venus and Adonis* is that of the hunter hunted; in this part of *The Rape of Lucrece* the ruiner is ruined.

Tarquin goes off with his spotted soul, bearing Lucrece's honour as his 'prisoner', and leaving the girl behind 'like a late-sacked island'; then Lucrece writes her series of poems to Night, to Opportunity, and to her mythological predecessor, Philomele. A modern reader could object that all this rhetoric is hardly in keeping with the events, but he must remember that these early poems are barns in which the young poet is storing up themes and metaphors for the future. They are virtuoso performances in which Shakespeare like a good musician is demonstrating both his repertoire and his skill with his instrument. The Troy cloth which follows them and occupies such a large section of the poem is possibly in the same tradition, but it may also have a deeper meaning.

The painted spectacle of the war before Troy that Lucrece studies and that Shakespeare describes has struck many critics as simply another rhetorical description that slows the movement of the poem until Collatine arrives and that gives the reader a chance to meditate on the tragedy. There have been various comments on whether or not Shakespeare had a real picture in mind; and if he did, the Italian painter, Giulio Romano, who painted Troy scenes, has been nominated as the most likely artist. The ecphrastic poetry of ancient and modern poets has been brought forward to account for Shakespeare's lines, and it has even been asserted that Shakespeare is attempting in this episode to distinguish in an aesthetic fashion between the task and skill of the artist in paint and verse.[27] All of these observations have been helpful in their ways, but the main questions are why the idea occurred to Shakespeare and what would a sixteenth-century reader see in the picture.

T. W. Baldwin has pointed to the commentaries of Marsus and Constantius on the Lucrece story in Ovid's *Fasti*[28] as the text that carried Shakespeare from Rome to Troy. In these commentaries, Lucrece is not only defended against the charges of St Augustine, but Tarquin is compared obliquely, by a quotation from the *Aeneid*, to Sinon, the betrayer of Troy. One hardly knows how a poet's imagination works, and Baldwin may be completely right; however, a few other matters might have brought this idea into Shakespeare's mind. Lucrece was, of course, a Trojan by ancestry, and the destruction of Troy was the greatest tragedy that she knew. She was also regularly associated in lists of noble women with Hecuba, that other faithful and suffering wife. There is finally the fact that the Renaissance attributed, until Goldast argued otherwise,[29] a poem on Philomela and a *De Excidio Trojae* to Ovid and that Shakespeare could have found these now rejected poems in the *Opera*. But we shall probably never know exactly how Shakespeare got from the rape of Lucrece, that fallen fortress of chastity, to the destruction of Troy.

Though we cannot explain the turns and halts of Shakespeare's imagination, we most certainly know that the Trojan episode in *The Rape of Lucrece* came from the first two books of the

Aeneid: the 'pictura inanis' from the first book, the fall of the city from the second. If we now think in terms of the Renaissance Vergil, we may be able to read a meaning into this section that may not be Shakespeare's but that suits the moral trend of his poem and may represent what a certain type of Renaissance reader saw in it. To introduce this last point, we must simply remember that the sixteenth century regarded Vergil as a superb moral poet and his hero as a man of high human perfection. In this regard they had, as we know, no quarrel with the Middle Ages; but even with this knowledge, we sometimes forget that a man of the Renaissance could read with the help of the experts the great allegory of the career of Aeneas. It is, then, not so much a question of how the Troy painting got into *Lucrece* or why it is there as what consonant meaning a man of the Renaissance might find in it.

Petrarch is always a good figure to stand at the door of any study of Renaissance intellectual attitudes, and in one of his letters he informs Frederico Aretino that the city of Troy is a symbol of the human body deep in sleep. Its gates are opened by sins that kill the defenders of the soul on the threshold. 'Relicta tergo mollitie, & antiqua coniunge ibi amissa, hoc est consuetudine voluptatum a prima aetate copulata, animo solus primum, sed virtute armatis.' 'Now all this tumult, this ruin, this destruction in which the voluptuous city, victim of its own passions, struggles between the fires kindled by libidinousness and the sword of anger occurs fitly at night to denote the darkness of human error and the blackness in which our life, buried in sleep and drenched in wine, is ignorantly and drunkenly immersed.' This is the tone of Petrarch's reading and he continues to match the poetry to the moral. The great horse is made by the evils of youth; and Laocoön or reason being overthrown, the 'infausta machina' is admitted conveying into the town Odysseus or 'wicked cunning', Neoptolemus or 'pride and vindictive ardour', and Menelaus or 'revenge'.[30]

Boccaccio, Petrarch's friend, always looked under 'the fitting veil of the fable for hidden truth' (sotto velame di favole appropriato, nascondere la verità),[31] and in his *Genealogy of the Gods*, he illustrates what he finds under this covering with a moral reading of the story of Perseus. He would obviously have approved of the letter to Aretino because, as he informs us, he looked into 'the core or literal sense' for the other allegorical significances.[32] The apparently medieval practices of both these poets were also followed by the humanist Collucio Salutati, who insisted on searching for 'the allegorical meanings in the traditional stories of the poets'.[33] A century later, the Florentine humanists, Ficino and Pico della Mirandola,[34] both recommend that the classical poets be read in terms of the four-fold exegesis of the twelfth-century theologians; and a member of their society, Landino, took it upon himself to provide such a reading of the *Aeneid*, a poem in which 'Vergil hid the most profound knowledge'. His *In Virgilii Opera Allegoria* was printed either in the *Quaestiones Camaldulenses* or as an appendix to the *Aeneid* at least twenty times between 1480 and 1596.

For Landino, Troy is the youthful life of man when reason slumbers and the senses rule; it is what philosophers call the 'natural state' and in this state the body reigns among fleshly pleasures. But some men discover, as they near maturity, that there is a road leading to the right which they must follow. To make plainer this notion of the divided way, Landino states that both Aeneas and Paris lived in Troy but followed separate courses. Paris preferred pleasure to virtue and perished with Troy; Aeneas, impelled by his mother, the higher Venus, left Troy to seek the truth and came eventually to Italy or divine sapience. One may object, Landino acknowledges, that Aeneas fought for Troy, but one must also admit that even though the night of passions surrounded him, he foresaw the fall of the city. For Aeneas was son of flesh (Anchises), but he also had a soul (Venus), and it is the death of his father as well as the wisdom of his mother that brings him in the end to perfection.[35]

We have only to remember Spenser's allegorical presentation of portions of the Troy story or Chapman's remarks on the Homeric allegory in the epistle to the *Odyssey*, to realize that Landino's formal symbolic reading is not a unique medieval retention. This impression of a strong sense of allegory in the Renaissance's interpretation of classical poets (aided, perhaps, by the discovery of some of the ancient moral and physical glosses on Homer) is given further emphasis by Fabrini's edition of the *Aeneid* in 1588. In this edition the Latin text is surrounded by the usual morass of an *apparatus criticus*, but the editor adds to the customary comments on syntax, history and so forth a separate 'allegorical exposition' that draws heavily on Landino's method and results. When, for instance, Venus pays her son a nocturnal visit (II, 489–504), Fabrini observes that this is the celestial Venus described by Plato, Pythagoras, Empedocles, and St Paul. She comes, he writes, to lead Aeneas away from Troy, the body of man besieged by pleasures and passions, in order that he may follow a divine course. Anchises (the flesh) naturally refuses to leave because he would rather die than give up his sensual desires, and so he must be carried off by force on the shoulders of the soul.[36] Fabrini's moral commentary omits much that is in Landino's, but what it accepts is elaborately annotated, and its basic conclusion is the same. Troy is the body which must be destroyed and abandoned so that the ideal man can gain the profits of a higher life.

Now there is absolutely no reason to believe that Shakespeare had any of Spenser's liking for overt allegory, but it is quite probable that he could allude to matters that had intrinsic allegorical values for his readers. The garden scene in *Richard II* connects symbolically with John of Gaunt's 'This other Eden;' and Falstaff, the 'old white-bearded Satan', takes us promptly to the Pauline 'homo vetus'. Neither of these suggestions are allegorical in the strict sense; but granted the intellectual inclinations of the audience, one cannot feel that corn was being sown on stony ground. I am moved to suppose, considering the nature of the central discussion and the symbolic signposts, that *The Rape of Lucrece* (although it is not an allegory in the same sense as Spenser's 'Muiopotomos') has certain sub-literal possibilities.

I cannot assume that Shakespeare knew the moral readings of Landino and Fabrini, but Lucrece, who compares the ravishment of her body with the fall of Troy, 'so my Troy did fall', seems to have intimations of this nature. Like the allegorizers of the *Aeneid* and, of course, in keeping with her historical utterances, she makes a careful distinction between her flesh and her soul:

> My body or my soul which was the dearer,
> When the one pure, the other made divine?
> Whose love of either to my self was nearer,
> When both were kept for heaven and Collatine?

But the house of her soul is 'sackt', her mansion 'batter'd', her temple 'corrupted'. There is but one thing left to do: she must leave. 'If in this blemisht fort I make some hole, Through which I may convay this troubled soule.'

In the allegories, Aeneas' Troy is equally ravaged by sins and sensations from without; and so on the advice of his mother, he departs to find divine wisdom. Lucrece's decision is similar, but, like Tarquin's amorous soldiership, morally improper. Her Troy is ruined by Tarquin-Sinon, and she believes that it must be annihilated to preserve the purity of her mind. Unfortunately she does not aspire to divine sapience but to pagan honour. Unled by the celestial Venus, her maculate body appears to control her decision more than her immaculate soul, which, according to her own statement, only endures in 'her poyson'd closet'. So while Brutus seems to have the last word in the pagan sense, it is really St Augustine (whose words fitted to Lucrece's tongue have earlier taken their place in the poem) who wins, in spite of Shakespeare's obvious sympathy for the lady, the debate between the classical and the Christian worlds.

NOTES

1. Jacobus Bergomensis, *De Claris Mulieribus* in *De memorabilibus et Claris Mulieribus* (Paris, 1521), p. 42*v*.

2. *Œuvres Complètes*, ed. De Queux de Saint-Hilaire (Paris, 1880), II, 336. Further lists are found at III, 294, 303; VII, 14, 289, and in Guillaume Alexis, 'Le Blason de Faulse Amours', *Œuvres Poétiques*, ed. Piaget and Picot (Paris, 1896), I, 214 as well as Charles d'Orléans, *Poésies*, ed. Champion (Paris, 1924), p. 191. Gower places Lucrece between Penelope and Alcestis in the *Confessio Amantis*, III, 2632–9.

3. 'Dialogi primo sopra Virgilio', *Opera* (Venice, 1740), II, 187.

4. Probus, *De Notis Romanorum Interpretandis*, ed. Tacuinus (Venice, 1525), p. lxxix *verso*.

5. Possibly the popular *Lucretia und Brutus* of Bullinger described in H. Galinsky, *Der Lucretia-Stoff in der Weltliteratur* (Breslau, 1932), pp. 76–80.

6. P. Camerarius, *Operae Horarum Subcesivarum, sive Meditationes Historicae* (Frankfort, 1609), p. 292. The poem according to Bayle (Lucretia) was written by Renatus Laurent de la Barre; it is printed in Latin and French in Estienne's *Apologie pour Hérodote*; the English version is from *A World of Wonders*, trans. R. Carew (1607), p. 101.

7. Tertullian, *Ad Martyres*, PL, I, 698–9; *De Exhortatione Castitatis*, PL, II, 929; *De Monogamia*, PL, II, 952 and Jerome, *Epistulae*, PL, XXI, 1051; *Adversus Jovinianum*, PL, XXIII, 294.

8. I, 19.

9. According to Camerarius, Bartolomi di Saliceto and Guillaume d'Oncieux, sixteenth-century jurists, excused Lucretia of any legal blame. The conventional position on her suicide is expressed by Justus Lipsius, *Manuductiones ad Stoicam Philosophiam* in *Opera* (Antwerp, 1637), III, 525. In the Constantius and Marsus edition of Ovid's *Fasti* (1527) the impossibility of Lucretia's fighting, flying, or crying for aid is emphasized (p. lxxxvii).

10. 'Orazione contra le Cortigiane', *Opera*, III, 208–11.

11. *Op. cit., loc. cit.* A comparison of Lucretia with the wife of Origiacon, who brought her husband the head of her ravisher is the subject of John Dickenson's Latin poem, 'De Lucretia Romana', in *Speculum Tragicum* (Leyden, 1605), pp. 234–5.

12. L. E. Dabney (*French Dramatic Literature in the Reign of Henri IV* (Austin, Texas, 1952), pp. 198–200) describes this manuscript play.

13. *Op. cit.* (Paris, 1638), pp. 76–7.

14. T. F. T. Dyer, *Folklore of Shakespeare* (1883), p. 189. The notion begins with Theophrastus, *Characteres*, 28, 5: see Erasmus, *Adagia*, I, 173; Alexander ab Alexandro, *Geniales Dies* (Paris, 1565), p. 275*v*.; Carolus Figulus, *Mustela* (Cologne, 1540); C. Gesner, *Historia Animalium* (Frankfort, 1603), I, 759–61.

15. A. Alciati, *Emblemata* (Leyden, 1593), CXXVI.

16. *Strozzi Poetae Pater et Filius* (Venice, 1513), II, 71*v*.–72*v*. U. Aldrovandus mentions poems on the same subject by Reusner, Mantuanus, and J. C. Scaliger, *De Quadrupedibus Digitatis* (Bologna, 1637), pp. 313, 319, 326. The weasel quite fittingly turns up in the pseudo-Ovidian 'Philomela'.

17. The earliest example is the πρῶτον μὲν στρατευτικωτάτους recorded by Athenaeus, 13,562. In Latin there is Propertius, 2, 12, 9–16; 3, 5, 1–2; 6, 40–2; 8, 31–4; 20, 19–20: Tibullus, I, 1, 75; 3, 64; 10, 53–6. Almost all classical examples have been gathered in Alfons Spies, *Militat Omnis Amans* (Tübingen, 1930).

18. *Amores*, 2, 9, 1–4; *Ars*, 1, 36–7; 2, 233–8, 671; 3, 3–4; *Rem.* 1–2, 158. See also Statius, *Silvae*, 1, 2, 61–7; Plautus, *Persa*, 2, 2, 49–50; *Truc.* 2, 1, 18–19. One of the more famous tropes is in Horace's recall to the colours at the age of fifty (4, 1, 1–2). The theme appears in the later Latins: Ausonius, *Opuscula*, ed. Schenkl (Berlin, 1883), p. 253; Venantius Fortunatus, *Opera poetica*, ed. Leo (Berlin, 1881), p. 125; Dracontius, *Romulea* in *Opera*, ed. Vollmer (Berlin, 1905), 6, 17–21 and 10, 338–9.

19. *Peirol d'Auvergne*, ed. Aston (Cambridge, 1953), p. 107; Aimeric de Peguilhan, *The Poems*, ed. Shepard and Chambers (Evanston, 1950), p. 101; *Piere Vidal*, ed. Anglade (Paris, 1923), p. 37; C. Appel, *Der Trobador Cadenet* (Halle, 1920), p. 44; Arnaut de Mareuil, *Les Poésies Lyriques*, ed. Johnston (Paris, 1935), p. 72; Bernart de Ventadorn, *Seine Lieder*, ed. Appel (Halle, 1915), pp. 23, 77–8, 199.

20. *Carmina Burana*, ed. Schmeller (Stuttgart, 1847), pp. 126–8, 135, 146, 184, 188, 198, 214.

21. See the poems of Lapo Gianni and Cino da Pistoia in *Rimatori del Dolce Stilnovo*, ed. Di Benedetto (Turin, 1925), pp. 95, 163.

22. Petrarch gives the story of Lucrece political emphasis in the third book of his *Africa* and places the lady in the *Trionfo della Pudicizia* (131–6) and in the sonnets (pp. 357, 504 of the Mestica edition, Florence, 1896). He uses the love-war motif in his sonnets (pp. 41, 141, 154, 156, 183–4, 203, 225), a theme common among his successors. Aretino, for example, can hardly write a sonnet without it, and it is popular among the French: see Louise Labé, *Œuvres Complètes*, ed. Boutens and De Grave (Maestricht, 1928), pp. 88–9; Guy de Tours, *Premières Œuvres*, ed. Blanchemain (Paris, 1879), pp. 70–1; Ronsard, *Œuvres*, ed. Vaganay (Paris, 1924), I, 4, 62, 96; III, 136, 352.

23. E. Wechssler, 'Frauendienst und Vassaltät', *Zeitschrift für französische Sprache und Literatur*, XXIV (1902), 176.

24. K. A. F. Mahn, *Die Werke der Troubadours* (Berlin, 1846–79), I, 6, v.

25. *Op. cit.*, ed. Langlois (Paris, 1914–24), V, 76–8.

26. *Les Faictz et Dictz*, ed. Dupire (Paris, 1937), II, 569–83.

27. *The Poems*, ed. Rollins (Philadelphia, 1938), pp. 224–7.

28. *On the Literary Genetics of Shakespere's Poems and Sonnets* (Urbana, 1950), pp. 144–5. A connection between Lucrece and Sinon is made by Fabrini in his *Opere* (1588) at *Aeneid*, 2, 79 when he observes that good and evil done under duress do not count and uses Lucrece as the counter-example. Jacobus Pontanus in his *Symbolarum libri XVII* (Augsburg, 1599), col. 837–8 compares Sinon to Zopyrus and Tarquin.

29. Both poems were regarded as genuine until the publication of the *Erotica et Amatoria Opusculi* (Frankfurt, 1610) in which Goldast assigns the 'Philomela' to either Albus Ovidius Juventinus or Julius Speratus and the 'De Excidio' to Benigne of Fleury.

30. *Opera* (Basel, 1554), pp. 872–3.

31. *Della Geneologia* (Venice, 1585), p. 233 *v*.

32. *Ibid.* p. 8.

33. R. H. Green, 'Classical Fable and English Poetry', *Critical Approaches to Mediaeval Literature* (New York, 1960), p. 120.

34. E. H. Gombrich, 'Icones Symbolicae', *Journal of the Warburg and Courtauld Institutes*, II (1948), 163–92.

35. Vergil, *Aeneidos*, ed. Hostensius (Basel, 1577), pp. 3001, 3004–8, 3011. Allusions to Vergil as an allegorist are found commonly at this time in prefaces to editions of the various works of Vergil and in some of the Italian critics. One of the most interesting is Celio Calcagnini, a contemporary of Landino's, who not only discusses the allegorical interpretation of ancient poetry (*Lectiones Antiquae* (Lyon, 1560), II, 555–9), but also criticizes Landino, and argues that Troy is not youth or the body but the world from which Aeneas rises on a three scale Neo-Platonic ladder (II, 429).

36. I have used the Venice edition of 1615.

AN ANATOMY OF
'THE PHOENIX AND THE TURTLE'

BY

ROBERT ELLRODT

I

'The Phoenix and the Turtle' had been nearly smothered in the dust of scholarly debate when a series of brilliant essays succeeded in rescuing it from a sadder fate than its heroes' eternal rest, 'enclos'd in cinders'. What radiance might have been lost in the controversy about biography, authenticity and sources the latest critics have fully recaptured.[1] Nevertheless the symbolical birds, to misquote Marvell, still wave in their plumes various light in different eyes. Thus A. Alvarez discovers in Shakespeare's argument 'a stringent logic' while F. T. Prince declares Shakespeare's use of analytic terminology 'free and rhapsodic, a kind of ethereal frenzy', in a poem which 'consists in a marriage between intense emotion, and almost unintelligible fantasy'.[2] To the same editor, nothing could be 'further from the methods of Donne's love-poetry than the method of this poem'. Yet 'The Phoenix and the Turtle' is included in Helen Gardner's anthology, *The Metaphysical Poets*, and Henri Fluchère would rank the poem in 'the highest tradition of "metaphysical" poetry'.[3] Now, these assertions, slightly qualified, may not prove actually inconsistent. But the obvious clash between such statements—and many more instances could be found—invites a resurvey. However loath one may feel to burden this lyrical flight with further plodding research, a re-examination of the bird symbolism and the 'Platonic' assumptions, supported by a fresh array of parallels, is required to avoid laying undue emphasis either on the poet's dependence on tradition or on his self-conscious originality in the handling of the Phoenix theme.

Shakespeare's contribution to *Loves Martyr* is unlikely to have been first conceived as a mere complimentary puff, as F. T. Prince surmises, allowing only 'a chance conjunction of images' to precipitate 'a sudden intensity of emotion in the poet'. Irony may be detected in the pieces signed by the 'Vatum Chorus', Marston and Jonson, but Shakespeare's poem never verges on burlesque.[4] The oracular utterance, though high-pitched, never suggests mock solemnity as in Ovid's playful elegy on his mistress' parrot.[5] Besides, though Shakespeare did take the notion of the Phoenix and the Turtle from *Loves Martyr*, he altered the story. The 'dead birds', who-ever they may be, leave no posterity although their love was not without offspring in Chester's poem.[6] Truth and Beauty vanish from the earth, the tone is throughout funereal and the theme of the Threnos not unlike that of Donne in *The First Anniversary*.[7] Sir Israel Gollancz, somewhat improbably, assumed that Shakespeare's lyric might have been 'originally written as an elegiac poem on some other love-story—a Phoenix and Turtle united in death and "leaving no posterity"'.[8] Three other hypotheses may be framed: (1) Shakespeare may have misread *Loves Martyr*: this, however, seems unlikely. (2) He may not have read Chester's poem at all: his connection with Sir John Salusbury was probably more remote than Jonson's. When requested to write a poem on the Phoenix and Turtle theme, he might have been merely told that they were a symbol of ideal love ending in death. (3) Lastly, the modification of the theme may have been deliberate, which seems to be the simplest and most satisfying explanation.

When claiming that no prospect of rebirth is suggested in the poem I am aware that Wilson Knight identifies 'the bird of loudest lay' with the Phoenix reborn from its ashes. This, indeed, is the only ground for his strange understatement when he describes as 'not obviously optimistic' a poem which begins in sadness and ends on a 'sigh'. He will grant, though, that the bird may be but a symbol of Shakespeare's own poetic creation (pp. 202–3, 194, 204). Yet nothing suggests that it arose from the mutual flame either as its natural offspring or as a poem inspired by the recorded experience. Baldwin's distinction between the mortal Phoenix and Turtle, the lovers for whom there is 'no hint of rebirth' and 'the immortal Phoenix' presiding at their funeral may not be unfounded but is hardly necessary. It rests on the assumption that the bird sitting 'on the sole Arabian tree' must be the Phoenix since that tree has been described by Lyly, Florio and Shakespeare himself as 'the phoenix' throne' (*Tempest*, III, iii, 23). But this was a distortion of the legend as related by Lactantius. It cannot be claimed that the tree was never 'vacant', since the Phoenix only sat on it for his dawn and death rites.[9] Besides, some time elapsed between his immolation and rebirth.[10] The 'herald sad' may surely be allowed to blow his trumpet from that tree. Lastly, as a 'trumpeter', he does not 'preside' at the funeral, as Baldwin and Wilson Knight assume: he is less important than the swan who acts the priest's part (ll. 13–16), an office devoted to the newborn Phoenix when he burnt his father's ashes on the altar of the Sun God in Heliopolis.[11]

II

To ascertain the meaning of the phoenix symbol in Shakespeare's poem, Renaissance adaptations of the myth must be considered rather than the time-honoured poems of Lactantius and Claudianus, though commentators have strangely ignored the latter. Many parallels, ranging from Michelangelo to Drayton, have been offered. Among these, Roydon's *Elegy for Astrophil*, first adduced by Sir Sidney Lee, has not been duly stressed in recent studies.[12] In the stanzas usually quoted (6–7), the Phoenix is but a mourner among the other birds assembled: eagle, turtle and swan. But his very fate calls to mind the hero's death and conveys the poet's sense of loss when the general sorrow

> Fired the Phoenix where she laid,
> Her ashes flying with the wind.
> So as I might with reason see
> That such a Phoenix ne'er should be.

Like Shakespeare and unlike Chester, Roydon therefore departs from the myth of rebirth to enhance the hero's praise. No such Phoenix will arise, though

> Haply the cinders driven about,
> May breed an offspring near that kind;
> But hardly a peer to that, I doubt.[13]

In the same elegy Roydon described Astrophel as a love poet and Stella as a nymph most rare (st. 22–7). Now, Astrophel's and Stella's well-known 'flame' became 'mutual' while remaining chaste. If Shakespeare was influenced by Roydon's elegy and thought of Sidney's Sonnets, he may well have had in mind a love relationship of this kind. But in the *Elegy for Astrophil* love and the phoenix myth are unconnected.

The Phoenix symbol in the love poetry of the Renaissance may be traced back to Petrarch's *Canzoniere*, the fountainhead whence flowed two different streams of conceits.[14] Generally, the Phoenix is feminine. Laura is, indeed, so insistently identified with the Arabian bird that the symbol might appear to be a hall-mark of Petrarchism. Emphasis is laid on the uniqueness and matchless beauty of a heavenly creature secure of immortality, crossing our path for a while, proud and lonely, and flying back to her far country.[15] Before this rare and unapproachable splendour one feels the tremulous awe and wonder of the poet. But from Phoenix-Laura to 'Phoenix-Stella' (*Astrophel*, XCII) the celestial glory somewhat faded into the light of common day. In their search for hyperboles the Elizabethan love poets on the whole were surprisingly chary of the phoenix symbol to heighten their praises of their ladies. Sidney himself and Dyer were satisfied with brief and random allusions, stressing, like Petrarch, beauty and rarity.[16]

In one instance only had Petrarch relied on the actual myth of rebirth. He then applied it to the lover. Just as the Phoenix, sitting on the topmost bough, turns towards the sun, so would his elevated thoughts turn to Laura and his passion take fire, burn to ashes and yet spring up anew (no. 135). The conceit of the ever-dying, ever-reviving lover was magnificently recast by Michelangelo.[17] But in riddles, epigrams and sonnets, from Pontanus to Thomas Lodge, Giles Fletcher and Drayton, it became little more than a rhetorical flourish.[18] A sonnet from William Smith's *Chloris* (1596) may be quoted since it offers one of the fullest Phoenix figures in lyrical poetry:

> The Phoenix fair which rich Arabia breeds,
> When wasting time expires her tragedy;
> No more on Phoebus' radiant rayes she feeds:
> But heapeth up great store of spicery;
>   And on a lofty tow'ring cedar tree,
> With heavenly substance, she herself consumes.
> From whence she young again appears to be,
> Out of the cinders of her peerless plumes.
>   So I, which long have frièd in love's flame,
> The fire, not made of spice, but sighs and tears,
> Revive again, in hope Disdain to shame,
> And put to flight the author of my fears.
>   Her eyes revive decaying life in me;
>   Though they augmentors of my thraldom be.[19]

The conventional association of the Phoenix with the renewed pangs of the lover may have half-consciously connected the myth of rebirth with torment rather than with triumph in the minds of many Elizabethan love poets. Donne's handling of the conceit will therefore appear all the more original. He retained the Petrarchan idea of the lover's death but made it a triumphant resurrection by boldly playing upon the erotic sense of the verb 'to die'. This ambiguity, though, must have been intended also in Chester's poem if the immolation did represent the consummation of wedded love. Donne introduced a further innovation in describing the two lovers as making up *one* Phoenix. This was no refinement of Petrarchism, but a new conceit, based both on the myth of rebirth and on the assumption of the bird's bisexuality. Metaphysical wit achieved a transmutation of the well-worn paradoxes of Lactantius.[20]

III

Shakespeare's Phoenix may now be securely 'pigeon-holed' in the tradition. On the one hand, it is of kin to Phoenix-Laura as a symbol of the beloved, the male turtle's 'queen'. 'Beauty'and 'rarity' or uniqueness are again emphasized. This agrees with the various tributes to Chester's She-Phoenix: 'Nature long time hath stor'd up vertue, fairenesse, Shaping the rest as foiles unto this Rarenesse' (*Loves Martyr*, pp. 178–9). Furthermore, this interpretation is consonant with Shakespeare's own Phoenix symbolism in *Timon* (II, ii, 29), *Antony and Cleopatra* (III, ii, 12), *Cymbeline* (I, vi, 17) and the *Tempest* (III, iii, 23).[21] On the other hand, Shakespeare is at one with Donne in availing himself of the Phoenix symbol to celebrate a mutual flame rather than an unreturned passion. The lovers' union, however, in accordance with the allegory of *Loves Martyr*, is typified not by the 'neutral' bird but by the mating of a female Phoenix with a male Turtle. The insistence on the 'two-in-one' theme still reminds us of Donne's later poems, but the union achieved is only spiritual.

The flame of perfect love burns all the brighter in an atmosphere of intense purity. Yet 'married chastity' (l. 61) could mean faithful married love to an Elizabethan[22] and the emphasis on chaste love may have no other meaning in Chester's poem, which seems to imply fruition and offspring. Physical intercourse is excluded in Shakespeare's lyric only by the assertion that ''twas not infirmity' that prevented the lovers from leaving 'posterity'. That chastity of this kind should be styled 'married' might still be puzzling. But the phrase can be understood in the light of sonnet CXVI: 'Let me not to the marriage of true minds Admit impediments.'

This and other parallels expanded by Wilson Knight raise a problem: was the fair youth of the sonnets Shakespeare's Phoenix? That he may have lurked in the poet's subconscious or even conscious mind, I am not prepared to deny. But, had the poem been *meant* to suggest a relationship of this type there would have been no need to point out that 'infirmity' was not responsible for the barrenness of the union. Wilson Knight is not justified in claiming that the bird symbolism suggests a confusion of the sexes. Though the Phoenix was male in Hesiod and Herodotus, Phoenix-Laura and Phoenix-Stella are unequivocally feminine. So is Chester's *Phoenix* 'analysde' by Jonson: Knight's reading only displays perverse ingenuity (pp. 188–9). One may further add that the legendary bird could be feminine in Elizabethan poetry even when 'she' typified a male lover or hero.[23] No ambiguity was intended: a female Phoenix could be a symbol of rarity irrespective of sex. As to the male turtle dove, though uncommon, it was not unprecedented. It appeared in one of the *Two Pastorals* 'made by Sir Philip Sidney upon his meeting with his two worthy friends and fellow poets, Sir Edward Dyer and M. Fulke Greville', first published in Davison's *Poetical Rhapsody* (1602) but written much earlier:

My two and I be met,
 A happy blessed trinity,
As three most jointly set
 In firmest band of unity.
  Join hearts and hands, so let it be,
  Make but one mind in bodies three.

And as the turtle Dove
 To mate with whom he liveth,
Such comfort fervent love
 Of you to my heart giveth.
  Join hands, &c.

Now joined be our hands,
 Let them be ne'er asunder,
But linked in binding bands
 By metamorphosed wonder.
  So should our severed bodies three
  As one for ever joined be.

From this daring insistence on close union in a poem about friendship, Wilson Knight, of course, might argue that a chaste homosexual love could have inspired 'The Phoenix and the Turtle'. The point need not be discussed since it is beyond proof. What matters is Shakespeare's poetic design. The mating of the Phoenix with a Turtle allowed him to bring together the extremes of love, constancy and chastity. The Turtle was a bird dedicated to Venus, yet chaste since it had but one mate in its life and therefore was a type of *absolute* constancy in married love.[24] The chastity of the Phoenix was absolute in a different way. Lactantius had praised it for 'knowing not the bonds of Venus' (l. 164). Claudianus had even declared it free from all the taints of our human world (*Phoenix*, l. 10). In *A Contention betwixt a Wife, a Widow, and a Maid*, a poetic dialogue by Sir John Davies, presented before Queen Elizabeth on 6 December 1602, the Turtle stood for love and truth, the Phoenix for maidenhead and 'oneness':

> *Wife*. The wife is as a turtle with her mate;
> *Widow*. The widow as the widow dove alone,
> Whose truth shines most in her forsaken state;
> *Maid*. The maid a Phoenix, and is still but one.[25]

To an Elizabethan, therefore, there must have been from the outset something of a paradox in mating the amorous and hymeneal Turtle with the virginal Phoenix.[26] In Chester's floundering allegory it may mean no more than the sacrifice of maidenhead to 'put on perfection, and a woman's name', to use Donne's words. But in Shakespeare's poem, through this very paradox, the bird symbolism becomes the fitting expression of the tension created by a certain type of 'Platonic' love.

IV

The reader, however, should be aware of the limits and the particular trend of the poet's Platonism. It invites no ascent along the well-known ladder leading up to the contemplation of the Heavenly Beauty, though a ray of it may flash through the flaming eyes of the Phoenix, her earthly reflection. The poet is concerned only with the perfect union achieved by the lovers' souls, an idea perhaps more closely related to Christian mysticism than genuine Platonism. Though the 'two-in-one' paradox may have been handled lightly by many love poets, the topic in itself was not 'far too slight', as Alvarez claims (p. 14), to support 'the logical structure of the poem'. It had engaged the attention of the best minds, the most thoughtful poets, from Ficino to Donne. In the *Commentarium in Convivium*, in Leone Ebreo's *Dialoghi d'Amore* and in Donne's later *Extasie*, (ll. 33–44), the oneness of the lovers *was* logically argued and stated in philosophical terms.[27] Shakespeare's restatement of it is of interest, because he made the truth his own, recreated the experience, revived the intuition. His perception of the paradox achieved originality when he substituted an immediate apprehension of unity for the Neoplatonic argument based on the assumption that each lover died in his own person to live in the beloved. Although the theory rested on a materialistic psychology, involving a transmission of spirits (*Commentarium*, II, 8; VII, 4), Shakespeare barely alludes to this doctrine when the Phoenix and the Turtle discern their mutual flame in each other's eyes (ll. 34–6). His intuition of the lovers' oneness, free from any psycho-physiological support, is stated in logical and ontological terms. It is, in fact, far more metaphysical than Ficino's. It may be so because the symbolical Phoenix and Turtle stand for universals and absolute values as well as individual lovers.

It would be tempting, therefore, to assume that Shakespeare was reaching out towards the genuine Platonic identification of the good, the true and the beautiful. Such an interpretation has been offered of sonnet CV:

> 'Fair, kind, and true', have often lived alone,
> Which three *till now* never kept seat in one.

But here the very turn of this compliment to the 'fair friend' shows that the poet was not concerned with the *timeless* identity of the Platonic principles. That all virtues or qualities should be united in one Phoenix creature or mistress was a commonplace in Renaissance love poetry. In significance, though not in seriousness, Shakespeare's sonnet hardly went beyond Nicholas Breton's '*Odd Conceit*' in his *Melancholic Humours* (1600): 'Wise, and kind, and fair, and true—Lovely live all these in you.' In 'The Phoenix and the Turtle', on the other hand, the solemnity of the tone, the cryptic language, tense and terse, are not alone responsible for the heightened awareness of paradox. The poet's theme is not the rational intuition of Platonism: it is the triumph of Love over Reason, as Lewis and Alvarez have noted. Shakespeare is not arguing.[28] He flies in the face of Reason with the blind confidence of sheer faith, by-passes her in a flashing intuition of utter transcendence. On these heights the 'two-in-one' paradox has specifically Christian connotations. Indeed, some of Shakespeare's statements would correctly apply only to the relationship between the persons of the Trinity.

This is no new remark. But the critic must steer clear of another pitfall. The scholastic echoes have been duly recognized,[29] but no theological construction should be forced upon the poem.

Through these concepts, Shakespeare seeks to transcend common experience, to pass into a realm 'All breathing human passion far above', but he nowhere suggests an allegory of religious mysteries or even of divine love. It is true that an allegory of this kind might well have been permitted by contemporary symbolism. That the Phoenix was a type of Christ is well known. One might add that the flock of birds following him after his rebirth represented the crowd of the elect.[30] Furthermore, the mystical significance of the turtle dove had a wide range, embracing Divine Sapience, the Blessed Virgin, the Church and the contemplative soul.[31] The Phoenix, though queenly in Shakespeare's poem, like Spenser's Sapience, *might* therefore stand for the second Person of the Trinity and the Turtle *might* represent either the Church betrothed to Christ, or the soul rapt in contemplation. This interpretation, however, would be flatly contradicted by their actual death and the sense of loss conveyed by the poem. Despite this, we must, of course, observe that a dim awareness of the mystical symbolism is induced by the religious phrasing and images of the poem. This would lurk in the mind of the contemporary reader, and the leap from an individual love relationship to absolute values would be made all the easier.

V

How freely the Renaissance mind could range in the field of symbolism is further illustrated by the most ambitious philosophical poem inspired by the Phoenix myth: *Le Phoenix de Jan Edouard du Monin*, published 'A Paris. Chez Guillaume Bichon' in 1585. So far unmentioned in connection with *Loves Martyr*, the poem deserves notice though no proof of influence can be offered. Chester and Chapman alone, or perhaps Marston in his more abstruse vein, might have been attracted by the ponderous though high-flown disquisitions of one who claimed to rival Ronsard and Du Bartas.[32] The author of the *Shadow of Night* could have enjoyed Du Monin's *Hymne de la Nuict* and would have welcomed his defence of obscurity.[33] He might have been undismayed by Du Monin's proud boast in the epistle prefixed to the *Phoenix*: 'entre soixante cinq mille vers de ma Muse, il ne s'en trouve mille qui ne soient batus au coin philosophique'. But Shakespeare is unlikely to have waded through the poem with what French he had. *Le Phoenix* is of interest not as a source, but as a very definite illustration of the principle of *Mehrdeutigkeit* applied by H. Straumann to 'The Phoenix and the Turtle'. The many levels of significance are not disguised under an allegory but plainly set forth. The Phoenix symbol is used to praise 'L'Illustrissime Phoenix de France', Charles de Bourbon, Archbishop of Rouen, a Catholic uncle of Henri IV whose claim to the throne was urged by the Guises. But it also expresses the excellence of Monarchy, as contrasted with Oligarchy and with Democracy: the mob is described as an 'Antiphoenix' (ff. 53–4). It serves a more personal end when Du Monin proudly poses as a lonely Phoenix among the poet-owls of his age (f. 15ᵛ). Religious symbolism is not wanting. Like the Phoenix, the Catholic Church is one, yet united with the 'greater Phoenix', 'ce Phoenix Christ unic' (f. 54ᵛ), which shows that Donne's 'Two Phoenixes' in his 1613 *Epithalamion* may not be so great 'an offence against tradition and poetry alike' as Wilson Knight claims (p. 207).

Du Monin has fused Christian theology and Neoplatonic philosophy. His God is the One of Plotinus. Divine unity is reflected in the human soul, 'Qui ne dement que peu d'un plumage mortel Le plumage admiré du Phoenix immortel' (f. 16ᵛ). The larger part of the poem elaborates 'la science de l'Humain Phoenix: "Le vrai Phoenix est l'âme humaine", "L'Arabie du Phoenix humain est le corps", "Le Phoenix humain doit suivre son Soleil Dieu", "L'Ame pour renaître comme le Phoenix doit se dépouiller de soi et s'investir des seuls merites de Christ son Soleil".' The parallel extends to bisexuality since Adam was first created both male and female (f. 35ᵛ). However dull and turgid the style may be, the note of exaltation rings true in the celebration of oneness. Du Monin's is not a passion for oneness in union, but the striving of the philosophic mind for unity, the rapturous assertion of God's and the Soul's and the World's oneness, the eager demonstration that the heavens, the planets and the seasons, the four elements and the four humours, and all the arts and sciences are but one. Further, it is the proud aspiration of the individual soul who

> thinkes he hath got
> To be a Phoenix, and that then can bee
> None of that kinde, of which he is, but hee.

> Donc, jalouse de l'Un, Muse uniquement une,
> De mon unique main fens cet unic Neptune
> Du Phoenix unic un, fais qu'un Phenix si bien
> M'unisse unic à soi, qu'un autre à l'Un n'ait rien:
> Que l'unique Phoenix de ma voix authentique
> Soit unique chanté par un Phoenix unique....[34]

VI

The originality of Shakespeare's handling of the Phoenix theme stands out more clearly from a comparison with other Phoenix poems in his own and previous ages.[35] The compositions of Lactantius and Claudianus were narrative and pictorial. Only in the closing lines did they muster the standard array of paradoxes which later poets marshalled to various ends. Du Monin aimed at writing metaphysical poetry. Yet he inserted a long narration of the myth among his abstract or allegorical disquisitions (ff. 5–11). The same trend may be discerned in lyrical poetry. Setting aside epigrammatic riddles or flashing conceits, one discovers that Petrarch and Pontanus, Ronsard and Drayton, whenever they expanded the Phoenix symbol, were apt to rely on pictorial features such as the bird's plumage, the death scene or the flight of the new Phoenix.[36] Now, a concrete evocation, even when intended as an allegory, would stir the imagination hardly more than a Euphuistic simile. Even in Shakespeare's age the bird was held to be legendary and Sebastian's belated acknowledgement in the *Tempest* (III, iii, 21) implied current disbelief.[37] Such incredulity would confine any pictorial treatment of the myth to rhetorical interest. But it would not affect Donne's 'metaphysical' handling of the 'Phoenix riddle', which is a mere idea. The very turn of the paradox in *The Canonization* shows that the fusion of the sexes in a perfect being able to regenerate itself is thought of as a myth only turned into truth by the union of the lovers. In the 1613 *Epithalamion* the poet openly disclaims the ornithological marvellous and once more describes the experience of the lovers as a higher prodigy than the legendary bird. Yet it is not unimportant that the very existence of the Phoenix should still have been a matter of debate.[38] Donne's open negation becomes a bold and modern assertion of the critical spirit. But, as a subject of controversy, the myth could still arouse perplexity and wonder.

By calling in question the ornithological miracle, Donne himself used it as a foil to the human miracle.

Shakespeare's approach was different. His very subject, the Phoenix and the Turtle, was a modification of the Phoenix myth which implied disbelief in, or at least disregard for, the time-honoured legend. Yet he is not merely dealing with 'bodied Ideas'. Birds are present from the first line to the last and some willing suspension of disbelief is required. It need not be romantic, for the symbolism is ruthlessly stripped of unessential detail. The Phoenix and the Turtle are not described. The very escort of the Phoenix was a mere flock of birds in earlier poems. Shakespeare availed himself of the convention to call attention to the values symbolized by his heroes or connected with their love. Eagle, crow and swan become emblems of royalty, chastity, holiness and poetry. The kingly eagle is further contrasted with the 'tyrant' birds of prey, and one may remember that eagle and phoenix symbolism often overlapped.[39] But the opening of the poem is also symbolic in a different way, more subtle than mere emblematic imagery. The puzzling bird of loudest lay is here to sound the note of hyperbole or exaltation in grief. Change 'loudest' into 'sweetest', which would better suit the reborn Phoenix, most melodious of singers:[40] both the loudness of lament and the magic of the line would be lost. The bird sits 'on the sole Arabian tree' chiefly to arouse wonder, to suggest remoteness and a towering isolation above a desert—a world left desolate by the Phoenix and Turtle's departure. The interplay of consonants and vowel sounds in the next stanzas is masterly. The 'er' sound conveys the sinister menace of the owl, while i's and u's for the swan in surplice white, a's for the 'sable' crow make up for ear and eye a symphony in black and white.

The appeal of the symbols to the sensuous imagination is superseded by an appeal to our intellectual imagination in the anthem. Shakespeare's handling of paradox is far more serious and philosophical than in the poems of Lactantius and Claudianus[41] or in the conceits of most sonneteers. The poet is genuinely concerned with ultimates. Yet the 'abstract allusiveness' of his approach (Alvarez, p. 13) brings him no nearer to Donne. In the poetry of Donne an immediate and particular experience is analysed abstractedly. In 'The Phoenix and the Turtle', despite the dramatic setting, one almost loses sight of the individuals involved when their love is described: the attention is focused on universals. Intellectually, Shakespeare is less inventive, less witty than Donne: he rings the changes on one idea instead of striking out fresh conceits from the traditional 'two-in-one' paradox. Donne would have inserted it in a new line of argument to account for a personal experience. Shakespeare's dialectic approach is original in a different way, through its very imprecision and ambiguity, heightening the sense of mystery. The sensitive comments of Alvarez and Prince on this point hardly leave room for further analysis. Some awkwardness arising from compression may even be acknowledged: it is not unfrequent in Shakespeare's rhymed verse of a more or less gnomic kind. The strange fascination exerted over the imagination by these abstract statements does not rest on intellectual power or penetration, but on their imperious finality. They evoke the inner response always awakened in the soul by an impassioned negation of duality. The Plotinian intuition of the One and the paradoxes of negative theology make a kindred appeal to the imaginative mind. In each case the sense of transcendence arises from an utter denial of common sense, an utter rejection of common experience.

After endeavouring to express this miraculous oneness, to realize vividly an unapprehended absolute, the poet could only maintain this exalted pitch by ending the 'tragic scene' on a further negation in the Threnos. Beauty, truth and rarity here enclosed in cinders lie, and any assurance, any hint of survival in a world beyond, is withheld. The rest is silence, and the finality of death is consciously emphasized: the Turtle's loyal breast *to eternity* doth rest. And since absolute Truth and Beauty are sunk below the furthest horizon of human ken, their withdrawal from this world must be total: 'Truth may seem, but cannot be: Beauty brag, but 'tis not she.' How shall we reconcile with this claim the final call to those that are 'either true or fair'? In this apparent contradiction lies the deeper meaning of the poem. Shakespeare has not been celebrating true lovers and beautiful creatures. He has been dreaming of Love and Constancy, Truth and Beauty, straining after the highest intensity, in which lies 'the excellence of every art' (Keats).

VII

The very mood of the poem, the aching sense that 'truth may seem but cannot be' for 'Love and Constancy is dead', would admirably suit the state of mind one may reasonably ascribe to Shakespeare in 1600–1. The latest commentators have hardly done justice to Heinrich Straumann's interpretation of the poem. His contention is that the union of Truth and Beauty achieved in the mutual flame of the Phoenix and the Turtle is contrasted with their present divorce in a world which may still hold lovers 'either true or fair', but cannot allow 'the pure union of the two qualities in one and the same woman'. In such a mood did Hamlet send Ophelia to a nunnery. In a mood hardly different did the dramatist in his later plays lodge 'beauty, truth and rarity' in *one* woman, *one* Phoenix-creature, miraculously preserved from this world's taints, like Marina among the bawds, Perdita among her flowers, Miranda on her desert island.[42]

NOTES

1. Heinrich Straumann, *Phönix und Taube* (Zürich, 1953); A. Alvarez, 'The Phoenix and the Turtle' in *Interpretations*, ed. John Wain (1955); G. Wilson Knight, *The Mutual Flame. On Shakespeare's 'Sonnets' and 'The Phoenix and the Turtle'* (1955); F. T. Prince, Introduction to the new Arden edition of *The Poems* (1960). The pregnant remarks of C. S. Lewis in his *English Literature in the Sixteenth Century* (Oxford, 1954), pp. 508–9, also deserve notice.

2. Alvarez, p. 8; Prince, p. xliv.

3. Prince, p. xliv; Fluchère, *Shakespeare, Poèmes* (Paris, 1959), p. 24.

4. Prince, pp. xlvi and xli.

5. That is why T. W. Baldwin's assertion that 'Shakespeare has taken his pattern from Ovid, *Amores*, II, 6' may be misleading: *On the Literary Genetics of Shakespeare's Poems and Sonnets* (Urbana, 1950), p. 364.

6. See *Loves Martyr*, pp. 132–4, and *Poems by Salusbury and Chester*, ed. Carleton Brown (1914), p. lx. Cf. Marston's 'description of a most exact wondrous creature, arising out of the Phoenix and Turtle Doves Ashes' (*Loves Martyr*, p. 177). Though this new Phoenix should be neither 'Man nor Woman', as Wilson Knight claims (see p. 183) the trend and tone of Shakespeare's poem would not agree with the 'happy Tragedy' of *Loves Martyr* and the other *Poeticall Essaies*.

7. As earlier noted by William Empson, *Some Versions of Pastoral* (1935), p. 139.

8. *T.L.S.* 26 January 1922, p. 56.

9. The phoenix sat on an unnamed tree for his morning rites (*Carmen de ave phoenice*, ll. 39–40), on a palm-tree or *phoinix*, for his death rites (ll. 69, 70). Both trees were lofty, but they towered above a grove of lesser trees.

According to Jean Hubaux and Maxime Leroy the two passages describe the same rites and the self-same tree; *Le Mythe du Phénix dans les Littératures Grecque et Latine* (Liège, 1939, pp. 148–50, 159). Elizabethan poets sometimes mentioned a cedar-tree: *Elegy for Astrophil*, st. 7; W. Smith, *Chloris*, sonnet XXIII.

10. Lactantius, ll. 98–108. To Christian interpreters of the myth the time would be three days as for the resurrection of Christ. Claudianus alone described the rebirth as instantaneous: *Phoenix*, ll. 65–71.

11. Lactantius, ll. 121–2; Claudianus, ll. 89–96.

12. Lee, *Life of Shakespeare* (1916 edition), p. 272.

13. Quoted from Bullen's *Some Longer Elizabethan Poems* (1903), p. 311.

14. Petrarch was mentioned by H. E. Rollins in his 1931 edition of *The Phoenix' Nest* and Wilson Knight has cited, but not analysed, nos. 185, 321, 323, omitting 135 and 210.

15. Canzoniere, 185, ll. 1–4, 12–14; 210, ll. 1–4; 321; 323, ll. 49–60.

16. See Dyer's 'Coridon to his Phillis' in *Englands Helicon* (1600).

17. See W. Knight's *Mutual Flame*, pp. 181–2.

18. See 'De Phoenice ave et de Amanti' in *Pontani Carmina*, ed. Soldati (Florence, 1902), II, 350; Lodge's *Phillis* (1593), XXV; Fletcher's *Licia* (1593), XV; Drayton's *Ideas Mirrour* (1594), 'Amours' 17 and 32. Drayton's alone have been previously cited.

19. Sonnet XXIII; S. Lee's *Elizabethan Sonnets* (1904), II, 336.

20. *Canonization*, 23–7; *Epithalamion on the Lady Elizabeth*, 18–28, 99–102. See Lactantius, 161–70. Cf. Symphosius, Aenigma XXXI, 'Phoenix'.

21. The myth of rebirth was used by the dramatist in the chronicle plays only, to suggest generation and perpetuity or dynastic continuity: *1 Henry VI*, IV, vii, 92; *1 Henry VI*, I, iv, 35; *Richard III*, IV, iv, 424; *Henry VIII*, V, v, 40. Shakespeare's Phoenix allusions have been recorded by Wilson Knight (*The Shakespearian Tempest*, Appendix A), but this distinction was not drawn and the accumulation of mere connotations often obscured the main significance.

22. See my *Neoplatonism in the Poetry of Spenser* (Geneva, 1960), pp. 55–6.

23. See Smith's Sonnet XXIII and Roydon's *Astrophil* quoted above.

24. *Alciati Emblemata*, XLVII; *Aldrovandi Ornithologiae Tomus Alter* (Bononiae, 1637), Lib. XV, c. IX.

25. Davison's *Poetical Rhapsody*, ed. Bullen, I, 22.

26. The same contradiction appears in the history of the Phoenix myth. The bird was first associated with Venus in the *Pterygion Phoenicis* of Laevius, some lines of which have been preserved in the *Ars Grammatica* of Charisius (IV, 6) and the *Saturnalia* of Macrobius (III, 8, 3), both available to the Elizabethans. On the development of the virginity symbol, see Hubaux-Leroy, pp. 3, 113–15.

27. *Commentarium*, II, 8; *Dialoghi*, ed. Caramella (Bari, 1929), pp. 30, 222.

28. In the Neoplatonic philosophy of love the standard paradox is not beyond proof. The lovers are one *and* two, since each dies in himself and lives in the beloved. This is logically explained on a psychological basis. In *The Phoenix and the Turtle* the lovers are '*neither* two nor one'. The negative makes the difference: it turns an intellectual paradox into an unintelligible mystery. Furthermore, that the selfsame should not be the same (l. 38) may be experienced or believed but eludes the grasp of the human understanding. Alvarez is therefore unjustified in claiming that the paradox is 'rationally accurate' and 'proves its point' (p. 8).

29. See J. V. Cunningham's article in *E.L.H.* XIX (1952), 265–76.

30. This may be traced to an anonymous expansion of Lactantius' *Carmen* in the ninth century: Hubaux-Leroy, p. 53.

31. Aldrovandus, *Ornithologiae Tomus Alter*, xv, ix, pp. 518–22.

32. See *L'Influence de Ronsard sur la Poésie Française* by M. Raymond (Paris, 1927), pp. 306–13.

33. *Nouvelles Œuvres* (1582), p. 128; *Phoenix*, f. 127ᵛ; *Uranologie* (1583), f. 207.

34. Donne, *First Anniversary*, 216–18; *Phoenix*, f. 42ʳ.

35. Price's suggestion that Poe or Mallarmé might 'help us to approach *The Phoenix and the Turtle*' as pure poetry, however sensitive and stimulating, might prove misleading in the perspective of literary history.

36. *Canzoniere*, 185, 321; *Pontani Carmina*; 'Eridanus', I, xi; *Ideas Mirrour*, 'Amour 6'; Ronsard, 'Panégyrique de la Renomée' in *Œuvres*, ed. Vaganay (Paris, 1923), IV, 419–20.

37. See D. C. Allen, 'Donne's Phoenix', *Modern Language Notes*, LXII (1947), 341–2.

38. Du Monin apparently believed in it since he argued that such a wondrous bird could not be wholly deprived of intellectual faculties (f. 11ᵛ).

39. Hubaux-Leroy, pp. 52, 58, 128–9.

40. See Baldwin, *Genetics of Shakespeare's Poems*, pp. 367–8.

41. Lactantius indeed asserted that 'the self was not the same' when he wrote: 'est eadem sed non eadem, quae est ipsa nec ipsa est.' But, unlike Shakespeare, he did not really call in question the principle of identity for the conceit only applied to the bird reborn from its ashes, a wonder in natural history but no contradiction in the realm of logic and ontology.

42. To read the poem in this perspective would require a longer development than the scope of this essay allows. This evolution of Shakespeare's sensibility is sketched in the third volume of my *Poètes Métaphysiques Anglais* (Paris, 1960), pp. 57–62.

SHAKESPEARE AND THE RITUALISTS

BY

ROBERT HAPGOOD

Gilbert Murray began his pioneer study of myth and ritual in Shakespeare, 'Hamlet and Orestes' (1914), by describing the reactions of two friends to whom he had shown his lecture: 'one friend has assured me that everyone knew it before; another has observed that most learned men, sooner or later, go a little mad on some subject or other, and that I am just about the right age to begin.' Since then, these contradictory criticisms of the approach Murray was inaugurating have been echoed many times. Philip Edwards, for example, has pronounced such interpretations of Shakespeare's last plays to be 'banal, trite, and colourless' (*Shakespeare Survey* II, p. 11), while William T. Hastings has found comparable interpretations in *Myth in the Later Plays of Shakespeare* to be forced, ingenious, startling, and lacking 'a sense of the ridiculous' (*Shakespeare Quarterly*, July 1950). Certainly there have been extravagances. Yet Murray was only the first in a long line of critics—both original and sane—who have found ritualistic qualities in Shakespeare; and, although it may be too soon to say that 'the use of anthropological methods has come to be taken for granted',[1] there are signs that these findings are receiving scholarly acceptance. The myth and ritual approach has thrown light on Shakespeare's histories, comedies, tragedies, and romances, illuminating lines, scenes, characters, rhythms and patterns of action, plays, groups of plays, and his whole 'idea of a theatre'.

This illumination, furthermore, has come from a great many directions. Since the terms 'ritualists' and 'myth and ritual approach' may seem to indicate a definite school of critics and a distinct set of methods, I should say at once that this is true only in a loose sense. Critics interested in myth and ritual have, of course, often influenced one another, but just as often they have worked independently and apparently without knowledge of other work along the same lines. To some, a concern with myth and ritual has been central; to others, it has been secondary or incidental. And there has been nearly as much diversity in methods as in critics. In their attempts to understand how ritualistic qualities came to be in Shakespeare and how they function there, critics have related them to a wide variety of contexts: to Elizabethan ceremonies, to the Elizabethan theatre and drama, to dramatic and literary traditions in general, to particular dramatic genres, to Shakespeare's artistic development, and to other elements in the work in which they appear. These contexts will provide the organizing principle for this survey.

ELIZABETHAN CEREMONIES

That Shakespeare's plays are full of folk-lore and custom has of course long been known. T. F. Thiselton Dyer's *Folk-lore of Shakespeare* (1884), although it needs bringing up to date, is still useful. To Thiselton Dyer, however, such passages were mere embellishments. What subsequent students have shown is that Shakespeare's knowledge of contemporary lore and custom could enter deeply into the plays, into character, scene, and imagery. In *The Royal Play of Macbeth* (1950), Henry Paul describes Macbeth as a 'conjurer and master of devils' of the sort

III

specified in King James's *Daemonologie* and interprets his tragedy, especially the necromantic scene, in these terms. William Montgomerie, although capable of suggesting that Hamlet may at one point 'be acting the part of the doctor of the folk-play' and of seeing in the final duel in *Hamlet* a 'tragic parody of the traditional sword dance', does bring out interesting resemblances between 'The Murder of Gonzago' and folk plays—the forgotten hobby horse, the dumb-show, Lucianus's damnable faces, Hamlet's 'mad' songs (*Folk-lore*, December, 1956). Alice Venezky demonstrates in *Pageantry on the Shakespearean Stage* (1951) Shakespeare's wide use of scenes and images drawn from contemporary pageantry—royal entries, pageants, street shows—and perceptively analyses their dramatic effects. She considers such matters as the 'mighty whiffler' in *Henry V*, Macbeth's dagger which 'marshall'st me the way that I was going', and Hamlet's employment of 'the whifflers and marshal of his usurped royal entry to describe his own dark and lonely journey *from* the kingdom:

> There's letters seal'd; and my two schoolfellows,
> Whom I will trust as I will adders fang'd,
> They bear the mandate; they must sweep my way
> And marshal me to knavery.   (III, iv, 202 ff.)

Unfortunately, she stops her survey of pageantry at 1603.

Contemporary ceremonial might also govern Shakespeare's conception of a whole play. The occasional character of *A Midsummer Night's Dream* is clear and generally recognized, the most elaborate interpretation of it as a piece of wedding pomp being Paul A. Olson's '*A Midsummer Night's Dream* and the Meaning of Court Marriage' (*E.L.H.*, June 1957). Similarly, Enid Welsford discerns in *Twelfth Night* 'the quintessence of the Saturnalia'; for 'Illyria is a country permeated with the spirit of the Feast of Fools, where identities are confused, "uncivil rule" applauded, cakes and ale successfully defended against virtuous onslaughts, and no harm is done' (*The Court Masque*, 1927, p. 251). Feste is a Lord of Misrule. To Leslie Hotson, it is Maria who is 'the mistress of revels'. But he agrees that Illyria is 'a land teeming with Christmas and Epiphany legend, folk customs, and traditional feasting, dance, jesting, and game' (*The First Night of Twelfth Night*, 1954, p. 160) and explains various allusions to holiday customs. For example, by pointing out that the day after Twelfth Night is Saint Distaff's day, he makes sense of the lines about Sir Andrew's hair:

To. ...it hangs like flax on a distaff; and I hope to see a housewife take thee between her legs and spin it off.
And. Faith, I'll home tomorrow, Sir Toby.

Less convincing is Janet Spens's attempt to line up five of the comedies with the five great folk festivals which Chambers describes in *The Medieval Stage*. Claiming that the plays sometimes served as 'aetiological myths' which explained the customs observed at these festivals, she relates *Twelfth Night* to the Winter Feast, *A Midsummer Night's Dream* to the High Summer Feast, *All's Well that Ends Well* to the Ploughing Feast, *As You Like It* to the Feast of the Beginning of Summer, and *The Winter's Tale* to the Harvest Feast. The parallels she draws, however, are dubious and tenuous—'Olivia's bereavement is a curious hint of the connection with the Feast of All Souls'—and do not begin to establish her assertion that 'after the composition of *The Two*

Gentlemen of Verona Shakespeare used a folk-play habitually as the nucleus of his comedies' (*Shakespeare's Relation to Tradition*, 1916, p. 38).

C. L. Barber makes such connections more persuasive by making them more general. In *Shakespeare's Festive Comedy* (1959) he observes that Elizabethan pleasure-seeking often took a saturnalian form—a celebration of misrule and carnival freedom, implying however an acceptance of 'every day' rule when the 'holiday' was over. He sums up this pattern in the formula 'from release to clarification', a pattern which he locates also in Shakespeare's comedies. That is why Sly mentions a 'comonty' in the same breath with 'a Christmas gambold or a tumbling trick': Shakespeare in his festive comedies 'gave the ritual pattern aesthetic actuality by discovering expressions of it in the fragmentary and incomplete gestures of daily life'.

The Elizabethan Theatre and Drama

Recent students of Shakespeare's theatre have found that it had a ritual dimension of its own. From his analysis of the inter-relationships between the tableaux vivants and the theatre, George R. Kernodle concludes in *From Art to Theatre* (1944):

Most of all, the Elizabethan stage had the atmosphere of a festival. The hangings, the painted architectural structure, the processions with banners and music, the special effects of soldiers assaulting castles, of kings holding courts, of gods and Virtues descending, of princes being welcomed at city gates—all created the spirit of a festival day when for the inauguration of the lord mayor or the progress of the queen or the return of a triumphant army the streets were decorated and street-shows were erected. The façade had on some occasions the appearance of a triumphal arch; on others, with black curtains hung for tragedies, it suggested a public ceremonial of mourning...(p. 151).

Of the drama itself, Clifford Leech has stated in *Shakespeare's Tragedies* (1950), p. 56, that 'In the fifty years from about 1575 to about 1625 the drama changed from a clearly ritual form to a predominantly documentary form'. In his article, 'Formalism and Illusion in Shakespearian Drama 1595–1598' (*Quarterly Journal of Speech*, December 1945), William G. McCollum has focused still more precisely on the moment of transition, finding that 'in the mid-nineties...the drama began to swing from formalism to illusion'. He goes even further than J. Dover Wilson (in the introduction to his edition), maintaining that the actor who plays the 'Christ-like' King Richard 'may be regarded as a priest commemorating the fall of the sacrificial victim...in a theatre converted for the purpose of the tragedy, into a kind of national church'. A certain amount of work has been done on Shakespeare's contemporaries which bears out these surveys. G. Wilson Knight has discussed Lyly's use of love myth (*Review of English Studies*, April 1939); Herbert Muller has made brief mention of ritual patterns in *The Spanish Tragedy* and *The Revenger's Tragedy* (*The Spirit of Tragedy*, 1956, pp. 159, 196); Northrup Frye in *Anatomy of Criticism* (1957) has sketched a tradition of 'green world' dramatists, 'established by Peele and developed by Greene and Lyly, which has affinities with the medieval tradition of the seasonal ritual-play'. But much more is needed.

Was Shakespeare's audience truly prepared to recognize a ritual dimension in his theatre? R. J. E. Tiddy decides in *The Mummer's Play* (1923) that 'except for *The Old Wives' Tale* the Elizabethan audience had lost the *primitive* feeling for fairy tale'. And John Crow, in his article on 'Folk-lore in Elizabethan Drama' (*Folk-lore*, September 1947), finds that 'the folk-lore world was in decay' and that there was 'a change of attitude toward folk-lore in Elizabethan authors', with Peele taking the old point of view and Shakespeare the new. Yet Douglas Hewitt points out that Puritan denunciations grouped 'popular stage-playes...sinfull, heathenish, lewde, ungodly spectacles' with pagan rites; and, in support of his interpretation of Lear as a scapegoat, he maintains that Shakespeare wrote 'at the last moment when this background of vague and misunderstood myth could combine with other belief and attitudes to produce the sense of inevitability and of the solidarity of the protagonists with their people which the finest tragedy demands' (*Review of English Studies*, January 1949). Paul N. Siegel in *Shakespearean Tragedy and the Elizabethan Compromise* (1957) agrees that the Elizabethan Londoner would have seen the resemblances of the 'comparatively innocent suffering' of Richard II, Hamlet, and Lear both to the passion of Christ and to that of the scapegoat in Elizabethan folk ceremonies; and he affirms that this recognition entered importantly into the tragic effect. Defining Shakespeare's intermediate position between Dante and our moderns, Philip Wheelwright observes that Shakespeare wrote 'at a time when a more sophisticated attitude toward myth is beginning to set in but before it has made such headway as to drain the myths of all vitality'.[2] In *The Idea of a Theater* Francis Fergusson speculates that the Elizabethan audience came to the Globe with a 'ritual expectancy' comparable to that of Athenians going to the Festival of Dionysus. In support of his interpretation of Falstaff as a scapegoat, J. I. M. Stewart explains that 'Falstaff's rejection and death are very sad, but Sir James Frazer would have classed them with the periodic Expulsion of Evils in a Material Vehicle, and discerned beneath the skin of Shakespeare's audience true brothers of the people of Leti, Moa, and Lakor'.[3]

At present, there is little evidence with which to test these opinions. It would be helpful to know more about the functions of drama in Elizabethan culture. Again, there have been surmises. G. Wilson Knight in *The Crown of Life* (1947) has felt that the drama held a position in Renaissance culture analogous to that of the Mass in medieval culture, and William Empson in *Some Versions of Pastoral* (1935) has expressed a similar view:

with nationalism and the disorder of religion the Renaissance Magnificent Man took the place of the patron saint, anyway on the stage...his death was somehow Christlike, somehow on his tribe's account, somehow like an atonement for the tribe that puts it in harmony with God or nature (p. 29).

But one wishes for a full-scale cultural anthropology of Elizabethan society, following perhaps the patterns in the Yale Human Relations Area Files.[4] Alfred Harbage's *Shakespeare and the Rival Traditions* (1952) has shown the way here. Insisting that Shakespeare's plays and the others written for the popular 'theatre of a nation' celebrated for the members of their audience 'the truths they lived by', Harbage in the second part of his book takes up these truths—'the divine plan', 'the dignity of man', 'sexual behaviour', 'wedded love', 'the commonweal'—as they are expressed both in the drama and—all too briefly—in prevailing belief and practice.[5]

DRAMATIC AND LITERARY TRADITIONS

G. Wilson Knight has done the most toward relating Shakespeare to the Christian origins of his dramatic tradition and to the Christian tradition generally. In *Principles of Shakespearian Production* (1936) he sees the Christian Mass as the 'central trunk' of Shakespearian tragedy:

Each of Shakespeare's tragic heroes is a miniature Christ. That is why I have urged the importance of Romeo's tragic *ascent*, his little Calvary. Richard II makes the comparison, and the analogy is pointed twice in *Timon*. Commentators from time to time make such a cross-reference in discussing *Lear*, suggested partly perhaps by his crown of country weeds (p. 231).

Roy Walker's book-length interpretations of *Hamlet* and *Macbeth* are in this spirit. In *Hamlet*, 'we are the spellbound witnesses of the crucifixion of the godlike in man'; in *Macbeth*, 'the murder of Duncan and its consequences are profoundly impregnated with the central tragedy of the Christian myth'. In his article on Shakespeare and the liturgy, L. A. Cormican finds that 'Shakespeare had, of course, no monopoly on the influences coming from Liturgy. But none of his contemporaries seem to have been as aware as he of the special fruitfulness and interest of these influences for dramatic purposes' (*Scrutiny*, Autumn, 1950, p. 196).

Although questioning the directness of descent of Shakespeare's drama from Christian ritual, J. A. Bryant nevertheless finds Shakespeare making use of biblical stories as analogues for his secular fables and in this way accounts for the 'ritual movement' in *The Winter's Tale* and *Richard II*.[6] He generalizes: 'Fundamentally Shakespeare's plays are explorations of mythic fragments, whereby the movement of the fable at hand, whether from English history, Roman history, Italian novella, or English fabliau, is revealed as participating by analogy in an action which, from the poet's point of view, is Christian, divine, and eternal.'

Taking up Bryant's suggestion, Roy Battenhouse has proposed that 'in general Shakespeare's tragedies rehearse various segments of the Old Adam analogue'.[7] Thus Othello is an analogue of Job, *Troilus and Cressida* of *Ecclesiastes*, and *Lear* 'of the Bible's story of mankind's journey toward revelation to a point as far as that journey can go short of the emergence of an adult New Adam'. He also finds in the tragedies a series of 'upside-down' parallels of Christian legend. Othello's scorn in telling Brabantio's men to put up their bright swords recalls but inverts Christ's humility in telling Peter to 'put up your sword into the sheath'; Romeo's cup of poison is 'a Thursday night last-supper, but the obverse of the Bible's', for Romeo's religion of love is a 'dark analogue of a supernatural love'. Yet if such analogies are more than distant echoes, if the tragedies are truly to be understood as Black Masses of self-idolatry, the effect of blasphemy would seem to overpower every other effect. Wilson Knight and Walker are much more convincing in bringing out the Christian reverberations of the contrasting banquet scenes in *Macbeth*; for here the effect of blasphemy is appropriate.

Following up his study of Shakespeare's narrative poems in *Mythology and the Renaissance Tradition* (1932), Douglas Bush in 'Classical Myths in Shakespeare's Plays'[8] concludes that Shakespeare's allusions 'range from Renaissance mythologizing to "myth"'. As instances of the latter he finds that in Portia's lines—'Peace, ho! the moon sleeps with Endymion and would not be awaked'—'myth is vivified by being humanized and re-created with imaginative "primitivism"'; that in *The Winter's Tale* Shakespeare's 'myth-making imagination—using the homely, authentic "waggon"—turns Proserpine and the goddesses into elements of the English spring'.

Going back to the Greeks and beyond, Gilbert Murray examines in 'Hamlet and Orestes' the curious resemblances between the Hamlet-saga and the Orestes-saga and traces both sagas to 'the world-wide ritual story of what we may call the Golden-Bough kings'. William H. Desmonde has followed the plot patterns of *Titus Andronicus* by way of Ovid to the Eleusinian mysteries (*International Journal of Psychoanalysis*, January–February, 1955). The most thorough study of such connections has been made by Herbert Weisinger.[9] He describes in detail the long development of the 'paradox of the fortunate fall', which he locates at the heart of tragedy, from its primitive origins to the tragedies of Shakespeare. By the time the basic ritual form became tragedy, he shows, many of its features had disappeared or were only implied—the death of the God, the sacred marriage, the triumphal procession, the settling of destinies—while new elements and emphases had been added, the most important of which was the hero's freedom of choice. In his article, Weisinger sums it up:

the structure of tragic form, as derived from the myth and ritual pattern may be diagrammed in this way: the tragic protagonist, in whom is subsumed the well-being of the people and the welfare of the state, engages in conflict with a representation of darkness and evil; a temporary defeat is inflicted on the tragic protagonist, but after shame and suffering he emerges triumphant as the symbol of the victory of light and good over darkness and evil, a victory sanctified by the covenant of the settling of destinies which reaffirms the well-being of the people and the welfare of the state (pp. 153–4).

This tragic pattern reached 'its most moving and significant expression' in *Othello*, where 'the opposites of good and evil in human nature are forcibly split' and the welfare of the people and state is jeopardized before the evil is purged, the good restored, and Othello enlightened. After that, Weisinger diagnoses, a process of disintegration immediately set in—perhaps from the moment Shakespeare realized that he had left Iago standing alive on the stage—so that in *Lear* and *Macbeth* he was unable 'to bear the burden of the tragic vision'.

At the farthest extreme of generalization are those who see in Shakespeare a prime instance of some single theme or pattern, derived from ritual origins, which dominates all literature. In *The White Goddess* (1948), Robert Graves half-playfully declares that the single grand theme of poetry is 'the life, death and resurrection of the Spirit of the Year, the Goddess's son and lover', and that 'the test of a poet's vision, one might say, is the accuracy of his portrayal of the White Goddess and of the island over which she rules'. She appears in Shakespeare as the Triple Hecate, as Cleopatra, as Sycorax, and—in that 'extraordinary mythographic jumble' *A Midsummer Night's Dream*—as 'tinselled Titania' coupled with the latter-day counterpart of 'Wild Ass Set-Dionysus', Bottom. In utter earnest,[10] Colin Still avers that in *The Tempest* 'Shakespeare wrote a dramatic version of the one theme which has appealed unfailingly to the imagination of mankind through all the ages'. This theme—'enshrined in all great art, myth and ritual'—is 'the Mystery of Redemption', 'the story of the upward struggle of the human spirit, individual or collective, out of the darkness of sin and error into the light of wisdom and truth'. *The Tempest* is Shakespeare's mystery play, directly comparable to Mystery and Morality plays and to pagan myth and ritual.

Recent writers—Wilson Knight, Fergusson, Heilman, Block—have honoured Still as a neglected pioneer, and his book does yield many insights. He is especially good on Sycorax and the tradition of the Evil Woman, and on the resemblances between the masque of Ceres and the Eleusinian mysteries. He may be right in linking Miranda's sleepiness with that of Persephone and other Sleeping Beauties. But he pushes his allegory much too hard. Miranda's proposal to her lover, for example, he sees as highly significant; he writes in *The Timeless Theme*: 'Her attitude is thus precisely that of Wisdom in ECCLESIASTICUS and of the Veiled Lady in the ZOHAR'

(p. 180). And, one must add, of numerous other Shakespearian heroines—Juliet, Rosalind, Helena, Olivia. As for his eternal and universal theme, Still himself points out only four works of literature other than *The Tempest* in which it appears (*The Divine Comedy*, *Aeneid VI*, *Paradise Regained*, and *Pilgrim's Progress*), and his definition of the myths in which it appears is circularly selective.

Graves and Still are only extremes of a strong tendency in modern criticism to read everything in terms of one 'monomyth' or another, usually involving sacrificial death and rebirth. In her article on 'ritual' in the *Encyclopedia of the Social Sciences*, Ruth Benedict writes:

Comparative study of ritual makes clear that a large number of themes have served in different cultures as the basis of the ritual complex. In most civilizations certain dominant themes are repetitiously elaborated in ritual after ritual.

Could it be that Shakespeare's plays and other great works of art in the Western tradition are just such repetitive elaborations of a few basic ritual themes? The possibility is not as alarming as it may appear. Admittedly explorations of the possibility have been guilty of many abuses. Finding a theme everywhere—whether it is there or not—is one abuse; there are already far too many 'symbolic' deaths and rebirths in contemporary criticism. Insisting that there is only *one* fundamental myth is another; different critics—in addition to Still and Graves—have already pointed out different 'monomyths'.[11] Stopping interpretation of a work at discovery of 'the myth' in it, is the worst abuse; properly, this discovery should be the starting-point for discriminating the unique qualities which give each work its identity.

Yet this approach, sensibly used, need not reduce or distort literary values. Rather, it can enlarge our sense of Shakespeare's universality, by making new connections with other works of literature and with the findings of modern psychology and anthropology. Its comprehensive sweep, on the other hand, can also help to define the limits of Shakespeare's apparently limitless genius. For example, Northrup Frye in *Anatomy of Criticism* postulates a 'central, unifying myth' of which romance, tragedy, satire and irony, and comedy are successive phases:

Agon or conflict is the basis or archetypal theme of romance, the radical of romance being a sequence of marvellous adventures. *Pathos* or catastrophe, whether in triumph or in defeat, is the archetypal theme of tragedy. *Sparagmos*, or the sense that heroism and effective action are absent, disorganized or foredoomed to defeat, and that confusion and anarchy reign over the world, is the archetypal theme of irony and satire. *Anagnorisis*, or recognition of a newborn society rising in triumph around a still somewhat mysterious hero and his bride, is the archetypal theme of comedy (p. 192).

He draws extensively on Shakespeare in his discussions of tragedy and comedy and their subphases, but hardly at all in his discussions of romance and of irony and satire—proportions which reflect, although exaggeratedly, Shakespeare's own. Frye's 'myth' thus provides an unusually extensive yet coherent set of literary possibilities against which Shakespeare's omissions and emphases may be appraised.

DRAMATIC GENRES

Many critics have felt that the ritual qualities of Shakespeare's plays derive from inherent attributes of the dramatic genres. In *Man in his Theatre* (1957) Samuel Selden admits that the 'theatre has evolved into various forms, few of which now bear much resemblance to the rituals and myths that were their ancestors', but he insists that 'the blood of descent is in them'. Describing the battle between summer and winter as 'from the beginning the central theme of drama', he accordingly finds that 'For Romeo, Juliet is Summer':

The heat of their love battles with the coldness of the hatred between their families. Hamlet is a prince of Light who struggles with the Darkness of his uncle and his nightmarish court (p. 32).

He finds the ritual pattern completed in these plays by a resurrection:

Hamlet in dying creates, and when he has passed leaves behind him an image of princeliness.... The fulfilment of the love of Romeo and Juliet rises out of their entombment (p. 59).

Like Selden, but less impressionistically, Northrup Frye in *Anatomy of Criticism* has recognized ritual qualities residual in the dramatic forms Shakespeare used. He explains that *The Winter's Tale*, for example, is 'more suggestive of ancient myths and rituals' than *The Two Gentlemen of Verona* because, 'As a result of expressing the inner forms of drama with increasing force and intensity, Shakespeare arrived in his last period at the bedrock of drama, the romantic spectacle out of which all the more specialized forms of drama, such as tragedy and social comedy, have come, and to which they recurrently return' (p. 117). This bedrock is the 'central unifying myth' already discussed. Again like Selden, Frye makes use of seasonal analogies, labelling the phases of his basic myth the mythoi of spring, summer, autumn, and winter. In Shakespeare's comedies, for example, he finds a recurring rhythmic movement from the normal world to a 'green world' —such as the forest scenes in *The Two Gentlemen of Verona*, *A Midsummer Night's Dream*, *As You Like It*—and back again. 'The green world', he feels, 'charges the comedies with a symbolism in which the comic resolution contains a suggestion of the old ritual pattern of the victory of summer over winter.'[12]

Clifford Leech also believes that dramatic forms retain attributes of the 'primitive dramatic act' (*Durham University Journal*, December 1937). Developing his distinction between 'drama as ritual' and 'drama as document', he explains that in ritual drama the playwright with his 'congregation', like the savage in his tribal dance, is 'going through a ceremony which is intended to convey his homage to a superior being'. He sees Shakespeare as such a playwright: his histories 'glorify the spirit of their country'; his tragedies render 'homage to the greatness, the invulnerability of the human spirit in face of the hostility of god and man'; his comedies pay 'homage to the superhuman force that sports kindly with men's lives'. A. P. Rossiter's analysis of Shakespeare's history plays gives Leech's idea more specific application (*Durham University Journal*, December 1938). Contrasting the first two parts of *Henry VI* with the last three and a half acts of part three and *Richard III*, he detects in the latter two a marked preference for ritual situations—formalized celebrations of pity, hate, 'the terrifying force of self-assertive energy which is Richard'. He takes as an example a passage from part three:

> *Richard*: Clifford, ask mercy and obtain no grace!
> *Edward*: Clifford, repent in bootless penitence!
> *Warwick*: Clifford, devise excuses for thy faults!
> *George*: While we devise fell tortures for thy faults.
> *Richard*: Thou didst love York, and I am son to York.

Edward: Thou pitiest Rutland, I will pity thee!
George: Where's Captain Margaret, to fence you now?

Clifford has been enemy to York, has killed Rutland, and has been protected by the militant queen Margaret; but since he is dead, these insults pass him by; and since the audience knows he is dead, these speeches are only a ritual of the bitter hatred bred by civil war. It is a war-dance of savages round a fallen foe... (p. 49).

Rossiter concludes, however, that Shakespeare after bringing this ritual method to a 'masterly peak' in *Richard III* abandoned it.

Other critics have found that certain patterns and rhythms within the dramatic forms possess ritual dimensions. Adopting Kenneth Burke's notion of a characteristically tragic rhythm of action which moves from purpose to passion to perception, Francis Fergusson in *The Idea of a Theatre* derives each moment in this pattern from ritual origins: he relates 'purpose' to the sacred combat between the old king and the new, 'passion' to the tearing asunder of the royal victim and the 'lamentation and/or rejoicing' which accompanied it, and 'perception' to the final epiphany of the god. He shows this rhythm operating in *Hamlet*, as in Oedipus, although in *Hamlet* the rhythm and its ritualistic import are complicated by ironic distortions and parallels:

Hamlet himself, though a prince, is without a throne; though a sufferer for the truth, he can appear in public as a mere infatuated or whimsical youth....It takes both Hamlet and Claudius to represent the royal victim of the tradition. Though the play has the general shape of the tragic rhythm, and the traditional parts of the plot, each part is presented in several ironically analogous versions (p. 118).

Nonetheless, he maintains, Shakespeare 'clings to the conception of the theatre as ritual'. In *Archetypal Patterns in Poetry* (1934), Maud Bodkin discovers in primitive attitudes toward the 'father-king' the same tensions and interactions between the impulses of self-assertion and submission that she takes to be 'the archetypal pattern corresponding to tragedy';

within the meaning communicated today to a sensitive reader or spectator of *Hamlet*, or *King Lear*... something is present corresponding to the emotional meaning that belonged to ancient rituals undertaken for the renewal of the life of the tribe (p. 85).

This is particularly true at the moment of the hero's death. She writes: 'Our exultation in the death of Hamlet is related in direct line of descent to the religious exultation felt by the primitive group that made sacrifice of the divine king.' Similarly, Kenneth Burke, in pursuit of that 'ritualistic form lurking behind a drama', has analysed *Othello* as a 'ritual of riddance...a requiem in which we participate at the ceremonious death of a portion of ourselves' (*Hudson Review*, Summer, 1951). In another of Burke's essays, Brutus is described as an 'expiative beast brought up for sacrifice...for it is Brutus that must die to absolve you of your stabbing an emperor who was deaf in one ear and whose wife was sterile'.[13] And T. R. Henn, in support of his assertion that 'tragedy presents an ordered ritual experience', points out in *The Harvest of Tragedy* (1956) that 'the kings of the Shakespearian history play are loaded at their end with a kind of collective responsibility for the many kinds of evil which have been freed (by whatever agencies) during their reign'.

Henn tries to work out a rationale of such associations by using as his guide Frazer's analysis of the rites for Carrying out Death:

We must therefore recognize two distinct and seemingly opposite features in these ceremonies: on the one hand sorrow for the death, and affection and respect for the dead; on the other hand, fear and hatred of the dead, and rejoicings at his death.

Using *King Lear* as one of his examples, Henn finds that a similar 'double tide is running in the spectator of the tragic pattern'. Consciously, the spectator identifies with the tragic hero, the saviour of the State, and regrets his misfortunes: Lear in a sense offers himself as a sacrifice 'for the sake of the unity which he has destroyed'. Yet, at the same time, the spectator unconsciously welcomes the hero's death as a release from this identification, as relief from 'the feeling of helplessness before superior strength now obeying its cyclic decline': in *King Lear* 'the waning powers of the Old King afford the normal pretext for his dethronement and death'.

There is much more still to be made of this analogy. Henn puts too much stress on the spectator's hostilities and not enough on his sympathies. His preference for the term 'release' rather than 'catharsis' points to his neglect in the tragic effect of what Wilson Knight calls the 'positive thrust of the sacrificial act'. Yet the association—not equation—of the death of the tragic hero with the sacrifice of the scapegoat king seems to me easily the soundest and most suggestive contribution which ritualists have made to date.

Shakespeare's Artistic Development

Other critics have held that Shakespeare in part arrived at the mythic and ritualistic qualities in his work independently, through the logic of his artistic development. Thomas Mann in *Essays of Three Decades* (1947) has observed:

when a writer has acquired the habit of regarding life as mythical and typical there comes a curious heightening of his artist temper, a new refreshment of his perceiving and shaping powers which otherwise occurs much later in life; for while in the life of the human race the mythical is an early and primitive stage, in the life of the individual it is a late and mature one (p. 422).

Mann expresses the view of many students of Shakespeare's last plays. In *The Crown of Life* Wilson Knight sees Shakespeare moving from problem plays and tragedies to 'myths of immortality' in his final plays, which are not 'to be read as pleasant fancies: rather as parables of a profound and glorious truth'. Knight sees Shakespeare working out a new mythology, which makes use of both pagan and Christian myths but recombines them in a new way, resulting—to use Bonamy Dobrée's phrase—in a Gospel According to St William. Numerous other critics have followed Knight's lead, and unquestionably it is in the interpretation of the last plays that ritualists have been most influential.[14] By offering an interpretation which includes—and welcomes—such striking features as the vision of Jupiter, the resurrection of Thaisa, Perdita's pastorals, and Hermione's 'resurrection', they have broadened and deepened our understanding of these plays. Yet in a way they have been too successful—to the point that the plays in their analyses have seemed to lose their literary character and to become literally myths. Colin Still's interpretation of *The Tempest* as a mystery play is a case in point. Richard Wincor has treated the romances as if they were merely 'festival plays' of the St George variety (*Shakespeare Quarterly*, October 1950); and Wilson Knight has proposed that incense be burned at their performances!

Knight's most interesting follower is D. G. James, who in *Scepticism and Poetry* (1937) accepts his view that the last plays seek to create a personal mythology but then argues that they fail: 'the making of a mythology is too great a work for one mind, though that mind be Shakespeare's'. He shows how Shakespeare's myths conflict—love with royalty, regeneration with evil—and how his myth of resurrection is weakened by attempts at plausibility. But he does not go on to consider that the qualities which produce the failure of the plays as a 'human mythology' might contribute to their success as works of art. For similar, though harsher, conflicts of myth with myth and of myth with fact occur in plays before the romances and with powerful effect.

This is Robert Heilman's point.[15] He follows Wheelright in considering 'the two Shakespearean key-myths' to be 'the myth of love and the myth of divine and earthly governance'. But he shows that Hamlet, Claudius, Othello, Iago, Lear violate the myth of love; that Claudius, Goneril, Regan, Edmund, Macbeth violate the myth of governance; and that a corrosive atmosphere pervades *Hamlet*, *Othello*, *Lear*, and *Macbeth*, an atmosphere of sceptical and calculating rationalism 'in revolt against the traditional, communal order of life'. The myths of love and governance at last triumph over their violators, villains and deluded heroes alike, but not until men and communities have been 'subjected to unbearable agonies'. For this reason he defines 'high Shakespearean tragedy as a study of the myth in crisis'. Only the Romances arrive at a serene 'reassertion or reaffirmation, or perhaps simply contemplation, of myth and mystery'.

There is thus a striking conjunction of opinion about the breaking up of the traditions of myth and ritual at the time of Shakespeare's greatest tragedies. Weisinger, coming all the way from the most primitive origins, places the break-up a little later than Heilman does but after *Othello* feels it to be more destructive than does Heilman. McCollum places the transition in the general dramatic tradition from 'formalism' to 'illusion' a little earlier, 1595–8; but Leech's broader view sees it taking place between 1575 and 1625. Does this breaking up of the mythic world view and its consequent conflicts between belief and scepticism, trust and calculation, mystery and fact have something to do with the power of the great tragedies? Heilman's brief essay certainly suggests that it does. It may well be that the great tragedies will prove to be an even more productive area for ritualistic studies than the Romances. For in the tragedies, critics will be compelled not only to identify the myth or ritual involved but also to relate it to the other parts of the work in which it appears.

OTHER ELEMENTS IN A WORK

Thus far, such studies have been relatively rare. A few critics, however, have already not only abstracted the element of myth or ritual from the work but also put it back again and observed what it contributes. The tragedies have received the most such attention. In *The Idea of a Theatre* Francis Fergusson has charted the interplay in *Hamlet* between scenes of ritual (the changing of the guard, Ophelia's funeral) and of improvisation (Hamlet's vaudeville bits with Polonius, the gravedigger). He shows how the alternating scenes of ritual and improvisation, with the play-within-a-play—both ritual and improvisation—at the centre, help to create the special tragic rhythm of the play. Brents Stirling in *The Unity of Shakespearean Tragedy* (1956) observes that in Shakespeare 'retreat into self is generally marked by ceremonial' and that 'the return of the outer world is often presented as a breaking of the ceremonial spell'. He finds that the hero's assumption of a ritualistic role is a prime factor in the 'false tragic sense' which deludes Shakespeare's tragic heroes:

Othello's self-contrived ritual tragedy ends with the sacrifice killing; Shakespeare's tragedy of Othello ends when Emilia tells the truth about the sacrifice and Othello understands it. Richard II sees the mirror ritual in the deposition scene as the true expression of his fall; Shakespeare modifies this *de casibus* pose by Richard's breaking of the glass, an act which discloses the erstwhile master of ceremony as a servant of egoistic passion (pp. 202–3).

M. M. Mahood in *Shakespeare's Wordplay* (1957) demonstrates how the many suggestions of the *amour-passion* myth work in *Romeo and Juliet*. Far from reducing the play to 'the *Liebestod* myth in dramatic form', the suggested myth—which is described in Denis de Rougemont's *L'Amour et l'Occident* (1939)—operates as one among various incompatible truths which the wordplay helps to clarify and bring into equilibrium. She points out important ways in which Shakespeare differs from the myth, finds that Shakespeare's treatment generally awakens 'detached judgment' as well as 'the implicated excitement we feel for myth', and feels that our sense of mythic fulfilment at the end is balanced by one of frustration: 'our final emotion is neither the satisfaction we should feel in the lovers' death if the play were a simple expression of the *Liebestod* theme, nor the dismay of seeing two lives thwarted and destroyed by vicious fates, but a tragic equilibrium which includes and transcends both these feelings' (p. 72). Deploring the excesses of 'ritual happy' critics, William Frost points out some of the artistic dangers of ceremony in drama: of losing personality in roles, of losing emotion in formulas, of losing truly dramatic effects in easy theatricality. But he shows also how Shakespeare transcends these difficulties in *King Lear*, how Lear's ritualistic abdication provides a point of reference for subsequent scenes, especially the final reunion of Lear and Cordelia, who by this time 'have passed beyond ritual altogether' (*Hudson Review*, Winter, 1957–8). Robert Elliott in *The Power of Satire* (1960), after tracing the satiric tradition from its origins in the magically powerful invective of ancient rituals, finds that Shakespeare's Timon seeks to play the satirist in just such a primitive way: he 'tries to preempt the full power of the archaic curse, calling on the gods, the heavens, the earth—and, as it were, the demonic power within himself—to confound the hated creature man'. Yet for all the force of Timon's denunciations, Elliott discerns, this primitive satirist is himself satirized by his creator: Shakespeare shows Timon's excessive hate, as well as his excessive love, to be folly.

Certain histories, romances, and comedies have also been approached in this way. Analysing the 'ceremonial or ritual form of writing' in *Richard II*, which he takes to be 'the very essence of the play', E. M. W. Tillyard in *Shakespeare's History Plays* (1944) fits Richard and his ceremonies into a general picture of ritualistic medievalism which usurping Bolingbroke pragmatically destroys. F. C. Tinkler relates the seasonal rhythms of *A Winter's Tale*—from winter to spring, with Perdita and Florizel 'almost vegetation deities'—to a pervasive set of tensions in the play— reason and intuition, court and country, individual and state (*Scrutiny*, March 1937). Warning against 'equating the literary form with primitive analogues', C. L. Barber in *Shakespeare's Festive Comedy* distinguishes between ritual patterns in *Henry IV* which fail dramatically and those which succeed. The sacrificial imagery surrounding the death of King Henry, for example, is effective as drama 'because it does not ask the audience to abandon any part of the awareness of the human, social situation which the play as a whole has expressed'. The expulsion of Falstaff fails precisely because its scapegoat imagery denies this full awareness, relying on an appeal to magic not fully validated by imagination.[16]

Harry Levin in *Contexts of Criticism* (1957) speaks in despair of an era in which Shakespeare's plays are regarded as so many 'ceremonials for a dying god'. And Wimsatt and Brooks conclude their history of literary criticism with an ominous vision: 'Surely the hugest cloudy symbol, the most threatening, of our last ten or fifteen years in criticism is the principle of criticism by myth and ritual origins.' This survey would suggest that at least as far as Shakespearian studies are concerned this alarm and despair are misplaced. Ritualists have been guilty of mistaking analogies for identities, of making claims far in excess of evidence, of trying to reduce literature to myth, of oversolemnity. But extravagant statements are not unknown among students of Shakespeare. Bradley, for example, could speak of the romantic comedies as 'the plays with Beatrice, and Jaques and Viola in them'. Caroline Spurgeon could see directly through her collections of images into the personality of Shakespeare the Christlike man, and other collectors of images have spoken of Shakespeare's plays simply as 'poems'. In these instances, the full productiveness of the approach has come when its object has been recognized as an element in a total work, not its essence. The recent tendencies among ritualists in this same direction give grounds for expecting this new approach to become equally productive.

NOTES

1. Haskell M. Block, 'Cultural Anthropology and Contemporary Literary Criticism', *Journal of Aesthetics and Art Criticism* (September 1952), p. 47. For additional general surveys, see Stanley Edgar Hyman, 'Myth, Ritual and Nonsense', *Kenyon Review* (Summer, 1949), *The Armed Vision* (1952), and 'The Ritual View of Myth and the Mythic', *Journal of American Folklore* (October–December 1955); John J. Gross, 'After Frazer; the Ritualistic Approach to Myth', *Western Humanities Review* (Autumn, 1951); John B. Vickery, '*The Golden Bough* and Modern Poetry', *Journal of Aesthetics and Art Criticism* (March 1957). For an unsympathetic survey, see Wallace W. Douglas, 'The Meanings of "Myth" in Modern Criticism', *Modern Philology* (May 1953). Douglas Bush has written a parody study of the Venus and Adonis myth in *Pride and Prejudice*, 'Mrs Bennet and the Dark Gods', *Sewannee Review* (Autumn, 1956).

2. 'Poetry, Myth, and Reality', *The Language of Poetry*, ed. A. Tate (1942), p. 22.

3. *Character and Motive in Shakespeare* (1949), pp. 138–9.

4. See George P. Murdock, *Outline of Cultural Materials*, 3rd rev. ed. (1950).

5. In his preface, Harbage remarks: 'I am actually presenting, by a process of fragmentation, just two plays—the popular play and the coterie play. I have toyed with the notion of calling the first the *archetype*, with the ideals it embodies *myths*, and the second the *anarchetype*, with its separatist and disintegrative features *contra-myths*; but I feel inexpert and self-conscious in using such language and must confine my sortie to the present remark.'

6. 'Shakespeare's Allegory: *The Winter's Tale*', *Sewanee Review* (Spring, 1955), and 'The Linked Analogies of *Richard II*', *Sewanee Review* (Summer, 1957).

7. 'Shakespearean Tragedy: A Christian Interpretation', in *The Tragic Vision and the Christian Faith*, ed. Nathan Scott, Jr. (1957).

8. In *Elizabethan and Jacobean Studies presented to F. P. Wilson* (1959).

9. In *Tragedy and the Paradox of the Fortunate Fall* (1953) and 'The Myth and Ritual Approach to Shakespearean Tragedy', *The Centennial Review of Arts and Science* (Spring, 1957).

10. In *Shakespeare's Mystery Play* (1921) and *The Timeless Theme* (1936).

11. Lord Raglan, who in *The Hero* (1936) finds a 22-phase pattern common to hero myths, devotes a chapter, 'Myth and the Historic Hero', to Hal and Falstaff. Joseph Campbell, *The Hero with a Thousand Faces* (1949), finds Hamlet a prime spokesman for the phase of disillusionment in 'the monomyth'.

12. 'The Argument of Comedy', *English Institute Essays, 1948* (1949), p. 68. Eric Bentley, *What is Theatre?* (1957), pp. 247–50, similarly feels that the comedies invoke 'seasonal myth'.

13. 'Antony in Behalf of the Play', *The Philosophy of Literary Form* (1941).

14. F. David Hoeniger, 'The Meaning of *The Winter's Tale*', *University of Toronto Quarterly* (October 1950); D. G. Bland, 'The Heroine and the Sea; An Aspect of Shakespeare's Last Plays', *Essays in Criticism* (January 1953); E. M. W. Tillyard, *Shakespeare's Last Plays* (1954); D. A. Traversi, *Shakespeare: the Last Phase* (1954).

15. 'The Lear World', *English Institute Essays, 1948* (1949). This essay is one of a group misleadingly titled 'Myth in the Later Plays of Shakespeare' which includes Northrup Frye's 'The Argument of Comedy', Leslie A. Fiedler's 'The Defense of the Illusion and the Creation of Myth', and Edward Hubler's 'Three Shakespearean Myths: Mutability, Plenitude, and Reputation'. None of these essays has much to say about the 'later' plays, and the last two essays use the term 'myth' in too special a sense to warrant discussion here.

16. Falstaff has been a favourite with ritualists. In addition to Barber and the studies by Stewart and Raglan already cited, see Wylie Sypher's long appendix in *Comedy* (1956), esp. pp. 214–26, and Philip Williams, 'The Birth and Death of Falstaff Reconsidered', *Shakespeare Quarterly* (Summer 1957).

ILLUSTRATIONS OF SOCIAL LIFE
IV: THE PLAGUE

BY

F. P. WILSON

London was ravaged by many an epidemic of bubonic plague before the last and greatest of them all, that of 1665. Major plagues which in their turn were called 'great' occurred in 1563, 1592–3, 1603 and 1625; and during Shakespeare's residence in London there were minor plagues in each year from 1606 till 1610. The effects upon the theatre were serious. In 1592 and 1593 companies were disbanded and reformed with bewildering speed, so that the tracing of Shakespeare's allegiance in these years is most difficult. The establishment in 1594 of the Lord Chamberlain's company, the most stable of all Elizabethan and early seventeenth-century companies, is a landmark in his life. It was secure enough to survive the great plague of 1603 and the minor plagues of 1606–10, though the London theatres were closed for nearly a year in 1603–4 and for some time in every year from 1606 to 1610—in 1608 and 1609 for many months. On 8 February 1604 the company received the special favour of a grant of £30 from its new patron King James for its maintenance and relief

being prohibited to presente any playes publiquelie in or neere London by reason of greate perill that might growe throughe the extraordinary Concourse and assemblie of people to a newe increase of the plague till it shall please god to settle the Cittie in a more perfecte health by way of his Maiesties free gifte.

Again, by a warrant of 26 April 1609 they were granted £40 'for their private practise in the time of infeccion' that they might the better act before the King during the Christmas holidays.

It would indeed be surprising if this fell disease had not left its mark on Shakespeare's plays. These lines in *Timon of Athens* (IV, iii, 109)

> a planetary plague, when Jove
> Will o'er some high-vic'd City, hang his poison
> In the sick air

allude to three of the causes to which according to orthodox opinion the plague was due. It was God's punishment for sin; it was engendered by a rotten and corrupt air (cf. also 'the plagues, that in the pendulous air Hang fated o'er men's faults', *Lear*, III, iv, 69); and a third cause was the conjunction of the stars and the aspect of the planets, especially when the planets 'In evil mixture to disorder wander' (*Troilus and Cressida*, I, iii, 95). Astrologers were not slow to observe that in 1603 there was a conjunction of Saturn and Jupiter in Sagittarius and just before that an eclipse of the sun.

Some of the innumerable remedies are given in Plate I, from a broadsheet in the Bodleian Library published *c.* 1603–10.[1] The fourth remedy may remind us that Prince Henry's sickness in 1612 seeming to lie in his head, they shaved him and applied warm cocks and pigeons newly killed; 'but with no successe' (J. Chamberlain, *Letters*, ed. McClure, I, 388). The cure for hydrophobia is not unlike. Take an old cock, pluck the feathers from its breech, and apply it to the bite. If the dog is mad the cock swells and dies; if the cock does not die, the dog is not mad (*teste* the Royal Society in its *Transactions* for 1687 (xiv, 410)).

Of the many orders imposed in time of plague by the magistrates of London nothing can be said here except in so far as Shakespeare refers to them.[2] Very much to the point is Berowne's speech in *Love's Labour's Lost*, v, ii, 419, a play written perhaps in 1594 when the experiences of 1592 and 1593 were still fresh in his mind:

> Write 'Lord have mercy on us' on those three;
> They are infected, in their hearts it lies;
> They have the plague, and caught it of your eyes:
> These lords are visited; you are not free,
> For the Lord's tokens on you do I see.

As elsewhere in Shakespeare the plague becomes by metaphor the plague of love. The verb 'visited' bears the special meaning 'infected with the plague'. In 'the Lord's tokens' he puns on the *petechiae* or spots which are one of the symptoms of bubonic plague, so called from their resemblance to the halfpenny or farthing tokens of cheap metal or leather issued by tradesmen. So in *Antony and Cleopatra* (iii, x, 9): 'the token'd pestilence Where death is sure.' They were often called 'God's tokens' because they were thought of as God's punishment for sin. Again, 'Lord have mercy upon us' refers to the best-known of plague-orders, remembered by all who have read Defoe's *Journal of the Plague Year* or the lyric which Nashe wrote during the plague of 1592 or 1593:

> Beauty is but a flowre,
> Which wrinckles will deuoure,
> Brightnesse falls from the ayre,
> Queenes haue died yong and faire,
> Dust hath closde Helens eye.
> I am sick, I must dye:
> 	Lord, haue mercy on vs.

A printed paper with these words was ordered to be set upon the door or lintel of an infected house immediately above a red cross fourteen inches long and broad to be painted on the door. Plate II A, from a woodcut on the title-page of Thomas Brewer's *Lord Have Mercy Upon Us* (1636),[3] suggests the form the paper took, although the border was in red ink and (in earlier years, if not later) a circle. Some commentators have argued that *Love's Labour's Lost* was written not earlier than 1592 on the ground that the inscription was first used in that year, but it was used from 1568 and possibly from 1563.

The regulation that the sound as well as the sick were to keep at home in an infected house had necessarily to be relaxed in times of heavy mortality when the sound were hardly sufficient to bury the dead. Then fever-maddened wretches ran from house to house infecting others. Benedick, says Beatrice, 'is sooner caught than the pestilence, and the taker runs presently mad' (i, i, 88). In *The Woman's Prize: or, The Tamer Tamed*, Fletcher's sequel to *The Taming of the Shrew*, Petruchio, falsely shut up by a ruse of his second wife, frightens away the watchmen with a fowling-piece (iii, v):

PLATE I

SVNDRÆ APPROOVED REMEDIES
againſt the Plague.

I.

A remedie againſt the Plague, ſent to the Lord Maior of London from King Henry the eight.

Take a handfull of Sage, a handfull of Elder leaues, a handful of redde Bramble leaues, ſtampe them all and ſtraine them through a fine cloth, with a quart of White wine and then take a quantitie of Ginger, and mingle them together, & ſo take a ſpoonefull of the ſame, and you ſhall be ſafe for foure and twentie daies: and ſo being nine times taken, ſhall be ſufficient for all the whole yeere by the grace of God. And if it be ſo that the party be ſtricken with the Plague before hee hath drunke of this medicine: Then take the water of Scabions a ſpoonefull and water of Betonie a ſpoonefull, and a quantitie of fine Treacle, and put them altogether, and cauſe him to drinke it, and it ſhall put out all the venome. If it fortune the Botche to appeare, then take the leaues of Brambles, Elder leaues, Muſtard ſeede, and ſtampe them altogether, and make a Plaiſter thereof, and lay it to the ſore, and it ſhall draw out the Uenome, and the partie ſhall be whole by the grace of God.

II.

A medicine taught vnto King Henrie the ſeuenth by his Phiſition againſt the Plague.

Take halfe a handfull of Rew, likewiſe of Mandragories, Feather-few, Sorrell, Burnet, and a quantitie of crops and rootes of Dragons, waſh them cleane, and ſeeth them with a ſoft fire in running water, from a Pottle to a Quarte, and then ſtraine them together through a cleane cloth: And if it be bitter, put thereto a quantitie of Suger-Candy, or of other Suger, and if this medicine bee vſed before the Purples doe ariſe: ye ſhall be whole by Gods grace.

III.

Another remedie.

Take three ſlips of Herbe grace, and ſixe ſpoonefuls of Vineger, and beate the ſame together, then ſtraine the iuyce out thereof, and put thereunto one ounce of fine Treacle, and one ounce of Suger, and ſtir it together, then ſet it ouer the fire, and make thereof a Sirrop, and put it in a Boxe cloſe: then take a Sage leafe, and euerie Morning faſting, ſpread as much as a Beane thereof vpon the ſame leafe, and ſo eate it. And if hee that taketh it, be infected it will driue it from his heart: and if the partie that taketh it Euening and Morning be not infected, it wil preſerue him for twentie foure houres after.

IIII.

Another.

Amongſt other excellent and approoued Medicines for the Peſtilence, there is none more worthy auaileable when the ſore doth appeare, then to take a Cocke, Pullet, or Chicken, and let the feathers of the taple of the higheſt pa ... ſucked off, till the rump: be bare, then holde the ſaide ... ce of the Pullet to the ſore, and the Pullet will gape and labour for life, and in the ende will die: then haue another Pullet, and do the like to the Patient, and if that die, yet ſtill apply the Patient with Pullets ſo longas any doe die: for when the Poyſon by the ſaide Chicken is drawen forth, the ſaid Chickens that be offered therunto will liue, then the ſore preſently will ſwage, and the partie forth-with recouereth: This Medicine is neceſſarie to driue the venome from the heart.

V.

A Plaiſter to draw the Sore to a head, and to breake it.

Take two Lyllie rootes, one handfull of ſower Dowe, two handfuls of Mallowes, one handfull of Linſeede, ſtampe all theſe together ſmall, and boyle it in a quarte of the Lees of Wine till it be thicke, then lay it an inch thicke vpon Leather, broader then the Sore, and let the borders of the Leather be plaſtered with Corbiers waxe, to make it cleaue: it ſhall bring out the Botch in twelue houres, and breake it ſhortly.

VI.

A drinke to be taken euery Morning for a preſeruatiue againſt the Plague, and for the voyding of infection.

Take Sauerie the quantitie of a handful, and boyle the ſame in a quart of good Wine vinegar, with a ſpoonefull of Graines being beaten, and put into the ſame: then drinke the ſame with a quantitie of Suger euery morning faſting.

VII.

Another drinke to be vſually drunke of euery one being infected.

Take Roſemarie the quantitie of eight or nine crops, then take of Marigolds being browne within, of Burnet, and of Bourage, euery one a handfull therof, let them be ſod in a quarte of ſtale Ale clariſyed: then put into it a cruſt of bread, a little whole Mace, and a quantitie of Suger, and let him drinke the ſame at all times during his ſickneſſe: ... ſo put Pimpernel in his broth.

VIII.

Another drinke againſt the Plague.

Take an ounce of Sorrell water, and as much Dragon water, a dragme of Treacle, and put thereto a dragme and a halfe of Powder imperial, & giue it to the Patient with Ale, within twenty foure houres after hee is infected, and hee ſhal with Gods grace eſcape and do well.

Imprinted at London by E. Allde for E. White, and are to be ſolde at the little North doore of Paules Church at the ſigne of the Gun.

'SUNDRIE APPROOVED REMEDIES AGAINST THE PLAGUE'

PLATE II

B. THE GALLANT

A. 'LORD HAVE MERCY UPON US'

PLATE III

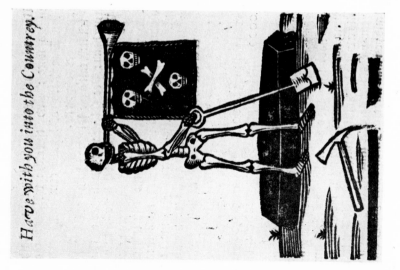

B. DEATH THE SKELETON

A. THE COUNTRYMAN AND HIS WIFE

PLATE IV

1602.　1603.

A TRVE REPORT OF ALL THE BVRIALS AND CHRISTNINGS

within the City of LONDON and the Liberties thereof, from the 23. of December, 1602. to the 22. of December, 1603. Whereunto is added the number of every severall Parish, from the 14. of Iuly, to the 22. of December, aswell within the Citie of LONDON and the Liberties thereof, as in other Parishes in the skirtes of the Citie, and out of the Freedome, adioyning to the Citie: According to the report made to the Kings most excellent Maiestie, by the Company of Parish Clearks of the same CITIE.

	Buried in all.	Of the plague	Christ- nings.
December 23	83	3	96
Ianuary 6	78	0	97
Ianuary 13	83	1	134
Ianuary 20	80	0	105
Ianuary 27	82	4	128
February 3	104	1	102
February 10	76	0	108
February 17	96	3	109
February 24	85	0	108
March 3	82	3	110
March 10	101	2	110
March 17	108	3	106
March 24	60	2	106
March 31	78	6	59
Aprill 7	66	4	143
Aprill 14	79	4	86
Aprill 21	98	8	84
Aprill 28	109	10	85
May 5	90	11	78
May 12	112	18	103
May 19	122	22	81
May 26	122	32	98
Iune 2	114	30	82
Iune 9	131	43	110
Iune 16	144	59	90
Iune 23	182	72	95
Iune 30	267	158	82
Iuly 7	445	263	89
Iuly 14	612	424	88

This weeke was the Out-parishes brought into be ioyned with the City and Liberties.

	Buried in all.	Of the plague	Christ- nings.
Iuly 21	1186	917	50
Iuly 28	1728	1396	138
August 4	2256	1922	115
August 11	2077	1745	110
August 18	3054	2713	95
August 25	2853	2539	127
September 1	3385	3035	97
September 8	3078	2724	105
September 15	3129	2818	89
September 22	2456	2195	90
September 29	1961	1732	81
October 6	1831	1641	71
October 13	1312	1146	73
October 20	766	642	67
October 27	625	508	75
Nouember 3	737	594	70
Nouember 10	585	442	65
Nouember 17	384	251	64
Nouember 24	198	105	58
December 1	223	102	64
December 8	163	55	72
December 15	200	96	71
December 22	168	74	70

The totall of all that hath beene buried
this yeare ———— 38244
Whereof of the Plague ———— 30578
Christnings ———— 4789

	Buried in all.	Of the plague		Buried in all.	Of the plague	London within the Walles.
Alhones in Woodstreet	183	164	Margrets Pattons	54	44	
Alhallowes Lumberstreet	109	98	Margrets Moyses	70	60	
Alhallowes the great	286	250	Margrets Lothbery	106	88	
Alhallowes the lesse	227	182	Martins in the Vintry	258	190	
Alhallowes Bredstreet	33	27	Martins Orgars	90	77	
Alhallowes stayings	123	103	Martins Iremonger lane	27	19	
Alhallowes the Wall	216	174	Martins at Ludgate	199	161	
Alhallowes Hony-lane	12	5	Martins Outwich	39	32	
Alhallowes Barking	390	339	Mary le Booe	26	24	
Alphage at Cripplegate	174	152	Mary Bothawe	35	31	
Androwes by the Wardrope	290	256	Mary at the hill	142	120	
Androwes Eastcheape	114	108	Mary Abchurch	124	110	
Androwes vndershaft	165	142	Mary Woolchurch	52	17	
Annes at Aldersgate	146	125	Mary Colchurch	10	8	
Annes Blacke Fryers	235	226	Mary Woolnoth	99	91	
Auntlins Parish	32	27	Mary Aldermary	60	68	
Austines Parish	92	78	Mary Aldermanbery	81	70	
Barthelmew at the Exch.	93	63	Mary Staynings	42	37	
Bennets at Pauls-Wharf	199	136	Mary Mountawe	51	45	
Bennets Grace-Church	40	30	Mary Sommersets	197	177	
Bennets Finck	95	78	Mathew Friday street	16	13	
Bennets Sherhogg	26	24	Maudlins Milke street	33	30	
Buttols Billingsgate	91	73	Maudlins by Olasishstreet	126	104	
Christ Church Parish	334	271	Mighels Basishawe	141	109	
Christophers Parish	41	35	Mighels Corne hill	130	91	
Clements by Eastcheape	48	40	Mighels in Woodstreet	156	137	
Dennis Backe Church	112	88	Mighels in the Ryall	100	79	
Dunstones in the East	227	197	Mighels in the Querne	61	46	
Edmunds in Lumbard-st.	78	67	Mighels Queene-hithe	138	105	
Ethelborow within Bishopsg.	163	124	Mighels Crooked lane	110	97	
S. Faithes	115	96	Mildreds Poultry	84	62	
S. Fosters in Foster-lane	94	81	Mildreds Bredstreet	45	33	
Gabriel Fan-Church	67	56	Nicholas Acons	41	32	
George Botolph lane	36	30	Nicholas Cole-abbay	147	103	
Gregories by Paules	272	217	Nicholas Olaues	83	69	
Hellens within Bishopsg.	98	83	Olaues in the Iury	41	33	
Iames by Garlike hithe	141	110	Olaues in Hartstreet	201	171	
Iohn Euangelist	9	5	Olaues in Siluer street	113	92	
Iohn Zacharies	131	118	Pancras by Soperlane	20	16	
Iohns in the Walbrooke	136	122	Peters in Cornehill	141	80	
Katherines Cree-Church	400	337	Peters in Cheape	58	37	
Katherine Colemans	190	167	Peters the poore in broadst.	44	39	
Laurence in the Iury	88	71	Peters at Pauls wharf	97	88	
Laurence Pountney	161	134	Stephens in Colemanstreet	363	315	
Leonards Foster-lane	250	210	Stephens in the Walbrook	24	20	
Leonards Eastcheape	54	39	Swithins at London-stone	120	95	
Magnus parish by the Bridge	109	76	Thomas Apostles	86	64	
Margrets New fishstreete	83	61	Trinity parish	116	108	

	Buried in all.	Of the plague		Buried in all.	Of the plague	London without the Walls, and with- in the Li- berties.
Androwes in Holborn	1191	1125	Dunstones in the West	510	412	
Barthelmew the lesse Smith	86	74	Georges in Southwarke	915	804	
Bartheimew the great Smith	195	165	Giles without Cripplegate	2408	1745	
Brides parish	933	805	Olaues in Southwark	2541	2383	
Buttols Algate	1413	1280	Sauiours in Southwarke	1914	1773	
Bridewell Precinct	108	105	Sepulchers parish	2223	1861	
Buttols Bishops	1228	1094	Thomas in Southwarke	249	221	
Buttols without Aldersg.	576	588	Trinity without the Minories	40	33	

	Buried in all.	Of the plague		Buried in all.	Of the plague	Out Pari- shes adioi- ning to the City.
Clements without Templeb.	662	501	Martins in the Fields	505	425	
Giles in the fields	456	402	Mary Whitechappell	1539	1352	
Iames at Clarkenwel	725	619	Magdalens in Barmondsey			
Katherines by the Tower	653	585	streete	597	562	
Leonards in Shordich	871	740	At the Pest-house	135	135	

Buried in all, within these 27 weekes ———— 33681.
Whereof, of the Plague ———— 29033.

Printed by Iohn Windet, Printer to the Honourable City of London.

BILL OF MORTALITY—YEARLY BILL FOR 1603

1 *Watch.* Let's quit him,
It may be it is trick: he's dangerous.
2 *Watch.* The devill take the hinmost, I cry.
Exit watch running.

The plague was a poor man's disease, finding its richest harvest in the rat-infested slums. Few men of note died or were said to have died of the plague in London. Mention Gavin Douglas, Holbein, Florio, John Fletcher, and the tale is almost taken. Any reader of John Chamberlain's letters will agree that smallpox was far more troublesome to the health and beauty of the well-to-do than the plague. Poor and rich alike tried to save themselves by flight, but for obvious reasons the rich were more successful. At the height of the infection London was deserted and grass grew in Cheapside. Ross's account of the state of Scotland (*Macbeth*, IV, iii, 166) exactly describes the lamentable condition of London in the terrible summer of 1603:

It cannot
Be call'd our Mother, but our Grave; where nothing
But who knows nothing, is once seen to smile:
Where sighs, and groans, and shrieks that rent the air
Are made, not mark'd: where violent sorrow seems
A modern ecstasy: the dead man's knell
Is there scarce ask'd for who, and good men's lives
Expire before the Flowers in their Caps,
Dying, or ere they sicken.

Many found in flight the death they sought to escape, and the pamphleteers tell gruesome or grimly humorous stories of the fate of many. Characteristic of the mood of the time are the three woodcuts (Plates II B, and III A and B) reproduced from *A Dialogue betwixt a Cittizen, and a poore Countrey-man and his Wife, in the Countrey* (1636).[4] Plates II B and III B provide a grim *memento mori*—a gallant in the pride of life metamorphosed into a skeleton with spade and mattock, and above the legend 'Have with you into the Countrey'. Plate III A shows the kind of reception a Londoner met with when he entered a country town or village. Often he was kept at bay with pitchforks and other rustic weapons, and at many towns no traveller was allowed to enter without a certificate that he had come from an uninfected district. Those who remained in the City complained bitterly of the 'runaways'—sometimes magistrates, clergymen, and doctors—who fled without thought for the wretches left behind. Among those who stayed at the post of duty was Thomas Lodge, poet, pamphleteer, and physician: but that was during the plague of 1625.

The bills of mortality are the chief source of information about the plague. Early in the sixteenth century the company of the parish-clerks of London were charged with the duty of delivering weekly to the Lord Mayor the numbers of the dead in each parish. An ordinance of 1555 required them to state 'the numbers of all the persons that do die and whereof they die': in practice the only disease differentiated before 1607 was that of the plague. For the causes of death the clerks were dependent on the searchers, officially 'honest and discreet matrons', two to each parish, but by all accounts ignorant and bribable. In *Romeo and Juliet* Friar John, suspected of being in an infected house, is shut up by the searchers and so prevented from carrying to

Romeo at Mantua the all-important letter from Friar Laurence. And so fearful are the citizens of Verona of the infection that no messenger can be found to return the letter to Friar Laurence. The earliest use of 'searcher' in this special sense cited by the *Oxford Dictionary* is from this play (v, ii, 8), but for the very earliest instance we must go back to the year in which the office was instituted, 1578. From 1607 till 1836, when the office was abolished by the Registration Act of that year, the searchers reported such dilucidations as 'Rising of the Lights', 'Meagrome', 'Suddenly', 'Plannet struck'.

On 14 July 1593 'the billes, briefes, notes and larges gyven out for the sicknes weekely or otherwise' were entered in the Stationers' Register to John Wolfe, then City printer (Arber, II, 634), and so far as is known his were the first bills of mortality to be printed. According to Thomas Nashe (ed. McKerrow, III, 89), Gabriel Harvey supplied them with an eloquent post-script. Very few sixteenth-century bills have survived, and all of these are in manuscript. Before the reign of Charles I, it is probable, they were printed only in plague years, when they became a topic of general conversation and would command a good sale in London and the country. Wolfe died in 1601, and the licence to print the bills passed on 1 August 1603 to John Windet, then City printer. When Windet died in 1611, William Stansby acquired his stock, including 'The bylls of those that dye of the Plague' and 'the briefes thereof' (Arber, III, 243, 467).

When in 1927 I searched for weekly bills printed before 1625, I could find very few. It is most remarkable that recently the Houghton Library, Harvard University, has been able to acquire some forty bills published in 1603 and 1604. For all but five weeks Harvard now has a complete run of weekly bills from 14 July 1603 till 12 April 1604 and from 24 May 1604 till 21 June 1604. The bill for the week 14–21 July 1603 is perhaps the earliest printed bill now known.

One of these Harvard bills is reproduced below (Plate IV) by generous permission of W. A. Jackson. The original measures $16\frac{1}{16}$ by $10\frac{5}{8}$ inches. The contents of this bill, popular because it gave the total mortality for the year, were known before from two reprints: (1) that at the end of a Dutch poem by Jacob Cool, nephew of Abraham Ortelius, *Den Staet van London in hare groote Peste*, published at Middelburg by Richard Schilders in 1606, an edition of which by J. van Dorsten and K. Schaap is announced from Leyden; and (2) that printed by Stansby in 1625 as a companion piece to his yearly bill for 1625 and reproduced in my book facing page 114. It will be seen that the bill gives the deaths and plague-deaths in each parish from 14 July to 22 December and the deaths, plague-deaths, and christenings in each week from the week ending 23 December 1602 to the week ending 22 December 1603. The out-parishes were first included during the week ending 21 July, and the addition of these suburbs with their teeming tenements accounts in part for the increase in that week from 612 to 1186 deaths in all, and from 424 to 917 of the plague.

The total mortality for the year is given as 38,244 with 30,578 of the plague. Add the out-lying districts of Westminster, Lambeth, Newington Butts, the Savoy, Stepney, Hackney, and Islington, and the total is swollen to 43,154 deaths, of which 35,104 were of the plague. In 1603 the population of London within the bills can hardly have been greater than 250,000 and was probably less, so that almost a sixth of the inhabitants perished in the year. In 1625 the figures were 63,001 and 41,313. 'This,' observed one writer in words to be proved false forty years later, 'This, to future Ages and Historiographers must needs be Kalendred the *Great Plague*.'

NOTES

1. Reproduced (in reduced facsimile) from a broadsheet in the Bodleian Library (Wood 276 a 32) by kind permission of Bodley's Librarian.

2. I examined them at length, with other matters, in *The Plague in Shakespeare's London* (Oxford, 1927).

3. Reproduced (in reduced facsimile) from the British Museum copy by kind permission. Other copies are in the Folger and Huntington Libraries.

4. Reproduced (in reduced facsimile) by kind permission of the Trustees of the Huntington Library. Another copy is in the Surgeon-General's Library, Washington, D.C.

THE SOEST PORTRAIT OF SHAKESPEARE

Students of Shakespeare portraiture will be interested to learn that a portrait of Shakespeare by Gerard Soest has recently been acquired by the Shakespeare Birthplace Trust at Stratford-upon-Avon.

The picture was painted probably somewhere between 1660 and 1680 and was engraved early in the eighteenth century.[1] It measures 29½ by 24½ inches, that is, just about life-size, and the subject is represented in a three-quarter view. The expression of the face is delicate, the beard and moustache slight and the hair curly and ample. The costume represents what the artist presumably thought Shakespeare would have been wearing in his lifetime and the collar at least suggests some possible relation to the Chandos portrait.

Quite apart from the early eighteenth-century engraving of Soest's picture of Shakespeare, stylistic evidence supports the attribution to Soest. Mr David Piper, Assistant Keeper of the National Portrait Gallery,[2] who has had an opportunity to examine it, informs me that Soest hardly ever signed his pictures, but that he is one of the easiest painters of his time to recognize. Mr Piper believes that the portrait is either Soest's original or a replica of it by himself.

The picture comes from the collections of Sir J. F. Grey and of the Earl of Stamford and was last seen in this country in the auction room at Christie's on 9 April 1954. Subsequently it went abroad and passed into the hands of a firm of art dealers in Lisbon, Portugal, from whom the Birthplace Trustees have purchased it. Very little attention was necessary to put the Shakespeare portrait into good order, and it has now been re-framed in a carved wood and gilt leaf moulding frame of early seventeenth-century date.

LEVI FOX

1. Norris, *Portraits of Shakespeare* (1885), pp. 201–3.
2. I should like to record my thanks to Mr Kingsley Adams, Director of the National Portrait Gallery, and to Mr David Piper, Assistant Keeper, for the interest thay have shown in this picture and for help given.

PLATE V

THE SOEST PORTRAIT OF SHAKESPEARE

PLATE VI

The final scene

'HAMLET', DUBROVNIK SUMMER FESTIVAL, 1961
Directed by M. Fotez

INTERNATIONAL NOTES

A selection has been made from the reports received from our correspondents, those which present material of a particularly interesting kind being printed in their entirety, or largely so. It should be emphasized that the choice of countries to be thus represented has depended on the nature of the information presented in the reports, not upon the importance of the countries concerned or upon the character of the reports themselves.

Australia

In 1960 there were the usual productions of plays set for the school examinations in the various States, including *Twelfth Night* (produced in Sydney by the Independent Theatre and the Sydney University Players, in Brisbane by the Repertory Theatre, and also in Adelaide), *Richard II* (the Independent Theatre, Sydney), *Hamlet* (Twelfth Night Theatre, Brisbane), *A Midsummer Night's Dream* (Kalgoorlie Repertory Club, in the Festival of Perth), *The Merchant of Venice* (Brisbane Arts Theatre, in both city and country) and *Julius Caesar* and *Richard III* (both in Adelaide). The National Institute of Dramatic Art in Sydney bravely essayed *Love's Labour's Lost* but the play had no great success either with the public or with academic critics.

On television, the National station, ABN 2, following its experimental productions of *Hamlet* and *Antony and Cleopatra* in 1959, presented *Richard II* and *Macbeth*. Nobody believes that the problems of performing Shakespeare on television have yet been solved; it is doubly a pity to find experiments now being confined to the plays that are familiar to schoolchildren.

Other pioneering included tours by two small companies of the Young Elizabethan Players (who visited all States except Western Australia to perform for schools and colleges special 75-minute condensed versions of chosen Shakespearian plays) and a ten-day tour of the remote north-western ports of Western Australia by a small group of three professional actors (who presented, in costume but without scenery, selected scenes from Shakespeare, as well as scenes from two Australian plays). The Western Australian project is thought to have meant that many residents, including Australian aborigines, saw live theatre for the first time.

It will be clear, however, that 1960 was a lean year so far as productions of Shakespeare in Australia were concerned and that professional performances in particular were few and undistinguished.   H. J. OLIVER

Austria

It is the sad duty of the reviewer to report the death on 5 November 1960, in Vienna, of Richard Flatter, the translator and author of several books and articles on Shakespeare. Richard Flatter devoted thirty years of his life to the rendering of Shakespeare's works, and since 1952 more than twenty of his versions have been performed in more than sixty theatres and over one hundred productions.

Flatter, however, was not only a brilliant translator, he was also a Shakespeare scholar and an expert in matters of the Elizabethan stage. His books (*Shakespeare's Producing Hand*, *Hamlet's Father* and *The Moor of Venice*) are the works of a scholar who had studied over many years problems concerned with the Elizabethan theatre, with acting, the editing of texts, and language. His most fascinating contribution towards an interpretation of Shakespeare is, perhaps, his volume of essays, *Triumph der Gnade* (1956), a work of fine understanding.

Flatter was able to produce his excellent translations because he was a poet himself. In the late thirties he wrote two plays and published a volume of original poetry (*Weg und Heimkehr*), a translation of Shakespeare's sonnets (1954), and an anthology of English lyrical poetry (*Die Fähre*).

It is the harmonious combination of these qualities that made him the most successful of the German translators of Shakespeare in the twentieth century. Through his efforts we have today a complete and modern Shake-speare translation that has taken the place of the romantic and distorted version of Schlegel–Tieck and the idealized text of Gundolf.

In 1960 the production of Shakespeare's comedies far outnumbered that of his tragedies, although the most memorable single production was that of *Henry IV* in the Burgtheater, Vienna. The first performance of *Henry IV* had taken place in 1782, when Parts I and II were played in the translation of F. L. Schröder in the course of one evening. In 1828 and 1829 another pro-duction followed, and this time the translation of F. Schreyvogel was used, the two parts of the play being performed on two successive nights. In 1851 an adapta-tion by H. Laube was presented (Parts I and II on one night), and in 1875 the two parts of the play were given on two nights in the translation of F. Dingelstedt; the same text was used for the production of 1890. A pro-duction in 1914 was the last a Vienna audience was to see before the 1960 production by Leopold Lindtberg, which used the translation of A. W. Schlegel. In this last production the two parts were combined into one sequence of twenty scenes. Whether Lindtberg suc-ceeded in fusing history, tragedy, and comedy, in keeping a proper balance among the various figures, scenes and accents, in making a uniform, dramatically effective piece while still producing Shakespeare remains a question. He was able to select from all levels of action material for the creation of an effective, powerful piece, but he shifted so many accents, so cut the parts and left out or modified characters that his version was remote from the original in many ways. To produce *Henry IV* on one night will always create these insurmountable problems. This *Henry IV* was produced as part of the whole series of Shakespearian histories, and is to be followed by *Henry V* in 1961.

Of the tragedies only *Othello* was produced (in the Landestheater, Innsbruck). The ever-growing apprecia-tion of Shakespeare's comic theatre is shown by the fact that half a dozen of the early comedies, praised for their combination of romance and boisterous humour, were selected for performance— *The Two Gentlemen of Verona* (Volkstheater, Vienna), *The Taming of the Shrew* (Akademie Mozarteum, Salzburg), *The Merry Wives of Windsor* (Festival Friesach, Carinthia), *Much Ado About Nothing* (Theatre in the Josef-stadt, Vienna), and, in-evitably, *A Midsummer Night's Dream* (Burgtheater Vienna and Landestheater Salzburg). In addition *Measure for Measure* was performed in the Stadttheater, Klagen-furt and *Cymbeline* in Graz.

SIEGFRIED KORNINGER

France

Jean-Louis Barrault has a keen sense of Shakespeare's history plays. The pages he devoted to *Henry IV* are penetrating and his introduction to a debate on his recent production of *Julius Caesar*, at the Odéon-Théâtre de France, revealed the same insight. He was conscious of a relationship between the conceptions which underlie the English history cycles and the Roman plays, and could discern in both a similar pattern of rebellion, strife and restoration of order. The pattern, of course, is not quite so clear as in the tetralogy ending with the death of Richard III, and the defeat of Brutus and Cassius cannot be so definitely interpreted in terms of judgment and retribution as in the case of Richard. All the same Barrault's way of bringing to bear his whole experience of the dramatist on the preparation of a single play was worthy of praise. In his direction, as in his own interpretation of the part of Cassius, he also showed an unusual awareness of a wealth of feelings of friendship and love, brought out by violence of conflict and tragic tension. The play was coldly received by most of the critics but the Odéon public responded favourably, and though I was conscious of some shortcomings (the women's parts were weak and the charming comedienne, Simone Valère, was unconvincing as Portia) I found the performance, on the whole, deeply moving.

Barrault is careful in choosing his translators. He had recourse to André Gide for *Hamlet* and *Antony and Cleopatra*. For *Caesar* he used the version of a dis-tinguished poet, Yves Bonnefoy. Balthus, a painter of considerable talent, was responsible for the settings. Barrault's idea was to provide Renaissance equivalents, in the plastic arts, for Shakespeare's poetic vision of the Romans. So the costumes were inspired by the triumph of Mantegna and the *décor*, used through the first part of the play, was strongly reminiscent of the Teatro Olimpico, with its triple perspective of streets. This structure had its beauty but did not help the movements of the Roman crowd, and it became very unconvincing when it had to be partly hidden for the scenes at Caesar's or Brutus's house. The second part, with its battle-scenes, moved more freely. Brutus's tent looked just a bit too much like the one in Piero della Francesca's Dream of Con-stantine. Barrault has an irresistible passion for panto-mime. He had some valid reasons for preferring a stylized to a realistic way of representing the fights; this might have been beautiful but it was overdone, and at times it looked a bit too much like Chinese opera. Besides it was not in keeping with Brutus's and Cassius's realistic way of committing suicide. Fortunately, this artiness and eclectism did not quite succeed in destroying the quality which resulted from Barrault's awareness of the play's deep motives and sources of emotion.

Barrault also revived, during the same season, André Obey's dramatic version of *The Rape of Lucretia*, which was originally produced in the early thirties by Michel Saint-Denis and a group of disciples of Jacques Copeau, the Compagnie des Quinze. The play was partly spoken and partly mimed. Two motionless figures, a man and a woman, one on each side of the stage, supplied respectively a narrative and a lyrical commentary of the action and expressed the unspoken thoughts of Tarquinus's and Lucretia's consciences. Much of the effect depended on the interplay between these two levels of the drama. Music performed on the stage (a lute on one side, percussion on the other) supported the two choral figures. André Barsacq provided settings and Elizabethan costumes.

Barrault is fascinated by Georges Feydeau's clever plots and low comedy. He gave another proof of his eclectism by rounding off the programme with *Mais n'te promène donc pas toute nue!*, a one-act play with an unfortunate title for the occasion, giving the critics an opportunity for a joke which they did not miss. Providing some comic relief at the end is in pure Comédie Française tradition, and an example of the cartesianism of the French: since their classical precepts proscribe the intermingling of comic and tragic scenes, they keep the light comedy for the end.

Maeterlinck made no concession to the comic muse when he adapted *'Tis Pity she's a Whore*: he suppressed the sub-plots entirely and gave the play a less objectionable title, *Annabella*. Since the days of Maeterlinck and Symbolism, *'Tis Pity* has been generally considered here one of the few dramas by contemporaries of Shakespeare which is worth knowing, not of course as a good play but as an extreme example of Renaissance violent and perverted passion. For this very reason it appealed to the taste of Lucchino Visconti, the Italian film director who produced it at the Théâtre de Paris. Nothing was spared in the way of brocade and silk and polished metal; it was a continual feast of colour and movement, among colonnades reminiscent of the Teatro Farnese in Parma. The music was by Gesualdo de Venosa and Frescobaldi. Romy Schneider and Alain Delon, who I am told are well known in the film world, took the parts of Anabella and Giovanni. Their beauty and youth and total inexperience of stage acting lent the incestuous couple a purity, an ignorance of good and evil which, though by accident, was convincing. Some other roles were hopelessly miscast and a few competent actors did not know

exactly what to do to maintain a balance. The adaptation, by Georges Baume, retained the sub-plots and gave a literal (and therefore misleading) translation of the title, using one of the rare words in the French language for which dots must be supplied. This may have had good advertising value. Baume's version was rather vulgar in tone; it did not matter very much as the important thing was obviously not the play, but Visconti's lavish display.

Another play by a contemporary of Shakespeare served as a basis for the production of *Edward II* by Roger Planchon at the Théâtre de la Cité in Villeurbanne. I understand that Planchon rewrote most of the text, but I shall not be able to give an account of the play before it is presented in Paris in November 1961.

Shakespeare's comedies are as popular as ever. *Twelfth Night* was given at the Vieux-Colombier, in an adaptation by Nicole and Jean Anouilh. Jean Le Poulain, the director, who also took the part of Malvolio, laid much emphasis on the clowning at the expense of the rest, thus neglecting the example Copeau had given on the same stage, almost fifty years ago, of a delicate balance between all the elements of the play. Some balance, however, was restored in favour of the poetry and romance by the music of Henri Sauget, the settings of Jacques Dupont, and Suzanne Flon's moving interpretation of the part of Viola.

Since the days when Firmin Gémier produced *The Taming of the Shrew* at the Odéon, there has been, in this country, a well-established tradition of horse-play for this lusty comedy, some of the favourite 'gags' being based on the idea that, in the Elizabethan theatre, settings were replaced by sign-boards and a minimum of stage property (*Julius Caesar* and *'Tis Pity* described above are examples of going to the other extreme). René Jauneau, who produced the play for the Centre Dramatique de l'Est, also toyed with this conception. The adaptation was by Henri Grangé, costumes and 'dispositifs scéniques' by M. H. Butel. Sixty performances were given in Strasbourg and neighbouring towns.

I have few details concerning Guy Parigot's *Othello*, the first Shakespearian venture of the Centre Dramatique de l'Ouest under his direction. The 'texte français' was by Charles Lecotteley, 'dispositifs' and costumes were by Claude Besson *Othello* was also given at the second festival of Provins; this open-air performance took place in an ancient cloister.

This year, once more, Mlle Rose-Marie Moudouès must be thanked for her assistance in the preparation of these notes.
JEAN JACQUOT

Germany

In 1960 Shakespeare's popularity on the German stage was again undiminished. There were more performances of his plays than of any other single author. Altogether twenty-three plays were performed in some ninety-seven new productions at eighty-seven theatres and there were twelve new productions of operas based on Shakespearian plays. The plays chosen for all these performances included most of the popular tragedies, comedies and histories, and also some of the less often performed works like *Cymbeline* and *Henry VIII* in Richard Flatter's adaptation, and *All's Well that Ends Well*.

Again producers have tried various new translations, among which those of Richard Flatter, Hans Rothe and Rudolf Schaller were used for more than thirty productions altogether. In Ulm J. J. Eschenburg's eighteenth-century translation of *The Taming of the Shrew* ('*Die Kunst, eine Widerbellerin zu zähmen*') had an interesting revival. But on the whole most producers decided in favour of the established translation by Schlegel–Tieck which was used for sixty-four productions.

Among the nine new productions of *Hamlet* that at Kassel may be mentioned. It was based on Hans Rothe's adaptation of the play which claims to present something like Shakespeare's own stage-version. There are numerous major changes in the accepted text; the first scene, for example, is left out completely since it is held that all the essential information it contains is provided by Horatio later in the play. Rothe's intention to simplify the drama and rid it of any inconsistencies has resulted in a rather shallow performance without any tragic power and effect.

Othello as a play seems to be in some danger of being ousted by Verdi's opera. In no case was Tieck's translation used, but several productions tried Schaller's new version. At Innsbruck Theodor von Zeyneck's translation was given a trial for the first time and seems to have met with a very favourable reception. *Romeo and Juliet* appears to have been more successful as a ballet and as an opera than in Shakespeare's original version.

There were only very few productions of the histories, one of which deserves to be specially noted. It was Richard Flatter's attempt to combine what he believes to be the only Shakespearian portions of *Henry VIII* and the anonymous *Sir Thomas More*. The resulting play, however, lacks dramatic unity and fails to be more than a rather loose sequence of historical pageants. The 'Burgtheater' Vienna has announced its intention to perform the whole of Shakespeare's histories within the next few years and has started with a very successful production of the two parts of *Henry IV* in one evening. Owing to the necessary cuts, however, the Falstaff scenes seemed to be unduly prominent.

As usual, the comedies had the lion's share and last year again the list was headed by *Twelfth Night*, followed by *A Midsummer Night's Dream*. It is interesting to note that more than half of the performances included Mendelssohn's music. *The Comedy of Errors* continues to be popular. In many productions the twins were played by only one actor which provided some extra fun, though it makes necessary some alterations in the text. Interestingly enough the 'dark' comedies are now far less popular than a few years ago; however, *Measure for Measure* was still performed at five theatres.

Another interesting, if perhaps not very successful, revival was a production of the apocryphal *The London Prodigal* at Rheydt. It was the first German performance in twenty-seven years.

Apart from all these productions four plays of Shakespeare's were presented either as wireless plays or on television. *King Lear* adapted by Wilhelm Semmelroth with Fritz Kortner as Lear was successful. On television, the performance of *Hamlet* on New Year's Day 1961 seems to have been particularly impressive. It was directed by Franz Peter Wirth with Maximilian Schell playing the part of Hamlet.　　KARL BRINKMANN
WOLFGANG CLEMEN

Greece

The following performances of the works of Shakespeare were given in the Greek language during 1960, either in Greece itself or by Greek companies on tour abroad:

The company of N. Chadjiskos played *The Taming of the Shrew* on 23 January at Limassol, Cyprus. This performance was repeated at Lefkosia and Ammochosto.

In Athens the National Theatre has since 1931 traditionally included one Shakespeare play in each annual programme. It must be noted that Shakespeare vies with our great classical authors in proving successful among all sections of the community. During 1960 the National Theatre staged two plays, *Richard III* and *The Merchant of Venice*. The new production of *Richard III* was by Alexis Minotis, who also played the part of Richard—a powerful interpretation, enriched through a fine actor's personality, and emphasizing the cruel nature of Gloucester. If anything were lacking in this performance, one might say it was the dimension of gloomy genius which characterizes Gloucester and gives him his secret charm. This, of course, is always the most difficult element of his character to supply. Minotis gave a similarly intense interpretation to the character of Shylock, playing in his own production of *The Merchant of Venice*. Here the general tone of the production tended to be more tragic than comic, for Minotis played Shylock with the weight which leading tragedians usually prefer to lend to this role. Beside him, the Portia of Vasso Manolidou was a figure of great charm.

ANGELOS TERZAKIS

Hungary

The popularity of Shakespeare continues undiminished on the Hungarian stage; indeed it seems to be on the increase both in Budapest and in the country. Owing to the great success of Shakespeare's plays the year before (as reported in volume 14 of *Shakespeare Survey*), the theatrical season of 1960–1 was dominated, as it were, by his dramas in the repertory theatres. The plays performed in Budapest in the latter season were the same as in 1959–60—*Richard III, Othello, Antony and Cleopatra, Twelfth Night, Much Ado About Nothing* and *The Merry Wives of Windsor* (these in the National Theatre) as well as *The Tempest* in the Madách Theatre. A revival of *A Midsummer Night's Dream* was added to last year's list late in 1960 in the National Theatre, which brought the number of currently played Shakespearian plays to eight in Budapest. Of these *Antony and Cleopatra* was by far the greatest success, achieving fifty performances in this season alone, with *Twelfth Night* coming second (thirty-five evenings) and *Much Ado* third (twenty-nine performances). With the National Theatre offering one hundred and fifty-one performances it may be stated without exaggeration that not a week has passed in the 1960–1 season in which there were not at least three performances of Shakespeare in the capital of the country.

Neither were the theatres of the provinces very far behind those of Budapest. In the theatre of Győr *Othello* was produced in 1960, the small stage forcing the director to cut out secondary matter and concentrate on the essentials of the plot. The quite young theatrical company of Szolnok staged a conservatively lyrical *Hamlet* in the same year. *Romeo and Juliet* was presented early in 1961 by the theatre of Miskolc while *The Taming of the Shrew*, that old favourite of Hungarian theatrical companies, was put on the stage of the small town of Eger. All these plays had fairly long runs in the country theatres, *The Taming* being produced eighteen times in the township of Eger and ten times in smaller localities of the neighbourhood, while *Romeo and Juliet* was given twenty-one times in Miskolc in the first half of 1961. The small villages not reached even by the provincial

theatres were catered for by the State Travelling Company (Déryné Állami Faluszinház, the activities of which were described in *Shakespeare Survey*, XII). In the 1960–1 season this company gave fifty-six performances of *The Taming* in as many backwoods localities.

Attempting to enlarge the audience for Shakespeare's plays, the Hungarian Broadcasting Corporation in Budapest started a series of studio broadcasts in 1960. The first play to be presented was *Hamlet*, followed some months later by *The Taming* and then by an almost entirely uncut *Julius Caesar*, a tragedy infrequently played on Hungarian stages.

Mention must be made of a publication indirectly connected with Shakespeare. The dramatic works of Shakespeare's contemporaries are just as much, if not more, overshadowed by his greatness in Hungary as in practically any other country. To redress the balance somewhat a three-volume collection, running to over two thousand pages, was published early in 1961 under the title *Angol reneszánsz drámák* ('Dramas of the English Renaissance'). The series contains twenty outstanding full-length dramatic works by practically all of Shakespeare's most important forerunners, contemporaries and followers, from the author of *Ralph Roister Doister* down to James Shirley. The verse translations, most of them very good, were made expressly for this series by the best living Hungarian poets and translators and will certainly be instrumental in popularizing the great age of English drama hitherto but insufficiently known here. Copious notes and introductions to each of the twenty plays, as well as an excellent general introduction to the collection by the editor, M. J. Szenczi of Budapest University, complete this most valuable work.

LADISLAS ORSZÁGH

India

India urgently needs a national theatre and a professional company of national actors. Whatever few theatrical troupes of nationwide importance existed up to the thirties of this century have been wiped out of existence by the tremendous progress which the film industry in this country has made during the last two decades. Credit therefore goes to the Shakespeare Society of St Stephen's College, Delhi, for doing at least one play of Shakespeare each year. The roles are all played by the students of this college and of a girl's college, and yet it is gratifying to note that the standard of production among these amateurs is high. Since its inception in 1924–5, the Society has with few breaks produced thirty-one plays altogether.

In November 1960 the Society played *The Merry Wives of Windsor*.

It was a straightforward production, consisting of the simplest possible curtain set, using its ten entrances and exits to enable actors to be anywhere in and around Windsor in the twinkling of an eye. Lights were dimmed to suggest the night that passes in the first half; and a second night was suggested to have passed in the fifteen minutes of the interval itself. On other occasions the passage of time was suggested by music. The role of Sir John Falstaff was played by Nigam Prakash, and Aruna Chatterji and Kiran Kapoor played Mistress Page and Mistress Ford respectively.

The play, which ran for three nights, was produced by William Jarvis assisted by David Summerscale.

H. S. D. MITHAL

Italy

1960 saw the completion of another Italian version of Shakespeare's theatre, Cesare Vico Lodovici's; the publisher Einaudi, who has been issuing his translations of single dramas over a number of years, has collected them in three magnificently produced volumes whose chief interest lies, however, not so much in the painstaking and praiseworthy work of the translator—who has tried to reconcile a literal rendering with the demands of the stage (making for terseness and economy of expression)—as in certain unusual features calculated to give a unique character to this edition. The plates are taken from drawings, prints and paintings of Henry Fuseli, the drawings being particularly effective, since that ambiguous Anglo-Swiss painter, who lived in a period no less stormy and torn by contrasting currents than ours, succeeded for the first time in seeing an aspect of Shakespeare which strongly appeals to us. As Richard David has said in one of the essays of *The Living Shakespeare* (edited by Robert Gittings, 1960), nowadays 'we are allergic to comedy. Life, we think, is full of strains and stresses...our mood is tragic, and only tragedy, or the bitter ironic comedy that is the counterpart of tragedy, can satisfy that mood. If we agree that Shakespeare is a great writer, it is of the author of *Hamlet* and *Lear* that we are thinking.' Now Shakespearian characters, as seen by Fuseli, a typical artist of the *Sturm und Drang* period, stretch, bend and twist like human catapults intent on tearing the walls of a narrow and suffocating world choked by that 'blanket of the dark' of which Lady Macbeth speaks. Fuseli's is a museum of galvanized statues of athletes, a cavalcade of furies, a rush into open graves, on prostrate bodies. In a lower key, the women of the comedies have serpentine motions,

Leonardo's enigmatic smile, and very often that black ribbon round their necks which was fashionable in the days of the Terror according to the macabre mode *à la guillotine*, almost as if they were sisters of that *Femme au collier de velours* who appears in the tales of Irving, Petrus Borel, and Alexandre Dumas. Giulio Carlo Argan, in an extremely penetrating essay on 'Fuseli, Shakespeare's Painter', has called attention to certain manneristic traits common to Shakespeare and Fuseli. Attuned to the English dramatist by a similar temper in the two ages, the Elizabethan and the *Sturm und Drang*, Fuseli was enabled to see in him 'a deeper sense beyond the ostensible drama: an intimation of the mysterial, initiatory, orphic character of the theatre'. Another unusual feature of this edition is the general introduction, consisting of Boris Pasternak's notes on Shakespeare instead of a full-dress professorial dissertation. Pasternak's notes are however a little disappointing: the Russian writer does little more than rehearse what has been often said about Shakespeare's realism.

Remarkable Shakespearian performances during the year have been given at Verona in July (*Romeo and Juliet* in Salvatore Quasimodo's version, in Signorio della Scala's courtyard), at the Roman theatre of Fiesole also in July (*Two Gentlemen* in Isabella Smith's version), and at the Great Theatre of Pompeii in August (*Antony and Cleopatra*). Franco Enriquez was the producer of the first and the third of these plays, Beppe Menegatto of the second. Gian Maria Volonté acted as Romeo at Verona, and as Octavius Caesar at Pompeii. Carla Gravina impersonated Juliet, Giancarlo Sbragia excelled in Mercutio's part. In the *Two Gentlemen of Verona* Maria Occhini was Julia, Osvaldo Ruggeri Proteus, Luca Ronconi Valentine, Paola Bacci Silvia, Alessandro Sperli the Duke of Milan, Giulio Brogi and Massimo Francovich respectively Speed and Launce, Armando Spadaro Thurio, Carlo Lima Eglamour—all young actors who achieved a remarkable success. In *Antony and Cleopatra* Elena Zareschi was Cleopatra, Giacomo Santuccio Antony, Otello Toso Enobarbus, José Greci Octavia, Maria Fiore Charmian. The reconcilement between Sextus Pompeius and Octavius Caesar with the following drunken orgy, Antony's impassioned address to the soldiers, and Cleopatra's anger at the news of the wedding of Antony and Octavia were particularly effective. The costumes, inspired by a painting of Paolo Veronese, were not altogether successful.

Samuel Johnson's *Preface to Shakespeare* and other Shakespearian writings were edited with an introduction and notes by Agostino Lombardo (Bari, Adriatica editrice, Biblioteca italiana di testi inglesi). Lombardo has published also remarkable essays on the imagery of *Antony and Cleopatra* (in the *English Miscellany*) and a long study of *Macbeth*.　　　　　MARIO PRAZ

Japan

The most important Shakespearian event in 1960 was the performance of *Othello* by actors who came from various fields of Japanese theatrical activity: in Japan actors and actresses have their own specialities, not in parts, but in dramatic categories, and it is not easy for them to move from one to another. In *Othello* the title-role was acted by Koshiro Matsumoto, an ambitious Kabuki actor, Iago by Masayuki Mori, a prominent actor of the genre of the modern straight play, and Desdemona by Michiyo Aratama, a cinema actress. This first attempt in a new production system by Tsuneari Fukuda, a producer and translator, was rather coldly received by critics, who disliked the heterogeneity of acting. Nevertheless, it was an attempt worthy of being tried and it will be repeated in future.

The popularity of Shakespeare has recently much increased here. Producers and actors who have recently visited England have gained knowledge and inspiration, while playgoers, who have become more or less familiar with the English manner of production, want, naturally, to see the 'original' stage. The possibility of a visit of the Old Vic or the Royal Shakespeare Theatre to Japan is much discussed here.

The Shakespeare Society of Japan has now been organized and started on its career on 23 April 1961. Already its members are making plans for the Fourth Centenary in 1964.　　　　　JIRO OZU

Kenya

Shakespeare's Birthday in East Africa was marked by the placing of floral tributes in the Shakespeare Corner of the Kenya National Theatre and a broadcast over the Kenya Broadcasting network at night.

The East African Shakespeare Festival productions included *The Winter's Tale* at the Kenya National Theatre and *A Midsummer Night's Dream* at Mombasa. Plans are being made for productions of *Twelfth Night* in Addis Ababa, of *Measure for Measure* and *Twelfth Night* in Nairobi and of *The Taming of the Shrew* at Mombasa.　　　　　A. J. R. MASTER

Poland

Among new Shakespearian translations there appeared *Cymbeline*, the ninth play put into Polish by Zofia Siwicka, who with indefatigable energy tries to score a third Polish record in translating the complete works of Shakespeare—following the example of her two predecessors in that field, Stanisław Koźmian and Leon Ulrich, who, by strange coincidence, were born and died during the same years of 1811–85. Her versions are highly appreciated and are being used on the Polish stage; her *Julius Caesar* at this moment is being performed in the theatre of the city of Łódź.

For the Fourth Centenary Polish scholars plan a set of studies and articles that will be printed in a special issue of the *Kwartalnik Neofilologiczny*.

The Polish interest in Shakespeare is steadily attested by many performances of Shakespeare's plays in Warsaw and all over the country in major cultural centres.
　　　　　STANISŁAW HELSZTYŃSKI

South Africa

During 1960 a number of useful contributions to Shakespearian criticism have appeared in literary journals. *Three Papers on Tragedy* by F. D. Sinclair was an independent publication by the University of South Africa; it contains studies on 'The Jacobean Anguish', 'The Meaning of *King Lear*' and 'Aristotle, Shakespeare, and Tragedy'. The first of these discusses the relevance of Jacobean tragedy to the restlessness and insecurity of our own time, with some observations on the place of Tourneur and *The Revenger's Tragedy*. The last shows that Shakespearian tragedy has fundamental divergences from the classical concepts, partly due to the intervention of Renaissance humanism.

E. Davis has a stimulating contribution on 'Shakespeare's Conception of Honour' in the March number of *English Studies in Africa*. There is a conflict in Shakespeare between conventional codes of morality and absolute notions of right and wrong. 'It is no small part of Shakespeare's greatness,' he says, 'that his conception of human honour is at once the least censorious and at the same time the most searching that any writer, religiously minded or not, has to offer.' In the same journal the undersigned contributes some views about 'Shakespeare and Religion'.

In *Theoria 14* (1960) Miss R. Rappoport raises some contentious matters in 'The Theme of Personal Integrity in *Othello*'; and in *Theoria 15*, of the same year, D. R. C. Marsh writes on 'The Conflict of Love and Responsibility in *Antony and Cleopatra*', the fruit of a sojourn in Pietermaritzburg gaol during the 1960 'Emergency'. Both discussions are worthy of study.
　　　　　A. C. PARTRIDGE

Sweden

Interest in Shakespeare is running high today in Sweden.

Last year's *Hamlet* at 'Dramaten' called forth much commentary and discussion. A valuable study was Lennart Josephson's 'En orientering om Hamlet'. It was followed by a number of articles in newspapers and periodicals.

A new *Hamlet* at Hälsingborg's Stadsteater (producer Frank Sundström) proved successful. The scenic pictures were fine, especially the opening with the dark sweeping clouds. The Ghost's voice—on tape!—was very effective. Bengt Virdestam was a brisk Hamlet, vigorous and supple in his movements as well as in his artistic treatment of the character. Sometimes new aspects seemed to open up in the old play. In Ophelia's songs there was a new tone. This was certainly due to the translation, by Björn Collinder. The skilled and learned translator of Greek tragedies, of *Kalevala* and of *Beowulf* has now tried his power on Shakespeare's tragedy. Of course it is not easy to measure oneself with Hagberg, but there are various ways of bringing new light to bear on the text, and Collinder's endeavours may be of great value to Swedish actors and readers.

Othello was acted at the new Stockholm Stadsteater. The setting, by Carl Johan Ström, was fine. A giant lighthouse tower, dominating the stage, was most effective. Objections may be raised against the rather slow pace in the acting, and a shortening of the text might have been advisable. Anders Ek, despite his power, uttered the lines in a rather cramped manner. Toivo Pawlo was a brilliant Iago—an underling, and a hard and clever intriguer.

The Gothenburg stage got its first *Antony and Cleopatra* in February 1961 at Stadsteatern. Hagberg's translation, revised by Alf Henriksson, was used. Hans Schalla, well known from the Bochum performances in 1955, was invited as producer.

Riksteatern, the national travelling company, has been touring with *A Midsummer Night's Dream* and *Taming of the Shrew* all over the country and even into Norway.

A comprehensive undertaking was Sveriges Radio's Shakespeare series. Seven plays (*Romeo and Juliet, Richard III, Hamlet, Julius Caesar, Othello, Macbeth* and *As You Like It*) have been presented, many of them in revivals. It must be said that this has brought Shakespeare nearer to large sections of the public.

NILS MOLIN

Switzerland

What Shakespearian theatrical activity there was in Switzerland in 1960 was partly due to the visits of a French and an English company. In June Lausanne had the privilege of seeing René Planchon's adaptation of the two parts of *Henry IV*, originally produced at Lyons and 'the major event of the 1959 Shakespeare season in Paris' (see *Shakespeare Survey*, XIII, p. 127). The Experimental Theatre Group of Cambridge University again toured most of our University towns with a performance of *As You Like It* which, if it was not considered as good as their *Hamlet* of the previous year, was acted with liveliness and intelligence.

Of the other Shakespearian productions, one at least deserves a special mention: in *King Lear* (at the Zürich Schauspielhaus in February) Gustav Knuth, the great tragic actor, was most impressive in his building up a convincing figure of the pitiable and powerful dotard turning, through his ordeal of extreme suffering and near-madness, into a love-redeemed soul, his and Cordelia's love irradiating in retrospect the whole tragedy.

To the Bern group of the Swiss–British Society Max Lüthi lectured in November on 'Spiel im Spiel und Imaginationsszenen bei Shakespeare'. The papers read at the Lausanne Conference of the International Association of University Professors of English in 1959 have now been published in a volume entitled 'English Studies Today, Second Series' (Francke Verlag Bern) which contains, besides Ian Duthie's 'Macbeth, A Study in Tragic Absurdity' and Josip Torbarina's 'On Translating Shakespeare', a searching discussion of Fredson Bowers's article on *sullied* or *solid Flesh* (see *Shakespeare Survey*, IX, pp. 44 *sqq.*) by F. W. Bateson. Two other papers in the same volume will be of great interest to students of the Jacobean drama, Jean Jacquot's 'Bussy d'Ambois and Chapman's Conception of Tragedy' and Clifford Leech's 'The Dramatic Style of John Fletcher'.

GEORGES BONNARD

Turkey

The annual Festival of Bergama (Pergamum) opened with *Othello* in Orhan Burian's Turkish version performed by the young players of the National Conservatoire of Ankara on 21 May at the ancient theatre of Aesclepion. The play was produced by Mahir Canova, and the title-role played by Kartal Tibet to Esin Avci's Desdemona and Bozkurt Kuruç's Iago. The same production was carried to the second-century Roman theatre of Aspendus in Southern Turkey, but the Festival was cancelled due to the political situation on 27 May.

The Municipal Theatre of Istanbul opened its season with a Shakespearian production as usual. This year

Irfan Şahinbaş's Turkish version of *King Lear* was chosen; this was followed by Miss Nur Sabuncu's translation of *The Shrew*. Mrs Perihan Tedü was responsible for the production of the former and Miss Şirin Devrim for the latter. Miss Devrim, who also impersonated Kate, used a very lively and acrobatic tempo in her production which was appreciated by the audience—although some newspaper critics blamed her for giving a non-traditional spirit to the play.

NUREDDIN SEVIN

U.S.A.

While Shakespeare has virtually disappeared from Broadway because of the smash-hit-or-catastrophe psychology that prevails on the professional stage, his plays have become the staple classic when one is acted on the community or educational stage, and the sole fare of at least ten Shakespeare Festivals throughout the nation. In the summer of 1960, about 400,000 devotees saw thirty productions of fifteen plays at thirteen summer theatres from Vermont to southern California.

Residents of the greater New York and southern New England area are fortunate in having the New York City Shakespeare Festival staged in the open air of Central Park and the American Shakespeare Festival in a beautiful theatre at Stratford, Connecticut. That there is a rivalry between the theatres must be admitted. There are thousands who brave the 175 miles round-trip to Stratford who would not be seen near the free Shakespeare Festival in New York; but the attitude of these aristocrats may well change shortly because the free festival seems to be getting the better reviews. At Stratford, with Katharine Hepburn starring in the roles of Cleopatra and Viola, the critics expected great performances, but frequently she fell short of this expectation; *The Tempest*, however, was praised with some reservations concerning a setting which detracted from the acting. Stratford has been called 'less elegant than showy', while Joseph Papp's free New York City Festival is winning praise with a bare open stage. *Henry V, Measure for Measure*, and *The Taming of the Shrew* were produced in a summer-long programme with concentration on the acting rather than on great names and striking settings. Staging these performances free of charge for 2000 nightly raises the expected financial problems, but patrons are apparently as willing to give of themselves as are the members of the company. A sizeable fund was raised by promoting 'An Evening of Shakespeare' with dinner served at $50 a plate! The City of New York is also finding out that Shakespeare is good for its citizens and has promised a permanent amphitheatre for the 1961 season.

At Ashland, Oregon, the 20th Shakespeare Festival ran for forty-one days with *The Taming of the Shrew, The Tempest, Richard II*, and *Julius Caesar*. San Diego's 11th Festival offered *Julius Caesar, As You Like It*, and *Hamlet*. In its eleven seasons the Old Globe replica has offered 455 performances of twenty-six plays to more than 157,000 spectators—an impressive record for a 400-seat theatre. A successful beginning in 1959 brought about a new annual Festival at the University of Vermont—the Champlain Shakespeare Festival. Here more than 5000 saw *1 Henry IV, Macbeth*, and *The Taming of the Shrew* during the month of August. The arena-type stage was effectively used by an impressive group of young actors. Elsewhere, there were two weeks of *1 Henry IV, Antony and Cleopatra*, and *Macbeth* at the beautiful Mary Rippon Theatre designed by George F. Reynolds at the University of Colorado, and five weeks at Akron, Ohio, where Arthur Lithgow, producer of the complete works at Antioch College from 1952 to 1956, is now managing director. Here the Plantagenet–Lancaster tetralogy was offered on the porch of a beautiful Tudor-style mansion.

The off-Broadway Phoenix Theatre has been annually offering some Shakespeare in New York City and earning well-deserved praise. This year its *1* and *2 Henry IV* were so well liked that they were again offered at the annual Cambridge Shakespeare Festival in July. Eric Berry's Falstaff was the most praised of all the characters.

Aside from such local productions as Barnard College's offering of the rarely produced *Pericles*, many people in widespread areas were fortunate in seeing the American Shakespeare Festival's *Winter's Tale* and *A Midsummer Night's Dream* (which toured many American cities from coast to coast) and the Player's Incorporated *Merchant of Venice*, which also toured widely.

LOUIS MARDER

U.S.S.R.

In the course of 1960 seventeen of Shakespeare's plays were performed in sixty-nine theatres of the Soviet Union. The first place is, as before, occupied by *Hamlet*—acted in thirteen theatres. A notable event in the stage-history of *Hamlet* in the U.S.S.R. is a new production by the Saratov Youth Theatre. The performance won a warm response not only from young spectators but from older theatre critics as well. The reviewers praised in particular A. Bysryakov's emotional and sincere Hamlet.

The Kiev Academic Drama Theatre showed in Moscow their recent production of *King Lear* in a new Ukrainian translation by M. Rylskii. The design by V. Meller met with general approval, and some of his inventions (for instance, the *décor* of the scene of Gloucester's blinding) were called a valuable contribution to the Soviet tradition of staging Shakespeare. But the interpretation of the title-role by M. Krushelnitzkii occasioned an important clash of opinion. The adherents of the Krushelnitzkii manner stressed his success in depicting Lear as a human being, while his opponents accused him of failing in the most tragic scenes. This controversy has led to a general discussion on realism and tragic exaggeration in *King Lear*.

The popularity of *King Lear* grows constantly in Moscow. The tragedy is still running in the Mossoviet Theatre, and N. Okhlopkov is to present a new production in the Mayakovskii Theatre with the well-known Polonius, Y. Sverdlin, in the title-role.

The most important landmark of Soviet Shakespearian study is the completing of the 8-volume edition of Shakespeare edited by A. Smirnov and A. Anikst. Another item of interest is the appearance of S. Nels's book *Shakespeare on the Soviet Stage*, a fruitful attempt to trace the development of Soviet productions of Shakespeare since 1917. The main theme of the new volume of *Shekspirovskii Sbornik* (*Shakespearian Miscellany*) is *Hamlet*; different aspects of the tragedy and its theatre interpretation are considered in articles by A. Anikst, I. Vertsman, N. Zubova and others; the volume contains also a review of recent Shakespearian studies in the U.S.S.R.

Recently a special Shakespearian Committee under R. Samarin was formed at the Institute of World Literature; its main aim is to co-ordinate Shakespearian activities in different republics of the Soviet Union. It is expected that scholars from different parts of the country as well as from England, the German Democratic Republic, Poland and other countries will contribute to the publications of the Committee.

An encouraging new development is the strengthening of international ties between Soviet and foreign scholars. Recently lectures on Shakespeare by A. Schlosser (G.D.R.), A. Kettle and Kenneth Muir (England) were delivered at Moscow University.   YURI SHVEDOV

Yugoslavia

Since the late V. Popović's report on Shakespearian activities in post-war Yugoslavia, published in the 1951 volume of *Shakespeare Survey*, these activities have become various and manifold. Shakespeare has always been very popular in this country, and in the last decade interest in his plays has manifested itself in numerous ways: many plays have been produced; new translations have appeared; three English theatrical companies have visited the country; several publications have been issued; and numerous public lectures have dealt with his work.

It is impossible to enumerate here all the plays which have been produced in various Yugoslav theatres. Suffice it to say that, as a rule, managers deem it almost indispensable to include in their annual repertory at least one of Shakespeare's works—a sound policy both because a Shakespeare play gives ample opportunity to all the participants to show their talents and artistic qualities, and because it generally attracts the public. Thus *King Lear* has had a run of ninety-five, and *Romeo and Juliet* of seventy-eight performances in the Yugoslav Dramatic Theatre in Belgrade in the last few years. This leading theatre has had less success with *Macbeth*, but just now it is scoring a much disputed success with *Richard III*: the audience, which keep filling the house to the last seat, seem to enjoy the play, while the journalistic criticism tends to find fault with the production. As a result there has been much discussion concerning the merits of the play and the shortcomings of the presentation: indeed the management of the Theatre has actually initiated a public inquiry: every visitor is requested to fill in a questionnaire, given him with the programme, stating his opinion of the performance, giving his reasons for approval or disapproval. Judging by the answers received, the audience seem to be very enthusiastic, and one or two critics have been asked to resign their posts! The present writer is inclined to add his vote to the *vox populi*, and grant due acknowledgement to the producer (M. Milošević), the protagonist (J. Miličević), the costume-designer (M. Glišić), the scenographer (M. Šerban), and all the other participants, for a high-standard presentation of this very popular 'history', which was given in a new Serbian translation by Ž. Simić and S. Pandurović.

In the same period, the Belgrade National Theatre has produced nine plays: *Othello* (two productions, fifty-five and sixteen nights each), *Hamlet* (twenty-five), *Much Ado About Nothing* (nineteen), *1* and *2 Henry IV* (twenty-two, the two dramas being played on successive nights), *The Merchant of Venice* (twenty-five), *Julius Caesar* (twenty-three), and *Twelfth Night* (twelve, still successfully running in B. Stupica's production); an English amateur company, the London Players, gave fragments from *The Merry Wives of Windsor*, *Romeo and*

Juliet, Hamlet, Twelfth Night and *Henry V* in 1951; the Stratford Royal Shakespeare Theatre gave four performances of *Titus Andronicus* (with Sir Laurence Olivier in the title-role) in 1957; and the Old Vic gave five performances of *Hamlet* (with John Neville) in 1959. These companies also visited Zagreb and Ljubljana. Needless to say, the 'house' was crowded on these latter occasions; had its seating-capacity (about one thousand) been much larger the tickets would still have been far from available for the very many prospective spectators. As an illustration of this, one might mention the letter which the students of the English Department of Belgrade University addressed to Sir Laurence, asking him for an extra performance. Owing to technical difficulties in the Theatre itself, arising from cramming too many performances into too short a space of time, this proved impossible, but Sir Laurence and Miss Vivian Leigh very generously gave a free informal recital of drama and poetry in a large university amphitheatre, over two thousand students attending. Later, two prominent Belgrade actors, R. Plaović and Lj. Jovanović, have followed suit, and have very kindly given similar recitals from Shakespeare's plays (in Serbian) for the students of the English Department.

The Belgrade Comic Theatre, although mostly concerned with modern works, has produced two plays, *As You Like It* and *The Taming of the Shrew*, and thus during the last decade no less than fifteen Shakespeare plays have been produced in Belgrade; sometimes three Shakespearian dramas were being enacted on the same night in the three main Belgrade theatres! It should be mentioned perhaps that the Yugoslav Dramatic Theatre, when on a tour in Poland in 1958, gave *King Lear*, with M. Živanović in the title-role, with much success.

The Croatian National Theatre in Zagreb has produced, since 1951, *Twelfth Night, The Merchant of Venice, King Lear* and *Hamlet*, while the Zagreb Dramatic Theatre has produced *The Winter's Tale* (produced by John Harrison as guest), *As You Like It* and *Macbeth*. Perhaps the most spectacular theatrical representations in the republic of Croatia are to be seen in Dubrovnik, at the Summer Play Festival, held there annually, in July and August, whose permanent feature has become *Hamlet*, produced by M. Fotez. Last summer, in the eleventh year of the Festival's life, it had its 100th performance. Enacted truly *à la belle étoile*, on the top terrace of the ancient fortress of Lovrienac, originally built in the eleventh century on a rock some 130 feet above the sea, it offers a rare and unique experience: within the original medieval structure, a slightly adapted auditorium can seat about 400 spectators; it provides an outer and an inner stage, as well as two upper stages, one above the other, formed by the original battlements; above is the vast starry sky, and down below the vast expanse of the Adriatic, whose waves can be heard booming against the rocky foundation. So far 40,000 spectators, of which more than half were foreigners from all over the world, have seen this wonderful performance of *Hamlet*, given of course in the Serbo-Croat language. The high popularity of the play enables the spectators to enjoy the performance although they may know nothing of the language in which it is delivered. Indeed there prevails an opinion that the Dubrovnik Summer Festival very much owes its international repute to this production of *Hamlet* in which some of the leading actors and actresses from various Yugoslav theatres have appeared. The performance has been very favourably reviewed in the world press. Thus, *The New York Times* (19 August 1959) writes: 'But the most spectacular setting of all is the place where *Hamlet* is performed.... The setting effortlessly conjures up the stony corridors and the ramparts of Elsinore itself. A spectator cannot escape becoming entranced with the seeming reality of the events unfolding in troubled Denmark.' *The Shakespeare Quarterly* (January 1954) considers it 'the most interesting performance of this tragedy in the world'.

Fotez staged yet another of Shakespeare's plays in Dubrovnik, *A Midsummer Night's Dream*, in 1954. It was presented in Gradac Park, on a natural stage amid olive-trees and cypresses, with an open view to the nearby sea glittering in the moonlight. The poetry of this Shakespearian fairy-tale found here an adequate and beautiful setting, and the two blended together into an unforgettable and charming impression of loveliness and beauty. Fotez's other Shakespearian productions include *As You Like It*, in Rijeka and Belgrade, *Hamlet*, in Sarajevo, and *The Taming of the Shrew*, in Osijek, Zadar and in Sosnoviec (Poland).

The Slovenian People's Theatre, in Ljubljana, has staged *Romeo and Juliet, Hamlet, 1* and *2 Henry IV, Henry V* and *A Midsummer Night's Dream*, all in B. Kreft's production. Kreft is not only a playwright himself and an experienced producer, but a Shakespearian scholar as well. An original feature of the *Henry V* production was the 'reviving' of Falstaff who, according to J. H. Walter (*Modern Language Review*, July 1946), 'must have appeared in the original version of *Henry V*'. Both M. Bor (the translator) in his analysis of the play, and Kreft in his scholarly introduction (*Henrik V*, Slovenska Matica, Ljubljana, 1959), agree with Walter that Shakespeare fulfilled 'the promise in the epilogue of *2 Henry IV* to continue the story "with Sir John in it"' (*King Henry V*, New Arden Edition, 1954), finding 'a convincing part of the former Falstaff's lines' in Pistol's speech which ends Act v, scene i. Accordingly Falstaff appeared in this Slovenian production, acted by P. Kovič, who of course played the same role in *Henry IV*.

After the death (1949) of the poet O. Župančič, who translated into Slovenian fifteen Shakespeare plays, his work in this field is being successfully continued by the poet and playwright M. Bor; so far he has translated *Richard III* (1955), *1* and *2 Henry IV* (1957), *Henry V* (1959) and *King John* (1960), all published by Slovenska Matica, in Ljubljana, with up-to-date notes by the translator and introductions by B. Kreft.

In Croatia, J. Torbarina has translated *Measure for Measure* (1957) and *Troilus and Cressida* (1960), both published by Matica Hrvatska, Zagreb, and has likewise supplied them with critical introductions and notes. The poet D. Andjelinović, who had already translated *Venus and Adonis* (Zagreb, 1950) and the *Sonnets* (Zagreb, 1951), has completed his translation of all Shakespeare's poems, and these were all issued in one volume by Matica Hrvatska, Zagreb in 1958.

Since Macedonia has become a people's republic within the Federacy of Yugoslavia, and the Macedonian language is recognized as a separate unit within the group of South Slavonic languages, there has sprung up a literature written in Macedonian. Besides original works, there have appeared many translations in that language, mainly from world classics, and among them are three of Shakespeare's plays—*As You Like It* (translated by V. Iljovski and I. Milčin, Skoplje, 1949), *Othello* (translated by B. Koneski, Skoplje) and *Hamlet* (translated by A. Šopov, Skoplje, 1960). All these versions, mainly from Serbo-Croat and Russian, are in verse, and have been successfully staged at the Macedonian National Theatre in Skoplje. The translator of *Hamlet*, who is a young poet, has been awarded the Macedonian Annual Prize for Literature for his successful rendering. So Shakespeare's immortal lines are to be read in yet one more language of the world—the Macedonian.

It may perhaps also be of interest to note here that two of Shakespeare's plays, *Hamlet* and *Julius Caesar*, translated into Albanian by F. S. Noli, have been published in Priština (in 1952 and 1953) for the sake of the Albanian minority in Yugoslavia.

Undoubtedly the most important achievement in the way of rendering Shakespeare in Yugoslavia has been accomplished in Belgrade by Ž. Simić, the translator and lexicographer, and S. Pandurović, the lately deceased Serbian poet. They have translated all Shakespeare's

tragedies, together with *Troilus and Cressida*, *Pericles*, and *Cymbeline*, and all the thirteen plays have been issued in one volume of some 1500 pages, together with introductory notes and commentaries, to which Ž. Jovanović has added an extensive and exhaustive bibliography of Serbian Shakespeariana. According to this, from 1864 to 1955 twenty-two plays have been translated into Serbian, of which there are fifty-three separate publications. The book, under the title *W. Shakespeare's Tragedies*, has been published by Narodna Knijiga, Cetinje, 1957. Simić and Pandurović have also translated *1* and *2 Henry IV* (1952), *King John* (1952) and *Richard II* (1953), all published by Nolit, in Belgrade.

B. Nedić and V. Zivojinović, in Belgrade, who had initiated a new series of translations in the post-war period, have so far added to their former efforts *The Winter's Tale* (1951), *Romeo and Juliet* (1951) and *Antony and Cleopatra* (1953).

Besides current reviews on the scenic representations of Shakespeare's plays, and the customary 'introductions' to their printed texts, there has been little writing in the way of original criticism or elucidation. However, in *Studia Romanica et Anglica* (Zagreb, December 1959) J. Torbarina has published two interesting articles: 'A Minor Crux in *Hamlet*', and 'On Rendering Shakespeare's Blank-Verse into Other Languages'. In the former of these he tried to give a new explanation of the line 'Observe his inclination in yourself' (*Hamlet*, II, i, 71) and to prove that it has been misinterpreted by almost all critics and mis-rendered by practically all translators, because both critics and translators saw in the line a typical Shakespearian 'ambiguity', and so overlooked the only true meaning of it. Torbarina says the line has only one meaning; it means exactly what it purports to say: 'Observe his inclination in yourself', i.e. in your own self, in your own mind, in your inner self. He supports his interpretation by referring to two other passages from Shakespeare which seem to throw light on the true meaning of the line: *Lear*, I, ii, 26 ff., and *Hamlet*, II, ii, 10–18.

In his second article Torbarina states that, on examining some older translations from Shakespeare in various languages, he has 'always been struck by the regularity, not to say rigidity, of their lines'; 'one has the impression that the development of the English blank-verse as a dramatic medium from *Gorboduc* to the plays of Marlowe and Shakespeare had never taken place'. The uniformity of verse in these translations 'precludes the possibility of feeling any difference between the plays written at various stages of Shakespeare's career'. However, now that knowledge of English is much more widely spread, he finds that 'tremendous advance has been made in the art of translating Shakespeare and in rendering more faithfully his blank-verse'.

B. Kreft, in Ljubljana, has written scholarly introductions to M. Bor's Slovenian translations of Shakespeare's 'histories'. Because of their grand conceptions, says Kreft, their host of tragic and comic characters, numerous events, deep analyses of individuals and society, with their virtues, sins, and blind passions, these ten dramatic rhapsodies stand side by side with Dante's *Divina Commedia* and Balzac's *Comédie Humaine*, and indeed might be named *A Royal Comedy*. With them Shakespeare undertook to solve one of the most difficult problems which mankind has been trying to solve from Plato's days to our own—the problem of the state, the governor, and the government. 'Among "histories" *Richard III* is like *Hamlet* among tragedies, because of its political problem; and although it is not a perfect work of art, like *Hamlet*, it still lives because it exposes tyranny.

A mere patriotic chronicle Shakespeare had turned into a drama with great political and ethical issues, actual even in our own troubled times.'

Kreft is also the author of a book on Pushkin and Shakespeare (*Puśkin in Shakespeare*, Ljubljana, 1952) in which he analyses Pushkin's views on drama and Shakespeare's eventual influence on him. Pushkin founded his theories mainly on Shakespeare, says Kreft, but beyond this he reached new and original conclusions; by way of romanticism and Shakespeare, he discovered and created a poetic, realistic historical tragedy. Therefore it is impossible to speak of an essential Shakespearian influence on Pushkin. It may only be said that Shakespeare's genius was an ideal, a starting point, from which Pushkin's genius went on to new and original conclusions. Pushkin's poetic realism, with his views on playwriting and his *Boris Godunov*, 'stands by the side of the romantic-baroque of Shakespeare'. B. NEDIĆ

SHAKESPEARE PRODUCTIONS IN THE UNITED KINGDOM: 1960

A LIST COMPILED FROM ITS RECORDS BY THE SHAKESPEARE MEMORIAL LIBRARY, BIRMINGHAM

JANUARY

1   *Twelfth Night:* The Playhouse, Sheffield. *Producer:* GEOFFREY OST.

FEBRUARY

1   *The Merchant of Venice:* S. T. G. Productions, Assembly Hall, Tunbridge Wells. *Producers:* PAXTON WHITEHEAD and BARBARA SYKES.

2   *Measure for Measure:* Oxford University Dramatic Society at the Playhouse, Oxford. *Producers:* MERLIN THOMAS and KENNETH LOACH.

3   *Much Ado About Nothing:* The Playhouse, Nottingham. *Producer:* VAL MAY.

8   *The Merchant of Venice:* Oldham Repertory Theatre Club, at the Coliseum, Oldham.

8   *Twelfth Night:* Colchester Repertory Theatre. *Producer:* WALLACE EVENNETT.

9   *The Merchant of Venice:* The Library Theatre, Manchester. *Producer:* DAVID SCASE.

16   *Henry IV, Part I:* Birmingham Repertory Theatre. *Producer:* BERNARD HEPTON.

22   *The Merchant of Venice:* The Renaissance Theatre Company, Her Majesty's Theatre, Barrow-in-Furness. *Producer:* DONALD SARTAIN.

22   *Henry IV, Part II:* Birmingham Repertory Theatre. *Producer:* BERNARD HEPTON.

25   *Henry V:* The Mermaid Theatre, London. *Producer:* JULIUS GELLNER.

27   *King Lear:* Eton College. *Producers:* R. PRIOR and R. J. G. PAYNE.

29   *The Merchant of Venice:* Ipswich Theatre. *Producer:* GEOFFREY EDWARDS.

MARCH

No date   *Twelfth Night:* Nottingham Playhouse Children's Theatre. *Producer:* R. D. MACDONALD.

7   *Hamlet:* Guildford Repertory Theatre. Producer not known.

7   *As You Like It:* The Playhouse, Salisbury. *Producer:* IAN MULLINS.

8   *Cymbeline:* The Marlowe Society, at the Arts Theatre, Cambridge. Producer and actors anonymous.

11   *A Midsummer Night's Dream:* The Norwich Players, at the Maddermarket Theatre, Norwich. Producer and actors anonymous.

15   *Twelfth Night:* The Marlowe Theatre, Canterbury. *Producer:* KENNETH PARROTT.

28   *The Merchant of Venice:* The Civic Playhouse, Bradford. *Producer:* MILLICENT ISHERWOOD.

APRIL

4   *Henry IV, Part I:* Theatre Royal, York. *Producer:* DONALD BODLEY.

5   *Two Gentlemen of Verona:* Shakespeare Memorial Theatre, Stratford-upon-Avon. *Producer:* PETER HALL.

11   *Henry IV, Part II:* Theatre Royal, York. *Producer:* DONALD BODLEY.

SHAKESPEARE PRODUCTIONS IN THE UNITED KINGDOM

APRIL

12   *Henry IV, Part I:* The Playhouse, Liverpool. *Producer:* WILLARD STOKER.

12   *The Merchant of Venice:* Shakespeare Memorial Theatre, Stratford-upon-Avon. *Producer:* MICHAEL LANGHAM.

26   *The Taming of the Shrew:* The Playhouse, Oxford. *Producer:* FRANK HAUSER.

MAY

2   *Henry IV, Part I:* Dundee Repertory Theatre. *Producer:* RAYMOND WESTWELL.

7   *Katharine and Petruchio (Garrick):* Festival Theatre, Pitlochry. *Producer:* JAMES ROOSE EVANS.

9   *The Merchant of Venice:* Queen's Theatre, Hornchurch. *Producer:* ANTHONY RICHARDSON.

9   *The Merchant of Venice:* Richmond Theatre. *Producer:* ALEXANDER DOVE.

11   *Much Ado About Nothing:* Castle Theatre, Farnham. *Producer:* GEORGE HARLAND.

17   *Twelfth Night:* Shakespeare Memorial Theatre. *Producer:* PETER HALL.

31   *Henry V:* The Old Vic Company, the Old Vic Theatre, London. *Producer:* JOHN NEVILLE.

JUNE

2   *The Tempest:* The Bankside Players at the Open-Air Theatre, Regent's Park, London. *Producer:* ROBERT ATKINS.

3   *A Midsummer Night's Dream:* Harrow School. *Producer:* RONALD WATKINS.

8   *A Midsummer Night's Dream:* The Royal Academy of Dramatic Arts at Hurley Manor, Surrey. *Producer:* ELLEN POLLOCK.

21   *The Taming of the Shrew:* Shakespeare Memorial Theatre, Stratford-upon-Avon. *Producer:* JOHN BARTON.

28   *The Comedy of Errors:* Bristol Old Vic Company at the Theatre Royal, Bristol. *Producer:* JOHN HALE.

JULY

22   *The Winter's Tale:* Stowe School. *Producer:* W. L. MCELWEE.

26   *Troilus and Cressida:* Shakespeare Memorial Theatre, Stratford-upon-Avon. *Producers:* PETER HALL and JOHN BARTON.

30   *As You Like it:* Exeter University Dramatic Society. *Producer:* EWART JOHNSON.

AUGUST

11   *Julius Caesar:* Youth Theatre at the Queen's Theatre, London. *Producer:* MICHAEL CROFT.

14   *Macbeth:* Hovenden Players at the Hovenden Theatre Club, London. *Producer:* VALERY HOVENDEN.

25   *Hamlet:* Birmingham University Guild Theatre Group at the Loft Theatre, Leamington. *Producer:* J. R. BROWN.

30   *The Winter's Tale:* Shakespeare Memorial Theatre, Stratford-upon-Avon. *Producer:* PETER WOOD.

SEPTEMBER

27   *Twelfth Night:* The Arts Theatre, Cambridge. *Producer:* WARIS HABIBULLAH.

27   *The Tempest:* The Bristol Old Vic Company at the Theatre Royal, Bristol.

OCTOBER

No date *King Lear:* Oxford University Lincoln College Players at the Playhouse, Oxford. *Producer:* PETER HUGHES.

3   *Hamlet:* The Citizens' Theatre, Glasgow. *Producer:* CALLUM MILL.

3   *The Taming of the Shrew:* Guildford Repertory Theatre. *Producer:* DAVID PAUL.

4   *Romeo and Juliet:* The Old Vic Company, The Old Vic Theatre, London. *Producer:* FRANCO ZEFFIRELLI.

4   *The Tempest:* Theatre Royal, Margate. *Producer:* JAMES GILLHOULEY.

4   *The Merchant of Venice:* The Playhouse, Nottingham. *Producer:* ANDRE VAN GYSEGHEM.

10   *Twelfth Night:* Theatre Royal, Lowestoft. *Producer:* EDGAR METCALF.

17   *As You Like It:* Colchester Repertory Theatre. *Producer:* RICHARD WORDSWORTH.

22   *The Tempest:* The Questors Theatre, London. *Producer:* JEFFREY SMITH.

24   *Hamlet:* The Pembroke Theatre, Croydon. *Producer:* ROBERT ATKINS.

24   *Twelfth Night:* The Repertory Theatre Club at the Coliseum, Oldham. *Producer:* CARL PAULSEN.

NOVEMBER

1   *As You Like It:* Library Theatre, Manchester. *Producer:* DAVID SCASE.

7   *Romeo and Juliet:* Theatre Royal, Lincoln (and at Scunthorpe and Rotherham). *Producer:* K. V. MOORE.

12   *The Merchant of Venice:* The Norwich Players at the Maddermarket Theatre, Norwich. *Producer:* IAN EMMERSON.

29   *Macbeth:* Fylde College Theatre Group at the Tower Circus, Blackpool.

DECEMBER

8   *Richard II:* The Arts Group, People's Theatre, Newcastle-on-Tyne. *Producer:* NICHOLAS WHITFIELD.

19   *Twelfth Night:* The Stratford-on-Avon Company, at the Aldwych Theatre, London. *Producer:* PETER HALL.

20   *A Midsummer Night's Dream:* The Old Vic Company, The Old Vic Theatre, London. *Producer:* MICHAEL LANGHAM.

S. FRANCO ZEFFIRELLI'S
ROMEO AND JULIET

BY

JOHN RUSSELL BROWN

An editorial in *Theatre Notebook* spoke of 'revelation', *The Observer* of 'revelation, even perhaps a revolution', and *Theatre World* of excitement, 'unity of presentation', and a 'reality which lifted one inescapably back to medieval Italy'.[1] These are examples of the enthusiastic reception which has kept Franco Zeffirelli's production of *Romeo and Juliet* in the repertory of a London or touring company of the Old Vic from 4 October 1960, into 1962, bringing them a greater success than they have enjoyed for more than a decade. Yet on the morning after its first-night, the critic of *The Times* spoke coldly of the performances, and in *The Sunday Times* Harold Hobson described a failure: to his disenchanted view, Romeo was 'well-spoken' but 'pasty-faced and sulky', Juliet flapped 'her arms about like a demented marionette'. After its season in London these conflicting reactions seem less remarkable: it was a production of unique and consistent achievement which exchanged a number of conventional virtues for others which are not often found in our presentations of Shakespeare. And it was effected with such intelligence, sympathy and authority that we can now take stock and ask how important these unusual virtues are for this play and, perhaps, for others.

*   *   *

The break with custom was clearest in Zeffirelli's visual presentation of Romeo. Audiences have come to expect a dark handsomeness, reminiscent of Sir Laurence Olivier in the production of 1935 (see Plate VII A). A white shirt is usually open at the neck; a dark wig accentuates a tall, noble brow; the eyes are made-up to appear large and deep. The pose chosen for official photographs usually suggests a lonely, haughty and brooding mind. With some additional swagger from the cloak Motley designed for him, Richard Johnson's Romeo at Stratford-upon-Avon in 1958 was in this tradition (see Plate VII B). Another recognizable but less common strain is the poetic: this is graceful, fluent, light. Michel Bernardy's Romeo for Saint-Denis's Strasbourg company in 1955 exemplified it, looking like some 'herald Mercury' (see Plate VII C). Both these traditions Zeffirelli broke. John Stride, his Romeo, wore no velvet; he had no wig, no cloak, no ornament; his shirt did not open at the neck (see Plate VII D). One of his costumes, devised by Peter Hall (the designer, not the director), seemed to be made of tweed, and none of them imposed grandiloquent postures; they were comfortable, hard-wearing, familiar clothes in greys and greyish-blues. In them, this Romeo could sit, squat, run or stroll; he could run his hand through his hair or look insignificant among a crowd. He was so little the gilded youth that it seemed odd that he should have a personal servant. Clearly, this director had paid less attention than usual to the opening words of the Prologue: 'Two households, both alike in dignity'; but in recompense he had avoided the meaningless gloss of 'fancy-dress' which many other Romeos assume with their splendid clothes. John Stride seemed to be English rather than Italianate, lively rather than sensuous; and he looked more convincingly in his teens than other actors of the part who have been equally young in fact.

To varying degrees all the young people in the play, except Paris, shared these qualities. Perhaps the Capulets were more richly dressed than the Montagues, but all the youth of Verona were at ease. Running and sauntering, they were immediately recognizable as unaffected teenagers; they ate apples and threw them, splashed each other with water, mocked, laughed, shouted; they became serious, sulked, were puzzled; they misunderstood confidently and expressed affection freely. Much of this behaviour has been seen before in Peter Hall's productions of *A Midsummer Night's Dream* and *The Two Gentlemen* at Stratford-upon-Avon,[2] but besides dispensing with the magnificent clothes that sat incongruously on Hall's Lysander or Silvia, Zeffirelli did not condescend towards his young lovers and did not underestimate them. He gave prominence to a sense of wonder, gentleness, strong affection, clear emotion and, sometimes, fine sentiment, as well as to high spirits and casual behaviour. His characters were exciting and affecting as less responsive heroines and heroes could never be.

For after the first visual surprise there were others. Despite the prodigality of the director's invention, the stage-business seemed to spring from the words spoken, often lending them, in return, immediacy, zest or delicacy. So the unpompous behaviour could catch the audience's interest for the characters and for the old story. In the balcony scene after Juliet (Miss Judi Dench) had been called away, there was a still silence on her return before she dared speak again or Romeo dared to come out of hiding: this was given meaning by Romeo's preceding soliloquy:

> I am afeard,
> Being in night, all this is but a dream,
> Too flattering-sweet to be substantial. (II, ii, 139–41)

And by illustrating their mutual sense of awe and fear, their response to the seemingly precarious nature of their new-found reality which at this time needs each other's presence to be substantiated, the still silence gave added force to the memory of Romeo's words. It also helped to prepare the audience for the direction and urgency of Juliet's following speech:

> If that thy bent of love be honourable,
> Thy purpose marriage, send me word tomorrow....

Words and stage-business together drew the audience into the dramatic illusion. Such should be the aim of all directors of plays, but Zeffirelli has been unusual among our contemporaries in unifying Shakespeare's words and an inventive, youthful and apparently spontaneous action. Again, as the lovers leave the stage with the Friar to be married, Romeo walked backwards so that he continued to face Juliet who was supported on the Friar's arm: Romeo was 'bewitched by the charm of looks' (II, Prol., 6) rapt in

> ...the imagined happiness that both
> Receive in either by this dear encounter. (II, vi, 28–9)

So the stage-business took its cue from the words spoken, and centred Romeo's interest, without respect to absurdity or other concerns, on his delight in love. As they met adversity and danger, phrases like 'Stand not amazed' (III, i, 139), ''Tis torture' (III, iii, 29), 'Blubbering and weeping'

(III, iii, 87) were all directly and convincingly related to the action, and consequently they were far more compelling than is customary in productions which deliberately court a sumptuous setting and exotic mood.

The street 'brawls' were realized in the same way. The fight between Mercutio and Tybalt had a mixture of daring and mockery which reflected the exaggeration of the text:

Consort! what, dost thou make us minstrels? an thou make minstrels of us, look to hear nothing but discords: here's my fiddlestick; here's that shall make you dance. 'Zounds, consort!   (III, i, 51–5)

Since few people in a modern audience can judge its fine points, the conventional duel usually appears either elegant and correct, or dangerous, or sometimes impassioned; it can hardly reflect the tone of this passage. Yet Zeffirelli made the fight high-spirited, like the words. Mercutio, gaining possession of both swords, used one as a whetstone for the other before handing Tybalt's back—stopping to wipe its handle with mocking ostentation. With such preparation, Romeo could respond to Mercutio's sour jests after he is wounded as casually as the text demands— 'Courage, man; the hurt cannot be much'—without appearing callow; the dying man's protestations could be taken as the holding up of an elaborate jest. Enacting the mood of the text in this way did not devalue the scene: the bragging turned to earnest all the more effectively with the suddenly involved and simple words of Romeo, 'I thought all for the best' (l. 109).

Visually, Zeffirelli's presentation of the young characters was remarkable, but not very original: he had gone further and was more consistent in a development already common—in less subtle and responsible hands, it is all too common. The greatest innovation of his production lay in unifying words and stage-business, in making the actors' speech as lively and fluent as their physical action. The result was that the dialogue did not appear the effect of study and care, but the natural idiom of the characters in the particular situations. It is a long time since Shakespeare's text has been so enfranchised. Juliet's 'I have forgot why I did call thee back' is often answered with rhetorical neatness, or passionate emphasis, or fanciful humour, in Romeo's 'Let me stand here till thou remember it' (II, ii, 171–2), but in this production the reply was frank and happy, appropriate to the quick sensations of the situation and suggesting a mutual response; the literary finesse of the text was not used to draw attention to itself but to give form and pressure to the dramatic moment. Or again, the interchange between the Friar and Romeo:

> *Fri.* . . . wast thou with Rosaline?
> *Rom.* With Rosaline, my ghostly father? no;
> I have forgot that name, and that name's woe.   (II, iii, 44–6)

was transformed by making Romeo blurt out 'I have forgot that name' as a sudden realization, a thought which had, at that instant, come to him for the first time: it was still an antithesis to the Friar's expectation, as a literary analysis of the speech could show, but its sudden clarity was represented and accentuated by the manner in which it was spoken.

Some critics complained that this treatment of the dialogue destroyed the 'poetry' of the play. But it would probably be truer to say that the poetry was rendered in an unfamiliar way. Zeffirelli has directed many operas, and turning to a Shakespeare production he ensured that many speeches were tuned with musical exactness. Changes of tempo, pitch and volume were used to strong dramatic effect. For example, when Romeo called 'Peace, peace!' at the climax of the Queen Mab speech, Mercutio's 'True' followed quickly and flatly, and then, changing the key, 'I talk of dreams...' was low and quiet, rapt in mood. This director knows more about musical speech than most of those working in our theatres today. There were, however, some notable lapses: Mercutio's speech and Juliet's potion soliloquy lost their cumulative effects because they were broken by too much stage-business (Juliet was made to writhe about in a red spot-light); the moments of incantatory stillness, which can have, in T. S. Eliot's words, a 'winged validity' beyond their immediate dramatic impulse, were surrendered for livelier effects; and the actors seldom delighted in the 'concord of sweet sounds'. But Zeffirelli's animated style of speech was appropriate to much of the dialogue of the young characters in the play: in its new dramatic life the 'poetry' showed its bravery, *élan*, gentleness. By making it sound like the natural idiom of the lovers and their companions, the director was restoring many of the original tones, the original freshness. In *Much Ado About Nothing*, Benedick says that Claudio was 'wont to speak plain and to the purpose, like an honest man and a soldier', but being turned lover he is 'turned orthography; his words are a very fantastical banquet, just so many strange dishes' (II, iii, 19–23). Romeo is such a lover: meeting with Mercutio after the balcony scene his verbal wit runs 'the wild-goose chase' and he is told: 'now art thou what thou art, by art as well as by nature' (II, iv, 94–5). The 'art' of much of the poetry in this play was surely intended to sound like a delighted and energetic response to immediate sensations, and in regaining this impression the actors responded in an appropriate way to the conscious artifice of their text. Their speaking reflected many of its moods, mixing humour with concern (as in Juliet's 'Swear not by the moon'), mockery with envy, passion with fear and hesitation. The metrical basis of the speech was sometimes insecure, but its colour and movement were often wonderfully accurate. Individual actors and actresses have achieved this dramatic life in Shake-spearian roles at the present day—Sir Laurence Olivier and Miss Dorothy Tutin are the most gifted and unfailing of them—but here the same quality was sustained through whole scenes. The director had treated wit, rhetoric and 'poetry' as an integral part of his production.

★   ★   ★

His success was chiefly with the young characters in the earlier part of the play. The first signs of merely routine handling were in the figures of authority. The Prince was given customary emphasis by two attendants with halberds, a voluminous gown and, by the standards of this production, rich accoutrements. On his first entry he stood right up-centre, and his words were accompanied by a muffled, rolling drum off-stage. But he lacked dramatic life comparable with that of the figures around him: the stage devices had added only an undefined impressiveness. This might be judged appropriate for his early appearance, but on his return after the death of Tybalt, when he stood down-stage centre, he still seemed out of touch with the other characters, for these hitherto agile and fluently organized figures immediately became fixed in postures at either side (see Plate IX A). In the last scene where the Prince finds himself implicated in the general sorrow and guilt ('for winking at your discords'), he stood unmoving, high above the heads of everyone else on the stage, and necessarily spoke in the earlier lifeless and formal manner. The director did attempt a more animated Friar, but here the business he invented seemed inapposite and occasionally impertinent: in the middle of his first speech a bell sounded off-stage and he stopped to kneel and cross himself, and when Juliet met Romeo at his cell he stepped between them to effect a comic collision involving all three figures—a kind of humour wholly different from that quieter kind written into the lines he speaks—and this stage-trick was repeated before the end of the short scene. In the last act, at the tomb, the Friar had such little relevance to the dramatic situation that he did not re-enter after he had left Juliet alone with Romeo's body: his speeches and all reference to him were cut.

While Zeffirelli had created an animating style for the story of the young lovers, he had not found a means of comparable liveliness to represent the authoritative figures which Shakespeare has made the centre of important scenes. In this, the production was like many others which have been seen in England recently: Sir Tyrone Guthrie's treatment of the King of France in *All's Well*, Peter Hall's of Priam in *Troilus*, and Tony Richardson's of the Duke of Venice in *Othello*, all shown at Stratford in recent years, are examples of the same malaise. Even when it was Romeo and Juliet who assumed new dignity and authority in confronting catastrophe, this director seemed unsure of touch. Juliet's 'Is there no pity sitting in the clouds...?' (III, v, 198) was said hurriedly, sitting on the floor, as if she needed no strength of mind to frame and speak this question. (One may contrast Alan Webb's dignified and affecting delivery of the comparable, 'O heavens, can you hear a good man groan, And not relent, or not compassion him?' from Peter Brook's production of *Titus Andronicus*.) Juliet's concluding line in this scene, with its authoritative and calm phrasing, 'If all else fail, myself have power to die', was said lightly on the point of running from the stage. Similarly, Romeo's stature in the final scene was belittled by failing to show his authority and compassion before the dead bodies of the other young men, as Shakespeare's text ensures: his description of Paris as 'One writ with me in sour misfortune's book' and:

> Tybalt, liest thou there in thy bloody sheet?
> O, what more favour can I do to thee,
> Than with that hand that cut thy youth in twain
> To sunder his that was thine enemy?
> Forgive me, cousin!

were both excised from the text used for this production, and no such effect was attempted.

Important moments of grief also seemed underplayed. The distraction, frustration and fear of the young lovers were well represented with nervous intensity; the fault here was that the cries and groans and other physical reactions were sometimes at odds with the technical demands of long speeches with elaborate syntax and rhetoric. It was the more general and more considered grief that seemed hollow. The mourning for Juliet when she is discovered as if dead was staged formally like the authoritative scenes (see Plate IX B), and anonymous servants were introduced mechanically, two at a time, to extend the tableau and so attempt to effect an impression of climax. This indeed is one old-fashioned way of responding to the formal nature of the verse. Elsewhere it might serve; but in this production it was in glaring contrast with the minutely and freshly motivated stage-business of adjacent scenes. The dramatic illusion previously established was lost in this presentation of general sorrow and was replaced with something that bore little or no resemblance to it. Romeo's address to the Apothecary showed the failure to represent a more considered grief. This is a speech of peculiar difficulty, for it must manifest complex reactions. In a vigorous handling, Zeffirelli concentrated on its agitation, so that his Romeo repeatedly struck and browbeat the 'caitiff wretch'. Here the difficulty was that this manner could not present consideration and compassion, responses that are implicit in:

> The world is not thy friend nor the world's law;
> The world affords no law to make thee rich;...

> There is thy gold, worse poison to men's souls,
> Doing more murders in this loathsome world,
> Than these poor compounds that thou mayst not sell...

> Farewell: buy food, and get thyself in flesh. (v, i, 72–84)

And the long and detailed description of the apothecary's shop and wares issued strangely from the mind of this Romeo, given over to turbulence and spite. The scene should surely be directed in a way that can show how grief *and* resolution have entered deeply into Romeo's soul, making him precise, understanding, compassionate, sharp, subtle and even cynical: it is a complex moment that cannot be presented by a simple pursuit of energetic expression.

The still moments of general or deliberate grief were, like the figures of authority, unsatisfactory. The concluding scene indicated how far Zeffirelli, despite his sympathetic handling of almost all of the earlier acts, failed to respond to Shakespeare's text in these matters. He cut a hundred and twenty consecutive lines, those from the last of Juliet's to the Prince's 'Where be these enemies?...'. The outcry of the people, the 'ambiguities', the concern to find the 'head' and 'true descent' of the calamity, the general suspicion in which the Prince at last finds himself implicated along with the others, the call for 'patience', the demand for 'rigour of severest law', were all sacrificed. The main reason for this was not shortage of time, for the scene was then extended by much interpolated silent business: anonymous servants embraced in pairs, symmetrically placed as a statuesque expression of general grief; mechanically, without being ordered to do so, they moved the bodies of Romeo and Juliet to the catafalque; in a slow procession, accompanied by singing off-stage, the supposedly reconciled families departed with composed neatness at opposite sides of the tomb, without a look at the dead bodies and without recognition of each other; Benvolio and the Nurse were then reintroduced to take silent farewells of the bodies; and, finally, to swelling music, the lights faded with impressive slowness until the curtain fell. The ending had been refashioned as a solemn, exotically illuminated dumb-show. In comparison with the animated interplay of words and action that had preceded it, this spectacle seemed empty and meaningless. The conclusion of a production that had gripped and moved its audience was pretentious, sentimental and vague.

Again it must be admitted that the discrepancy was not unexpected. Professional producers in recent years have all cut something from the last scene of *Romeo and Juliet*. Glen Byam Shaw, directing at Stratford-upon-Avon in 1954 and 1958, cut the dialogue between the Friar and Balthazar as the former approached the tomb, cut lines on the entry of the watch, delayed the Prince's entry, so that he had no need to repeat his question, and eliminated some of his orders; he also cut a few lines of the Friar's explanation and the whole of the depositions of Balthazar and Paris's page. The Stratford production of 1945 cut the Friar's last speech from forty lines to six; that of 1941 omitted the Friar altogether after he had left Juliet; and Peter Brook's pro-

PLATE VII

A. Laurence Olivier

B. Richard Johnson

C. Michel Bernardy

D. John Stride

THE VISUAL PRESENTATION OF ROMEO

PLATE VIII

The Balcony Scene: John Stride as Romeo, Judi Dench as Juliet

'ROMEO AND JULIET', OLD VIC THEATRE, 1960
Directed by Franco Zeffirelli, scenery by Franco Zeffirelli, costumes by Peter J. Hall

PLATE IX

A. The Prince after the death of Tybalt

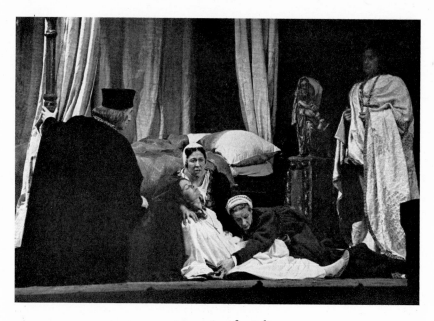

B. Mourning for Juliet

'ROMEO AND JULIET'

PLATE X

The first brawl

'ROMEO AND JULIET'

duction of 1947 deleted everything after Juliet's last words and, then, simply brought on the Chorus to conclude with a few of the Prince's last lines (and yet on this occasion there was time enough in the course of the play for introducing a negro servant, an Arab, a carpet seller, a 'man with a drum' and various other extra attractions).[3]

Directors working in the English theatre do not respond to Shakespeare's presentation of authority and responsibility and of understanding, compassionate grief. This is surely a loss. The Prince's acknowledgement of complicity is Shakespeare's addition to the story as he found it in Arthur Brooke's narrative poem, *The Tragical History of Romeus and Juliet*. Moreover we know that Shakespeare was deeply concerned with the ways in which responsibility is learnt in adversity. The theme recurs at important crises in plays throughout his career: it is found when Richard the Second is imprisoned and when Henry the Fifth prays before Agincourt, and later, when Lear, Pericles, Cymbeline, Leontes and Prospero become suppliants. Such a climax in *Romeo and Juliet* needs the development of the preceding hundred and twenty lines which Zeffirelli cut. And these lines have important dramatic interests to present on their own account. Compared with Arthur Brooke, who gave Juliet two long speeches immediately before her death, and with Otway, Cibber and Garrick, who revised the play in the seventeenth and eighteenth centuries and invented final speeches for the heroine, Shakespeare has hustled her last moments; he allowed her only the briefest possible utterances and brought the busy watchmen on stage immediately afterwards. Shakespeare gave time and words and action at this important culmination of the tragedy to the crowded stage as one after another of the characters kneel as 'parties of suspicion' and as the two families stand silently listening. The Friar's long speech is so tightly written that it is difficult for a director to do anything but keep it almost intact or cut it out entirely; its very texture shows that it cannot represent a slackening of interest in the dramatist but rather a determination to show the manifold ways in which small, over-confident human decisions had worked together with some kind of destiny, that 'greater power than we can contradict'. Shakespeare's complicated and highly-worked last movement of the tragedy suggests that, however powerful destiny may seem, man and a Prince among men react to catastrophe with a sifting of responsibility and a demand for justice:

> Go hence, to have more talk of these sad things;
> Some shall be pardon'd, and some punished.

Zeffirelli's change to dignified dumb-shows of grief could not endow these words with the socially responsible, seemingly endless particularity of Shakespeare's full text. To present *Romeo and Juliet* satisfactorily it is necessary to find a style which can sustain the dramatic life of the entire last scene and of those earlier moments of authority and responsibility and of compassionate, understanding grief which prepare for this conclusion.

$$\ast \qquad \ast \qquad \ast$$

In part the shortcomings of this production may have been due to a lack of sympathy, for several of the less successful passages are known to be capable of lively presentation. In part it was probably due to a weakness in the metrical control of speech, for most of these moments involve sustained utterance or counter-pointed phrases. It may also be bound up with the timing of the production as a whole.

At the very end the director used a slow pace in order to make the invented conclusion impressive, but this was after he had hurried some speeches which demand time to give the impression of consideration and after he had cut much from the second half of the play: III, iv and IV, iv were cut completely, the beginning of IV, ii, the musicians from IV, v, the first twenty-three lines of the important scene of Romeo in Mantua. It looks as if the earlier Acts had been given too easy a rein. Discounting two intervals, the performance lasted two hours and fifty minutes: the first part, up to the end of II, ii, took an hour; the second part, up to the end of III, i, took forty minutes; and this left but an hour and ten minutes for most of Act III and the whole of Acts IV and V. It may well be that Zeffirelli purposely tried to speed up Acts III, IV and V, sensing that the tempo had become too slack.

The beginning was slow in order to establish characters and atmosphere. For example, Romeo's first entrance was long and silent accompanied by shouting and laughter off-stage; it showed his solitary, self-absorbed nature at the cost of narrative pressure. To introduce Mercutio with Benvolio for II, iv, time was taken to show them lounging in the street and encountering two casual passers-by who had left the stage before the first of Shakespeare's words had been spoken. After the Prince had pronounced judgement for the death of Tybalt, the stage emptied very slowly until only the Chorus was left and then he closed the scene by slowly walking the full depth of the deserted stage and, again slowly, lifting his hands in a gesture of despair. Some of the long pauses were made in order to enforce the lively manner of speech and action, but the style of acting was not the chief cause of slowness: that was rather the scenic realism. Twice a curtain rose to show the stage covered with smoke giving a hazy impression and to singing or calling and a whole crowd of stage-dressing supernumeraries. Two sets of curtains were used within the proscenium (visible in Plate X) so that the scenery could be changed on every possible occasion, even if to disclose merely 'another part of the streets' or 'another room in Capulet's house'. Some of the changes marvellously mirrored the change of mood implicit in the text: the most effective was to Juliet's bedroom with pale blue walls and a tall bed furnished with the same blue and white, making these colours dominant for the first time and giving a sense of space, femininity and domestic peace. But all too many scene-changes were trivial in effect, one being only more or less commodious than the other or cumbersomely providing a large and by no means essential property, like the desk for Friar Lawrence placed before an all but meaningless back-drop.

The audience and critics generally admired the settings which were designed by Zeffirelli himself—although their mechanism and scenic realism were often old-fashioned in contrast to the style of acting. But on reflection we may question their usefulness and tact. With a simpler, but not necessarily less evocative or less changeable setting, the new, alert style of action and speaking might have made an even greater impact and the 'realism' centre more in the human behaviour on which the story and the tragedy depends. By the same means, the tempo could have been more brisk. This would have answered the motif of 'sudden haste' which is found in Shakespeare's text repeatedly, and with insistence:

It is too rash, too unadvised, too sudden: Too like the lightning. . . .on a sudden one hath wounded me, That's by me wounded. . . . Tybalt, that an hour Hath been my kinsman. . . .let Romeo hence in haste. . . .Hie to your chamber. . . .Hie you, make haste. . .hie hence, be gone, away! . . .Come, stir, stir, stir!

...Uncomfortable time, why camest thou now...?...O mischief, thou art swift....Stay not to question...then I'll be brief.

Such phrases are found in almost every scene after the first few and are not without significance. The pace, or momentum, of events can help to represent the 'star-crossed' elements of the love story and so enable Romeo and Juliet to appear to be fighting with growing urgency against an increasingly complex concatenation of misfortunes, against a narrative logic that seems to emanate from 'inauspicious stars' beyond man's control. The speedier overall tempo which a simpler setting would have permitted could have aided this element of the tragedy.

And, to return to the earlier and even more important point, a simpler setting with a brisker pace would have allowed the director to give the breathing time which is necessary in Acts III, IV and V for presenting the theme of responsibility and the deeper understanding which men learn through this catastrophe. The young characters of this production were so compellingly alive that the loss of the full play is the more unfortunate. It would be a pity if Zeffirelli's unity of speech and action, his enfranchisement of the elaborate dialogue as the natural idiom of the characters of the play, were to be associated in the public's mind with a tragedy which seemed to have lost its momentum and lifelike qualities half-way through performance.

NOTES

1. *Theatre Notebook*, XV (1961), 75; *The Observer* (9 October 1960); *Theatre World* (November 1960).
2. Reviewed in *Shakespeare Survey*, XIII (1960) and XIV (1961).
3. The prompt-books of these productions are in the library of the Royal Shakespeare Theatre, Stratford-upon-Avon.

THE YEAR'S CONTRIBUTIONS TO SHAKESPEARIAN STUDY

1. CRITICAL STUDIES

reviewed by BERNARD HARRIS

'Shakespeare is a dead issue' decides T. J. B. Spencer,[1] and the words will alarm alike the incautious critic and the indolent reviewer. The remark is elegaic, however, rather than contentious—a threnody for the lost spirit of detraction in writing about Shakespeare. The lecture does more than remind us by frequent and (literally) far-fetched quotation that 'the discussion of Shakespeare has been, in the past, far more defensive than is commonly supposed': we are reminded, forcefully, that the history of Shakespeare criticism is more than 'an account of the books written about him', or 'a record of progress', or 'a chronicle of opinion', that indeed 'It also has connections with literature, with the production of poetry'.

From Dryden's time onwards Shakespeare has been a live issue. And we misinterpret the admiration of our writers for Shakespeare unless we bear in mind that their feelings have been mixed. It has been inconvenient for them that his plays have normally been interpreted in accordance with the dominant literary form of each period.

Thus the early nineteenth century regarded his writings as 'the self-revelations of a great personality'; for the Victorians, whose dominant literary form was the serious moralizing novel, Shakespeare's plays were assumed to be (as objects of criticism) something like *Middlemarch*.

And in the twentieth century, in a post-symbolist world, when the kind of literary work which (if not dominant) receives the most attention from serious criticism is—how shall I describe it?—the rather fragmentary and indirect revelation of the nature of man and the human dilemma, with outcroppings of the *philosophia perennis*, preserving perhaps a certain Christian (or at least traditional) steadiness in a world in which all coherence is going—it is natural, I say, for our critics to regard the plays (as objects of criticism) as less like *Middlemarch* and more like *The Waste Land*. This, at any rate, is the unspoken assumption in much of the most striking Shakespeare criticism of the last thirty years, and explains some of its peculiarities.

It is a poor augury for the next thirty years that Spencer should conclude that 'the spectacle afforded by modern criticism is the shadow-boxing of rival bardolaters. Shakespeare is a dead issue. The resistance to his magnificent tyranny is over; and with it has gone something of the vigour and excitement and courage of Shakespeare criticism.'

It is encouraging to report that these qualities are not destitute in John Bayley's *The Characters of Love*,[2] which treats of *Troilus and Criseyde*, *Othello* and *The Golden Bowl*, in terms (respectively)

---

[1] *The Tyranny of Shakespeare* (British Academy Annual Shakespeare Lecture, 1959; Oxford University Press, 1960).

[2] Constable, 1960.

of love's code, identity and knowledge. These are thin terms, however, for the rich sensibility which the book conveys in its analysis of human personality. Bayley believes that an author's success in approaching the theme of love is 'closely linked with his attitude towards his own characters', and comments that 'The writers whom we admire today do not appear to love their characters, and the critics who appraise their books show no signs of doing so either.... Characters, it seems, are no longer objects of affection. The literary personality has gone down in the world.' Bayley is not so much concerned to say why—he acknowledges that there are 'plenty of reasons for our lack of confidence in personality and our lack of respect for it', among them our awareness of Freudian psychology and our awareness of history—his book is much more preoccupied with 'asserting an extremely simple point—the supremacy of personality in the greatest literature'.

Such a statement is the more welcome because it is so long overdue, and because it is made in full awareness of the nature of the implications it will carry for the sophisticated reader. The author compares himself modestly with Fluellen as an artist in ingenious comparison, agrees that 'the whole direction of this book may seem to be towards a rather futile kind of literary primitivism, a nostalgia for the past', and thus skilfully removes the fuses from any such charges.

To approach *Othello* in terms of the novel may seem to be asking for trouble. Not only is it usually taken to be the most simply and obviously dramatic of Shakespeare's tragedies but the whole idea of discussing the tragedies and their characters in terms of fiction is now very much frowned upon. It is an approach associated with Bradley's classic on Shakespearean tragedy, and though Bradley's perceptions are still respected his critical premises are not.

And of the most famous question which Bradley asked, Bayley retorts 'But perhaps the time has come to ask ourselves whether this sort of query is really quite so absurd as it sounds' since its 'great virtue' is that 'it takes for granted the scope and completeness of Shakespeare's tragic setting, and also his success in conveying the wider consciousness of his major figures as well as their dramatic and functional personality'. The point is pressed home boldly: 'There is a sense in which the highest compliment we can pay to Shakespeare is to discuss his great plays as if they were also great novels.' The 'also' needs more emphasis; Bayley is well aware of the 'possible relevance of four basic critical approaches to character in Shakespeare', those of 'our approach to real life, or—by a slight extension of sophistication—to the novel', then from the standpoint of Elizabethan dramatic and ethical convention, again from considerations of dramatic function, and finally the perception of character 'in a metaphysical light', with the proviso that such approaches 'apply of course to the whole play as well as to the characters in it'. There is much to commend in a study which makes such extensive use of the first approach to a poem, a play and a novel which have in common the theme of love, are seen as '*tours de force* of personality', and whose characters 'make possible their special sort of success'.

The critical atmosphere is undoubtedly lifting a little; we are almost out of *The Waste Land* and clear of the climate of *Middlemarch*. The human emphasis comes through strongly in John Lawlor's[1] rejection of the word 'vision' with its suggestion of 'a region of truth permanently

---

[1] *The Tragic Sense in Shakespeare* (Chatto and Windus, 1960).

accessible to the dramatist-sage to which the persons and actions of the drama are ultimately referred'—

I therefore speak of 'sense' rather than 'vision', for it seems to me that the central truths offered by the Shakespearian imagination are things felt, groped towards and finally held to. They are not the mountain peak to which the traveller lifts his eyes, but the rock to which a drowning man clings. I speak, of course, of the persons of the plays: it is in and through them that we reach the Shakespearian tragic imagination, and not otherwise.

The tone of these books by Bayley and Lawlor is utterly different, yet their central concerns are manifestly comparable. Bayley passes over what he describes as 'the dogmatic', 'the whole truth' and 'the romantic' approaches to his theme, in favour of what he discerns as 'the neutrality of love', which 'implies a mode of creation particularly necessary to love as a theme, because the idea of the artist as holding a balance between opposing forces...is one most clearly brought out by this theme'. For Lawlor this is part of 'the decisively Shakespearian contribution to tragic art', whereby 'Shakespeare's very mode of presentation, his characteristic handling of his themes, is in and through the co-existence of opposites'. Lawlor's own mode of presentation is somewhat akin to the method of scholastic disputation, which moves through repeated questions, definitions and redefinitions to decisive conclusions. There is reflection here of what the author ascribes to Shakespeare in terms of a 'characteristically medieval cast of mind which would look for definition between opposites, the thesis and antithesis of that dialectical habit which is possibly the greatest single factor in forming the Shakespearian outlook'. The factors of thesis and antithesis for the tetralogy of Richard II—Henry IV—Henry V are appearance and reality; for Hamlet that of man as agent or patient of his destiny; for Romeo and Juliet and Othello the twin aspects of accident and design; for Macbeth the natural and supernatural; for Lear, in which 'certain deep-rooted characteristics' of Shakespeare's outlook receive 'a unique and collective weight', the idea of justice is explored and asserted in terms of the truth of imagination. The book rests its case in the conviction that 'Shakespeare's greatest contributions to tragic experience, the distinctive emphasis the tragic has in his working imagination, are on the side of the natural. The bedrock of understanding is in shared experience....' Examination of the tensions and shifting balances in the plays 'have all revealed the inadequacy of man setting up on his own': and so, by refinement and resolution of argument, we reach the conclusion that

Shakespeare's greatest single gift is an unwearied sense of the natural tie—the utter punishment of separate existence on the one hand; on the other, the endlessly fruitful possibilities once the human circle holds. No man seems to have responded more fully to natural affection as an irresistible power—a mighty current...that must be ruthlessly earthed before final disaster begins to be a possibility; and which, given only an ordinary room, can leap unimaginable gaps. The power of the natural bond is the only final reality; and as such it illuminates and sustains all else.

The extension of this natural bond to its contractual and social implications is demonstrated in a fine study by J. Stampfer[1] of 'The Catharsis of King Lear' which is seen to lie 'in the challenge

---

[1] *Shakespeare Survey*, XIII (Cambridge University Press, 1960), 1–10.

of Lear's subsequent death to the penance and spiritual transcendence that culminates the play's second movement'. The challenge is this:

All men, in all societies, make, as it were, a covenant with society in their earliest infancy. By this covenant, the dawning human consciousness accepts society's deepest ordinances, beliefs, and moral standards in exchange for a promise of whatever rewards and blessings society offers....But given the contingency of human life, that covenant is constantly broken by corruption within and without.

When the play opens Lear 'embodies all that man looks forward to in a world in which, ultimately, nothing is secure'. When he dies 'the uttermost that can happen to man has happened', and with his death an audience 'shares and releases the most private and constricting fear to which mankind is subject, the fear that penance is impossible, that the covenant, once broken, can never be re-established, because its partner has no charity, resilience, or harmony—the fear... that we inhabit an imbecile universe'.

A similar sobering honesty is behind J. K. Walton's[1] interpretation of 'Lear's last speech', in which 'Lear dies with the effort of realizing to the full the implications' of Cordelia's silence; and in a concise but exploratory article Winifred Nowottny[2] takes up the theme of a 'contrast of dimension' as a characteristic of the play's tragic vision, and with admirable coherence analyses the linguistic art of a play 'in which the minor characters are used to support the language of the hero, who must use language not as the adequate register of experience, but as evidence that his experience is beyond language's scope'. The 'cultural diversity' of *Hamlet's* vocabulary, the 'deeply emotive vocabulary' of *Macbeth*, the 'iridescence of physical and affective experience' in *Othello*, could only have obscured, in *Lear*, the 'terror of a universe whose few simple pillars fall ruining'.

The modern and fearful preoccupation with *Lear* admits of very different insights and offered solutions. Leo Kirschbaum[3] turns our attention to the growth of Albany from 'nonentity to greatness' in *Lear*, so that the end of the play becomes dominated by a genial giant 'great in psychological strength, great in physical power, great in speech, great in piety and morality.... And *King Lear* is often described as totally dark!'. Further comfort is offered by R. P. Adams,[4] who relates 'King Lear's Revenges' to those moments when 'the Shakespearean hero typically elects action requiring all of his *virtu* and strength, requiring total involvement in life's affairs, even though what is to come is fearfully unsure': 'to revenge is to suffer' and thus Lear becomes 'credibly redeemable through that suffering'. Whichever way we turn in criticism of *Lear* we encounter the problem of pain, the acceptability or non-acceptability of punishment. As A. P. Rossiter[5] said,

I take occasion to quote Bradley here. He labours to believe that the gods *are* just: that a moral principle re-establishes itself at the end of *King Lear*; and yet he writes: 'to assert that he deserved to suffer what he did suffer is to do violence not merely to language but to any healthy moral sense'. On the next page he says: 'Let us put aside the ideas of justice and merit...' and '...it seems to me that what Shakespeare had to do was to put aside those ideas, in order to become a Shakespearian, not an Elizabethan, *tragedian*'.

---

[1] *Shakespeare Survey*, XIII (Cambridge University Press, 1960), pp. 11–19.
[2] *Ibid.* pp. 49–57.   [3] *Ibid.* pp. 20–9.
[4] *Modern Language Quarterly*, XXI (1960), 223–7.   [5] *Angel with Horns* (Longmans, 1961).

This comment is typical of the many fruitful asides to be found in this posthumous collection (edited by Graham Storey) of Rossiter's lectures, which range most fruitfully in the histories perhaps, but are always—if unevenly—provocative on every play they touch. Rossiter's remark has critical application too; for many critics fail to put aside their own ideas in favour of those more directly offered by the plays. J. A. Bryant Jr.[1] is clear in his preferences, arguing that 'Profitable as it is to consider Shakespeare's plays as studies in human relations or as reflections of the Elizabethan world picture, we are lingering on the periphery when we limit our attention to such matters'. Fundamentally, for Bryant, Shakespeare's plays are 'developments of the great archetypal myths of the human race...participating by analogy in an action which, from the poet's point of view, is Christian, divine, and eternal'. There are many incidental correctives to be found to such thinking in current criticism. R. H. West,[2] in a study of 'Sex and Pessimism in *King Lear*', observes that 'The given morality of *King Lear* suits Christianity, certainly, and no doubt it suits many other creeds, but to feel its force in the play does not require a Christian account of it nor any account that fits into a system'. The play must be allowed Bradley's 'painful mystery'; 'the goodness of the good children gives no explanation of the evil of the evil, and only partial reassurance', so that 'The given morality...does not exhaust the sophistication of the author about generation!'

This distinction between the 'given' and its extension is part of the concern of Clifford Leech's[3] full and important essay on 'The "Capability" of Shakespeare', important equally for the producer and the reader of his plays, and stressing again and again that 'we must not expect a rigid consistency' from Shakespeare, but must 'be prepared for a variety of intellectual impulses to be manifested'. Leech argues that

in choosing to write plays that belong to the traditional Kinds, Shakespeare was entering into a more durable relationship with a particular *Weltanschauung* than the term '*negative* capability' would imply. His adherence to a tragic or a comic view of the universe seems never total, always subject to the impulsion of non-tragic consolation, non-comic disturbance: nevertheless, within the compass of the play his commitment to a tragic or a comic view may be profound. In writing tragedy and comedy he joins hands with all others who have worked in those Kinds: he makes the tragic affirmation and the comic denial that, in general terms, have been made before him and will be made again. Tragedy and comedy, as modes of perception determining the general pattern of the thing perceived, regulate the poet's responses to the world and receive his (not total but) firm allegiance.

The admirably lucid statements of this essay keep in proportion the theatrical condition of Shakespeare's art, reject the notions of the 'governing idea', the simple 'meaning' or the 'complete performance', in preference for the 'moment to moment' improvisation of a 'kind of drama rich in the individuality of its men and women'. It ought not to be possible to write on this large subject without reference to this study; and after reading it the need to write will be less apparent.

Meanwhile, before turning to treatments of other kinds and of individual plays, two short

---

[1] *Hippolyta's View: Some Christian Aspects of Shakespeare's Plays* (University of Kentucky Press, 1961). For a short and effective treatment of this large theme see an editorial by A. C. Partridge, 'Shakespeare and Religion', in *English Studies in Africa*, 3 (1960), 1–7.

[2] *Shakespeare Quarterly*, XI (1960), 55–60.   [3] *Ibid.* pp. 123–36.

accounts and a general work on Shakespeare's tragedies must be remarked. Peter Ure[1] chose for his inaugural lecture the theme of the 'Inward Self' of the tragic hero in Shakespeare, accepting the necessity of 'some useful limitation' in speaking of 'inner and outer, the "real self" which the reader or the audience alone is privileged to see, and the outward man which the other characters in his drama see'; this is a good discussion, in summary terms, of how 'Richard II's self is annulled, Othello's remains unchanged, Lear's is radically transformed, and the real nature of Coriolanus's self is revealed beneath its appearances'. Maynard Mack,[2] in what he describes as a 'modest supplement' to Bradley's 'pioneering analysis' of the construction of Shakespeare's tragedies, takes up the discussion of the 'vertebrate characteristics' which the different tragedies share. Among them are 'the residue of hyperbole' in the tragic hero, the 'opposing voice' of the hero's foil, devices of play construction and 'ways of recording the progress of "inward action"'—such as the hero's journeying, the 'mirror scenes' of the opening episodes of the plays and those of the recapitulation of themes. For Mack, 'the most important thing that happens in a Shakespearian tragedy is that the hero follows a cycle of change, which is, in part, psychic change', constituted in three phases. The hero is delineated first, and then, in a second phase of 'conflict, crisis and falling action' the one certain development is that 'the hero tends to become his own antithesis' and one of the 'symbolic elements' of this phase is the hero's experience of madness. The third phase is 'a recovery of sorts...perhaps even a species of synthesis'. This is but the skeleton of Mack's thought about construction in an essay which is persuasive and flexible—not dogmatic—about Shakespeare's modes of 'indirection' in the tragedies.

William Rosen[3] has written with new perception about structure and story in Shakespearian tragedy, keeping firm hold upon immediate and apprehensible dramatic values. This is an extremely sane, well-annotated account of *Lear*, *Macbeth*, *Antony and Cleopatra* and *Coriolanus*, which concentrates on the plays' 'dramatic techniques; more specifically, it investigates how the point of view of an audience is established towards the protagonist'. The distinction drawn between the first two of these plays and the latter two is put into these words:

King Lear acquires an identity; Macbeth loses his humanity and descends to the bestial. One journeys to find himself, the other, to lose himself. In both plays, however, an audience sees events primarily from within the protagonist's own consciousness. This is true neither of *Antony and Cleopatra* nor of *Coriolanus*, where our view of the protagonists is primarily from without, through the eyes of *raisonneurs* who subject them to relentless analysis. Because Antony, Cleopatra, and Coriolanus have little insight into themselves, commentators provide the understanding they lack.

Rosen is able to make a just claim that he has not 'treated the problem of point of view in a single-minded fashion because drama is more than technique and more than form...great tragedy, in the last analysis, issues from a unique vision that encompasses problems of value and personality'. It is one of the virtues of this book that it keeps the new interest in character within the framework of dramatically achieved and humanly centred values; this is a human not a transcendental Cleopatra, for instance, and though it is acknowledged that Lear progresses from nothingness to see 'beyond the world of pomp, state, contractual obligations', yet here 'His

---

[1] *Shakespeare and the Inward Self of the Tragic Hero* (University of Durham, 1961).
[2] In *Jacobean Theatre* (Edward Arnold, 1960), pp. 11–41.
[3] *Shakespeare and the Craft of Tragedy* (Harvard University Press, 1960).

vision is of truth or perfection or blessedness, not the center of a flower or blinding light, but a secular vision of love and the community of mankind'.

Bertrand Evans[1] has attempted 'an approach to the comedies through one of Shakespeare's notable dramaturgical characteristics—his uses of awareness and control'. Evans argues that dramatists may be classified 'in a rather fundamental way according to their preferences in the handling of the relative awarenesses of audience and participants', and distinguishes three possible methods, those of an audience less informed than the participants, equally aware or more aware. The first way is that of 'mystery' writers; the second is held to be the normal or standard way of story-tellers; the third is claimed to be Shakespeare's, and to be his consistently alone. Evans begins with the rather intimidating statistics that 'the seventeen comedies and romances include 297 scenes, in 170 of which an arrangement of discrepant awareness is the indispensable condition of dramatic effect...we hold significant advantage over participants during those scenes'. We are also told that of the 277 persons in the comedies '151 stand occasionally, frequently, or steadily in a condition of exploitable ignorance'. Evans believes that 'what most emerges from the present study is a view of Shakespeare as the shrewdest of dramatic engineers'. Those of us who have long been taking this on trust will be glad to have it confirmed in detail, but it must be admitted that the unremitting attention to the same characteristic and unceasing use of the same terminology is in great danger of imposing a sense of similarity upon essentially dissimilar structures. What is of some surprise, however, is that preoccupation with the technique of exploitable awareness should reveal a progress in Shakespeare's art strictly in accordance with old-fashioned biographically based accounts. The book takes us in its chapter divisions through the 'First Explorations' of his early comedies, on to 'The Way Found' of *A Midsummer-Night's Dream* and *The Merchant of Venice*, through 'The Approach to the Summit' of *Much Ado*, *As You Like It*, and *The Merry Wives*, to 'The Fruits of the Sport' in *Twelfth Night*. We then decline through the dark comedies, find consolation in *Measure for Measure*, rise through the 'Planetary Romances' to the dramatic satisfactions of *The Tempest*, which 'replacing the more dazzling cross-plays of the comedies, are the last benefits yielded by exploitation of the discrepancy between the participants' ignorance and our Olympian vision'. It is perhaps a pity that the romances are treated in a book whose method and interest are much more strongly engaged in those 'dazzling cross-plays' of the mature comedies, for the best chapters seem to be very obviously those where Shakespeare's developing interest becomes most explicitly the author's own, particularly those on the *Dream*, *As You Like It*, and *The Merry Wives*, while *Twelfth Night* largely eludes this type of analysis. Read as a series of studies, rather than a continuously conducted argument, however, the book has more attraction and constantly offers concise comparisons of theme and effect; for instance, we note that

In the world of *Much Ado* all is astir, for its people will not suffer it to stand motionless for a moment. Twelve active practisers, nine amateur, three professional, deceiving one another and being deceived in turn, keep Messina bustling. Beside it the world of *As You Like It* is still and golden, and most of its inhabitants would be content if some of its moments endured for ever: Jacques weeping with the stricken deer, 'Ganymede' being wooed by Orlando, Duke Senior hearing Amiens sing, Phebe being chided by 'Ganymede'. While Oliver sleeps, the serpent will not sting nor the lioness claw him.

---

[1] *Shakespeare's Comedies* (Oxford University Press, 1960).

It is in comparisons of this kind that Evans's single-minded approach seems effective and most attractively written.

Sitansu Maitra[1] displays an equal single-mindedness in dealing with Shakespeare's comedies: a compressed account of the 'English Renaissance' is followed by a short study of the emergence of the 'New Individual', and the treatment of this individual in Shakespearian comedy is the concern of the principal chapter. Shakespeare's comedies 'present his vision of the New Individual moving about in search of fulfilment of the new value of constancy in love'. We are warned that the 'abstract term individual must not create the impression that it is only one kind of individual that Shakespeare studies', but the study is too compressed to prevent this happening. Yet despite some creative misprints ('love at first sigh'), and some uncertainties of English idiom ('any Tom, Dick or John') the book covers much profitable ground in its attempt to delineate the 'individual sex love that the typical Renaissance comedy cultivates', that kind of love found 'between Bassanio and Portia or even between Campaspe and Apelles or between Sapho and Phao'.

John Vyvyan[2] has examined Shakespeare's early plays in relation to 'the medieval philosophy of love', but it must be observed that his findings of detail are no more successful than Maitra's general conclusions, and perhaps less so. In the most developed chapter of the book Vyvyan finds Shakespeare dealing with the problems formulated in *The Romaunt of the Rose*, and freshly answering them. His reading of Shakespeare's plays in the light of this allegory, however, is dark indeed. In *The Two Gentlemen of Verona* Shakespeare 'is writing an allegory as well as a play', in which Valentine's captaincy of the outlaws is seen mysteriously as giving special stress to the 'parable': who is Sylvia? she is 'more than a girl in a play; she is also a symbol of the eternal Beauty'. This study is much less coherent than Vyvyan's *Shakespearean Ethic* and carries the eccentric aspects of that work to extremes, hunting the spiritual significance in every *double entendre* and disregarding the secular. When Mercutio and Benvolio lose Romeo on the way from the Capulets' ball, it is because 'The Romeo they are looking for, in fact, exists no more'. By his climbing the wall and disappearing we are to understand 'his conversion'—'the ape is dead'.

In turning to treatments of individual plays—of which, again, *Hamlet* has alone earned a book to itself—we encounter a very different connotation for 'religious drama' and its applicability as a description of Shakespearian tragedy. L. C. Knights's[3] concern is remote from Vyvyan's platonizing (though some incidental views are quoted with approval) and dissents from H. F. D. Kitto's interpretation on a major point. *Hamlet* does indeed show the 'working out of inexorable laws...but with this difference: we are required not only to *watch* the august working out of the law which the dramatist's understanding of spiritual and psychological truth enables him to put before us; we are required to enter imaginatively into the spiritual and psychological states with which the given experience is confronted'. The difficulty for Knights is in entering imaginatively into a state of being which he finds corrupt and paralysed: 'Hamlet does not merely see the evil about him, does not merely react to it with loathing and rejection, he allows his vision to activate something within himself—say, if you like, his own feeling of corruption—

[1] *Shakespeare's Comic Idea* (Calcutta: K. L. Mukhopadhyay, 1960).
[2] *Shakespeare and the Rose of Love* (Chatto and Windus, 1960).
[3] *An Approach to Hamlet* (Chatto and Windus, 1961).

and so to produce that state of near paralysis that so perplexes him.' Hamlet's final readiness is only 'to meet his death in playing the part of the avenger' and the 'awareness that he embodies is at best an intermediate stage of the spirit, at worst a blind alley'. Rossiter found a not dissimilar 'central "moral" theme' for this play:

To bring the 'native hue of resolution' to bear on life, and to make the deeper findings of 'pale thought' effective in the world of living men, the thinker must come down to that world. By coming down to that world, he accepts its terms, its ways of making things happen; accepts the necessity of managing affairs by making levers of men's weaknesses, and so necessarily tends to live in a world, not of men, but of machines.

And though, for Rossiter, 'Hamlet's profoundest intuitions of nobility, goodness, value, truth are without validity....Yet Hamlet's fineness is noble, though all life confute its efficacy. And much life does. That is why the play is a tragedy, and symbolizes the conflict between two antinomies, the contradictions I have called "circumstances" and "inner values".' Beside such a modern resolution of the difficulty John Wasson's[1] view that 'no sooner does Hamlet...place himself in the hands of Providence than Providence arranges for him to accomplish his purpose' seems almost immoral. More fashionably, Thomas Greene[2] believes that 'Nowhere in the play is it indicated that any synthesis is possible', indeed, 'it is inevitable that Hamlet dies in our eyes a lesser man. He has begun to lose the tragic dimensions which have made him memorable.' For Leo Kirschbaum,[3] acting 'In Defense of Guildenstern and Rosencrantz', such tragic dimensions must be radically adjusted: the 'moral accuser makes us nervous...we feel...that he is being more destructive than remedial'; by the end of the play 'the Prince has almost wrecked the given society in which he lives'. In fact, 'to the extent that a civilized person disengages himself from the exclusive Hamlet viewpoint to that extent he passes out of the world of infantile idealism'. The writer assures us that he has 'never been more serious in my life'. But then so too, fifty years ago, was Christopher Welch[4] when he lectured the Musical Association on 'Hamlet and the Recorder', bringing before them 'the views of a flute-player' and assuming it not necessary to 'dwell on the leading incidents of the play'.

Among Shakespeare's other tragedies, *Macbeth* appears to have drawn most attention this year—and it is of a diverse nature. M. M. Badawi[5] analyses the 'numerous instances of euphemism and circumlocution' in it, first, to define 'the attitude of both Macbeth and Lady Macbeth to the murder of Duncan', and then to relate the evil of the Witches to that of Macbeth and Lady Macbeth. He notes that 'the reluctance or inability to call a terrible thing by its real name, which is after all what lies behind euphemism and circumlocution, reveals an ingrained fear of the right word,...essentially a habit of the primitive mind'. Aleksander Nejgebauer[6] has reopened the discussion of the authorship of the Hecate scenes in *Macbeth* and attempted a reconstruction based on 'bibliographical considerations and arguments on an elementary content

[1] 'Hamlet's Second Chance', *Research Studies*, XXVIII (1960), 117–24.
[2] 'The Postures of Hamlet', *Shakespeare Quarterly*, XI (1960), 357–66.
[3] *Two Lectures on Shakespeare* (B. H. Blackwell, Oxford, 1961).
[4] *Lectures on the Recorder* (Oxford University Press, reprinted 1961).
[5] *Euphemism and Circumlocution in 'Macbeth'* (Alexandria University Press, 1959).
[6] 'On Hecat in *Macbeth*' (Novi Sad, 1960).

level'. Arun Kumar Dasgupta[1] comments on 'the multitudinous seas incarnadine' with the aid of Leonardo da Vinci's *Notebooks*, linking the image of blood and sea as forming part of the analogy between microcosm and macrocosm. John Harvey[2] has provided some sensible introductory comments on the play for use in upper forms of schools. A note by Isabel Hyde[3] questions whether in 'discounting the effect of Macbeth's use of imagery' Kenneth Muir has not 'surely misinterpreted the nature of the tragedy'. She argues that it is 'no mere convention of poetic drama that makes Macbeth express his thoughts and feelings in powerful imagery, but part of Shakespeare's fundamental conception of the tragedy'. (Rossiter's lecture opens boldly 'Macbeth, like *Richard III*, is best interpreted through its themes and imagery, not through "character" (contrast *Othello*); and after a consideration of order, kingship and "the state of man" in the Histories'. The images stressed here are those of concord and 'unity of Nature'.)

Among discussions of the love-tragedies is a skilful account by Harry Levin[4] of the structural and linguistic interplay in the 'Form and Formality of *Romeo and Juliet*'. There is a tendency to proliferate comparisons as in the comment that the contraries of the plot 'are reinforced on the plane of imagery by omnipresent reminders of light and darkness, youth and age, and many other antitheses subsumed by the all-embracing one of Eros and Thanatos, the *leitmotif* of the *Liebestod*, the myth of the tryst in the tomb': but there is also recognition that 'Against this insistence upon polarity, at every level, the mutuality of the lovers stands out, the one organic relation amid an overplus of stylized expressions and attitudes'. The mutuality of the loves of Othello and Desdemona is seen by Terence Hawkes[5] as 'a communion of souls rather than of bodies, as the whole story of their wooing shows'. The 'gradual poisoning of the "higher" world of Desdemona by the rational "lower" world of Iago is the main theme of the play'. In 'A new source for *Othello*?' Paul N. Siegal[6] brings out some details from Fenton's *Certaine Tragicall Discourses*, one story of which concerns an 'Albanoys captaine' who kills his innocent wife in jealousy. Allan D. Bloom[7] removes the play altogether from these regions of Elizabethan reference, finding the two 'Venetian plays' Shakespeare's explicit treatment of 'the possibility of an interracial, inter-faith society'. But Othello's 'guise of universality' is a lie, and Desdemona's death is 'in large measure due to her own errors': we may take her side over the deceit of her father, but 'perhaps from a...highest standpoint we must come to the defense of civil society.... Marriage is a part of political life, of civil society.' To objections by Burckhardt Bloom[8] reiterates the 'relevance of the tradition of political philosophy for the interpretation of Shakespeare'. We come nearer to dramatic relevance with Leonard Prager[9] on the subject of the Clown. Not content with the notion of simple 'comic relief', Prager examines the two

[1] A Note on *Macbeth*, II, ii, 61–3.

[2] *Macbeth (Notes on English Literature*: Oxford, Basil Blackwell, 1960). A series of filmstrips made by Educational Productions Ltd, despite some over-broad generalizations in the accompanying notes, may well have a useful appeal for a young audience. The least accurate supporting material is that for the films on the Elizabethan theatre and on Shakespeare's biography; but ten plays are skilfully abridged and the pictures are attractive.

[3] '*Macbeth*: A Problem', *English*, XIII (1960), 91–4.   [4] *Shakespeare Quarterly*, XI (1960), 3–11.

[5] 'Iago's Use of Reason', *Studies in Philology*, LVIII (1961), 160–9.

[6] *P.M.L.A.* LXXV (1960).

[7] 'Cosmopolitan Man and the Political Community: An Interpretation of *Othello*', *American Political Science Review*, LIV (1960), 130–57.

[8] *Ibid.* pp. 471–3.   [9] *Shakespeare Quarterly*, XI (1960), 94–6.

appearances of Othello's servant; in III, i he is instructed to send away the musicians, and his 'crude quibbles center on the theme of cacophony', thus 'Othello will not hear music, will not be soothed, brought back into harmony with himself'; and in III, iv the Clown's pun on 'lie' (to 'fabricate' and 'to dwell') 'introduces a rash of lying on the part of *all* the major characters', and thus the pun is 'a pointer directing the audience to the significant action which follows the quibbling'. One may admit as much without being easily capable of resolving the awkward facts that the Clown 'appears twice, speaking a total of a dozen lines, and is not especially humorous'; he seems a superfluous signpost.

A full and considered statement has come from L. J. Mills[1] on the question of 'Cleopatra's Tragedy', seeking not to keep in balance the posed problems of Rome and Egypt, or the struggles of the triumvirate, nor even the love of Antony and Cleopatra, but rather to follow out in much detail the appearances of Cleopatra in the play as a series of relating clues to the nature of her individual tragedy. Mills goes back to E. E. Stoll as nearer to the text of the play and the evidence of the action in asserting the natural figure of the final scene: 'to have Cleopatra glorified and transfigured is to forgive her treatment of Antony.... If the tragedy of Antony and the tragedy of Cleopatra are to interact to intensify each other, it is necessary *not* to have a transfiguration of Cleopatra.... That she does change somewhat, that she does attain some realization of what Antony was, is to be recognized. That she did not realize it earlier, and to a much greater degree, is her tragedy: the too little and the too late.' It may be necessary to ask for a similar objectivity about Antony.

The identity of 'The Tragic Hero in *Julius Caesar*' is investigated yet again by Anne Paolucci,[2] who decides that 'Brutus is misled into mistaking the *potential* Caesar for the *actual* Caesar, and the play is nothing more than a slow Sophoclean self-revelation on the part of Brutus that not Caesar but he himself has sinned against the gods'.

Interest in Shakespeare's English history plays seems concerned with rather more varied aspects of structure, imagery and character. In 'A little more than a little' R. J. Dorius[3] notes that 'collaboration of plot, character, and thematic imagery to create a unity of tone and meaning is so intimate in these plays that a word or metaphor can be said to be deepened into character or extended into plot'. The principal concentration of an interesting article is upon the development of 'themes of good husbandry and extravagance through the metaphoric language' of *Richard II*, *1 and 2 Henry IV*, and *Henry V*. S. K. Heninger Jr.[4] writes rather crudely about 'Richard's metaphorical mouthings' and 'claim to be a sun-king', in tracing the analogy of the latter phrase. Such unsubtle writing is scarcely likely to engage very closely with a highly rhetorical play. Equally, Julia C. Van de Water[5] appears to have undertaken to reduce the stature of the Bastard in *King John* from dislike of 'an increasing tendency on the part of commentators to exaggerate both his function and his merits'. But no very cogent reasons emerge for disregarding one of the most obviously attractive characters in that play. More positive thought has gone into Sidney T. Fisher's[6] 'Letter to a University Librarian on Sir John Falstaff'. This argues that the name 'Falstaff' is one of 'a remarkable company: Pistol, Shallow, Silence, Fang, Snare, Mouldy, Shadow, Wart, Feeble, Bullcalf, Mistress Quickly, Sampson Stock-fish,

[1] *Shakespeare Quarterly*, XI (1960), pp. 147–62.
[2] *Ibid.* pp. 329–33.
[3] *Ibid.* pp. 13–26.
[4] *Ibid.* pp. 319–27.
[5] *Ibid.* pp. 137–46.
[6] Montreal: Redpath Press, 1960.

Doll Tearsheet, Nell Night-work'; and concludes that 'Surely the name is simply a made-up word from "staff", the male generative organ, and "fall", to droop'. Evidence is cited in support from Jonson and Wycherley, as well as from the plays of Shakespeare. Apart from this entertaining item, it must be remarked that very little of the current criticism of either the history plays or the problem comedies has anything of the vigour of chapters devoted to these works in Rossiter's volume: the lecture on 'Ambivalence: The Dialectic of the Histories' was a public performance of spirit, scarcely repeated on the page but still vigorous, and the tough thinking on the problem comedies is not easily located elsewhere. John Wasson[1] considers *Measure for Measure* 'A play of incontinence'; he seems remarkably satisfied that there are only a few 'unsolved problems' left about the play, 'the most important being concerned with character interpretation', and that 'the major concerns of the play center on the incontinent acts of Claudio and Angelo'. J. P. Cutts[2] contributes a note on 'Perfect Contrition', commenting that 'The whole scene between the Friar and Juliet seems to me to be for all practical stage purposes the scene of the confessional *in extenso*'; the latter half of the note should be read in conjunction with E. Schanzer's article on the marriage-contracts in *Survey 14*. Gunnar Sjogren[3] suggests that the setting of *Measure for Measure* may be located in Vienne, not in Vienna, on the grounds that certain topographical details are in accord. *Troilus and Cressida* has occasioned a note by Albert Gerard[4] who feels that 'the central idea which is the basis of its structure and the principle of its unity is the disintegration of the values...built up in the course of its first part'. Robert Y. Turner[5] approaches the problem of critical dissatisfaction with *All's Well* by means of the dramatic conventions of the late sixteenth century. He suggests that Shakespeare adopted such conventions 'more literally than in any play written after his apprenticeship in the early 1590's, and, as a consequence, produced a comedy more of an age than for all time'. Too much relationship is discovered, however, with 'prodigal son comedies'; modern discontent would seem to have little basis if the case against *All's Well* rested on the lost currency of a simple parable.

The sonnets, though not the poems, of Shakespeare have been the subject of criticism and suggestion. F. T. Prince[6] has provided an account in condensed form of the sonnet form from Wyatt to Shakespeare; Brents Stirling[7] has proposed a relationship between eleven sonnet stanzas not previously associated as a group; and B. C. Southam[8] has inverted a traditional interpretation of sonnet CXLVI, claiming that it is 'pleading for the life of the body as against the rigorous asceticism which glorifies the life of the spirit at the expense of the vitality and richness of sensuous experience'. The humanist Shakespeare is back again with us, in company with his repersonalized characters.

The publication of new translations and republication of older versions continues; this year has seen volume 4 of G. Meri's[9] Estonian version of Shakespeare, containing *The Merchant of*

[1] *English Literary History*, 27 (1960), 262–75.   [2] *Notes & Queries* (November 1960), pp. 416–19.

[3] 'The Setting of *Measure for Measure*', *Revue de Litterature Comparée* (Paris: Didier, 1961).

[4] 'Meaning and Structure in *Troilus and Cressida*', *English Studies*, XL (1959).

[5] 'Dramatic Conventions in *All's Well that Ends Well*', *P.M.L.A.* LXXV, 5 (1960), 497–502.

[6] In *Elizabethan Poetry* (Edward Arnold, 1960), pp. 11–29.

[7] 'A Shakespeare Sonnet Group', *P.M.L.A.* LXXV, 4 (1960), 340–9.

[8] 'Shakespeare's Christian Sonnet? No. 146', *Shakespeare Quarterly*, XI (1960), 67–71.

[9] *William Shakespeare*, Komoodiad II (Eesti Riiklik Kirjastus, 1960).

Venice, Much Ado, As You Like It, Twelfth Night, Troilus and Cressida, All's Well that Ends Well, and *Measure for Measure,* while volume I of a new edition of F-Victor Hugo's[1] French translation has appeared, containing twelve plays and with introduction, and notes, by J. B. Fort. Nico Kiasashvili[2] has written a short account in English of Shakespeare in Georgia, and the Avril-Juin 1960 issue of *Études Anglaises*[3] was wholly devoted to *Shakespeare en France.* Eugenio Gomes[4] has provided a book on *Shakespeare No Brasil.*

The range of even this selected list of foreign activity may well furnish a final question: Allardyce Nicoll[5] asks 'What do we do with Shakespeare?' The present popularity of Shakespeare in the theatre has never been experienced before, 'yet on the one hand much scholarly criticism engages itself in discovering virtues which have rarely, if ever, been grasped in performance, and on the other hand many stage directors have been busily occupied either in subordinating Shakespeare's language...or in imposing on his works ideas of their own'. There is needed 'a realization that stage and study, having equal interest in him, must work in harmony—an appreciation of the basic sources of his power, accompanied by a resolution not to obscure these but to build upon them constantly'.

2. SHAKESPEARE'S LIFE, TIMES AND STAGE

reviewed by W. MOELWYN MERCHANT

This year has been spared the wilder extravagances in Shakespearian biography. F. E. Halliday usefully summarizes the known facts in the pleasantly illustrated *Life of Shakespeare*[6] and it is unfortunate that he extended his brief to interpretation. He is not happy in his account of Shakespeare's marriage, shaky in the chronology of the plays—essential data in his biographical method—and disastrous in his occasional sallies into criticism. Not uncharacteristic is the opening of chapter VI where biography is tied to criticism: 'the death of Hamnet was a blow that had bruised the very centre of his being...so that...he turned to themes that matched the temporary cynicism of his outlook.' *The Merchant of Venice* is a 'heartless comedy of revenge about a vindictive Jew and a company of Christian adventurers'. These are unfortunate blots on a work that was needed.

Robert Gittings explores the identity of 'the rival poet' in the sonnets (a theme largely omitted from J. B. Leishman's *Themes and Variations in Shakespeare's Sonnets,* consideration of which will have to be postponed until *Survey 16*). Gittings's attempt to identify the rival poet as Gervase Markham is in fact the least valuable part of this lively and scholarly work.[7] It is essentially a poet's book (happily produced within a month or two of his verse-play for 'Son et Lumière', *This Tower my Prison,* a study of the guilt of Frances Howard and Robert Carr in the murder of Overbury). Gittings examines the sonnets and *Love's Labour's Lost,* with Guilpin's *Skialetheia* and Markham's *Devoreux* in the course of his quest for the rival; sensitive literary perceptions

[1] *Théâtre Complet de Shakespeare* (Paris: Garnier, 1961).
[2] *Anglo-Soviet Journal,* XXI (1960), 19–22.
[3] Paris: Didier, 1960.
[4] Ministério de Educação e Cultura, 1960.
[5] *Shakespeare-Jahrbuch,* 96 (1960), 35–46.
[6] Gerald Duckworth, 1961.
[7] *Shakespeare's Rival* (Heinemann, 1960, with plates).

are backed by precise historical citation, justifying the major intention of the book: 'the theatre of any age must have its thread of topicality, and it was typical of Shakespeare to lavish great care upon it. That is why any study of the day-to-day situations in which he may have found himself involved can be so revealing.' By this token, in a small matter, it would be pleasant to have confirmation of M. W. Jones's conjecture[1] that Shakespeare doubled the parts of Adam and William in *As You Like It*.

In a small but important volume Kenneth Muir examines critically the evidence for Shakespeare's collaboration in *Edward III, Pericles, The Two Noble Kinsmen* and the lost *Cardenio*.[2] Though his methods are scrupulously conservative, Muir finds strong evidence of Shakespeare's hand even where he goes on to stress (in his conclusions on *The Two Noble Kinsmen* and *Cardenio*) that the plays 'add nothing to his reputation'. The arguments are so tersely put that they cannot be summarized with profit here; what needs stressing is the method of the book, each play (except *Cardenio*, for obvious reasons) given two chapters, the first textual, the second critically analytical and depending for its interest and importance not on the extraneous fact of the authorship of the play treated, but on the literary value of the play as it stands; the three plays treated in this way leave Muir's hands with increased stature, while the book itself assists in breaking down the damaging and unnecessary distinction between the textual and critical scholar. The authorship of *Pericles* is considered in some detail by F. D. Hoeniger,[3] who suggests a humble place (in II, i and II, iii) for the collaboration of John Day; and in justice it must be said further that the thesis is put forward both modestly and with a tacit questioning of the value of textual parallels as a whole.

The sources of the plays have earned extended treatment during the year. Most notable has been Geoffrey Bullough's reaching the half-way mark of the *Narrative and Dramatic Sources of Shakespeare*, with the third volume, on 'The Earlier English History Plays: *Henry II, Richard III, Richard II*'.[4] This volume involved difficult decisions of inclusion and compression. 'Ideally one would print a complete parallel text of Fabyan, Hall (or Grafton), Holinshed and Stow for each reign, to enable the reader to make up his own mind about the degree and nature of Shakespeare's indebtedness to these authors.' Though this degree of completeness was clearly impracticable, the reader of this volume is enabled to read considerable portions of all these chroniclers, together with substantial portions of the 'literary analogues', *A Myrroure for Magistrates*, Daniel, and *Woodstock*. Bullough's full and judicious introduction to each play establishes the quality of the borrowing and the degree of Shakespeare's manipulation of the material. Moreover the homogeneity of theme and material in this volume, with the general introduction on 'Historical Authorities available to Shakespeare', raise even more important questions of historiography. Bullough's conclusion is that Shakespeare 'was so steeped in [Hall's] ideas, and fortified no doubt by acquaintance with the Anglican Homilies and such literary works as *The Mirror for Magistrates*...that he was already fully conscious of the moral scheme working through what Hall termed "the Great Discord"'. This matter is extended in Kenneth Muir's article, 'Source Problems in the Histories',[5] in which he promises, in the second volume of his *Sources*, a general discussion of Shakespeare's reading in Seneca, Ovid, the Bible,

[1] *Shakespeare Quarterly*, XI (1960), 87–8.　　　　[2] *Shakespeare as Collaborator* (Methuen, 1960).
[3] 'How Significant are Textual Parallels? A new Author for *Pericles*?', *Shakespeare Quarterly*, XI (1960), 27–38.
[4] Routledge and Kegan Paul, 1960.　　　　[5] *Shakespeare-Jahrbuch*, 96 (1960), 35–46.

etc.; in the present article he treats the source problems of *Richard II* and gives his general conclusion: 'I have come round, somewhat unwillingly, to the view that Shakespeare's imagination worked most successfully when it was stimulated by his reading and that he read any relevant book on which he could lay his hands.' C. T. Prouty, in the same volume of the *Jahrbuch*, offers more general 'Observations on Shakespeare's Sources', and a warning against a too 'scientific' examination of source material. Returning to the argument of his *Sources of Much Ado* (1950) he claims that 'the Renaissance doctrine of imitation has been generally disregarded by those writing on Shakespeare's sources'; hence 'the accumulation of sources is not an end in itself...we must know what a given work meant in its time both in respect to its subject matter and its critical bases; secondly, using this knowledge, we must try to ascertain Shakespeare's reaction to both aspects'. In an important examination of *Rosalynde* as the source of *As You Like It*,[1] Marco Mincoff also establishes a general principle: 'an author's rejections are often as important as his actual borrowings'; from this standpoint he draws attention to the commentators' odd assumption that *As You Like It* is primarily 'an inquiry into pastoral', for Shakespeare has omitted much of Lodge's arcadianism and, more positively, has developed matters which were not Lodge's concern, 'love's foolishness and the clash between appearance and reality'. Relationships of a rather different quality are analysed by Barbara H. C. de Mendonça in 'The Influence of *Gorboduc* on *King Lear*'.[2] Noting that the numerous plot-sources of *Lear* have none of the tragic tone of Shakespeare's play, she argues some interesting parallels between the matter and temper of *Lear* and *Gorboduc* and claims that 'the older play seems to provide the stimulus which aroused Shakespeare's poetic vision', acting as a catalytic agent on the diversity of source material. Paul N. Siegel[3] cites Geoffrey Fenton's *Certaine Tragicall Discourses* (1567), translating from Belleforest's French version of Bandello, as an additional source for *Othello*; this story of a captain who kills his wife from jealousy, kissing her at the point of death 'as Judas kissed our Lord', reinforces Siegel's former argument (*Shakespearian Tragedy and the Elizabethan Compromise*, 1957) concerning a conscious parallel between Othello and Judas. Ernest Schanzer[4] asks where Shakespeare can have heard of Cleopatra's marriage to her brother Ptolemy (I, iv, 6, 16–17), since Plutarch does not mention it. He refers to Chaucer's *Legend of Good Women* as the probable source: 'After the deth of Tholome the kyng...Regned his queene Cleopataras'; for Shakespeare had drawn on the *Legend* at least twice before (in *A Midsummer-Night's Dream* and *The Merchant of Venice*). C. C. Seronsy carries further the tale of Shakespeare's borrowings from Daniel[5] with two more citations from *Queenes Arcadia* (1605). Robert R. Reed Jr. assumes the character of Shrimp in Munday's *John a Kent*[6] to be a prototype of Ariel both in the multifariousness of his acts of magic and in the complexity of his nature as an inhabitant of more than one element.

There have been four studies of dramatic plot and structure during the year. The briefest but most suggestive is Allardyce Nicoll's 'Tragical-Comical-Historical-Pastoral'.[7] He notes that drama is peculiar in its nomenclature, with a steady trend towards defining dramatic categories.

---

[1] 'What Shakespeare did to *Rosalynd*', *Shakespeare-Jahrbuch*, 96 (1960), 34–46.
[2] *Shakespeare Survey*, XIII (1960), 41–8. [3] *P.M.L.A.* LXXV, 4 (1960), 480.
[4] *Notes & Queries* (September 1960), pp. 335–6. [5] *Notes & Queries* (September 1960), pp. 328–9.
[6] *Shakespeare Quarterly*, XI (1960), 61–6.
[7] *Bulletin of the John Rylands Library*, 43, 1 (September 1960), 70–87.

With the establishment of the first public theatre in 1576 no further works were described as 'interludes', while there was a crystallizing of the forms 'comedy' and 'tragedy' in descriptive use, and the emergence of 'history'. Nicoll concludes: 'Shakespeare clearly put the categories of plays into Polonius's mouth as a joke; yet often we may suspect that Shakespeare's jokes were directed at least partly towards himself. He, it seems, was responsible for establishing "history" as a generic term, and it looks as though Polonius's tragical-historical was indeed first used for the world's most famous play—*The Tragicall Historie of Hamlet*.' Ernst Theodor Sehrt in *Der dramatische Auftakt in der elisabethanischen Tragödie* (Göttingen, 1960), makes an exhaustive examination of the introductory scenes in Elizabethan tragedy, analysing pre-Shakespearian forms in pantomime, prologue and induction as a study preliminary to a critical account of these forms in Shakespeare's Histories and Tragedies. Of particular interest is Sehrt's handling of audience psychology and the quick involvement of the audience in the theme and temper of the play. Arthur Brown also relates 'The Play within a Play'[1] to the audience's awareness of illusion. 'At its best it can give an extra depth, almost an extra dimension to the play of which it forms a part; for a time some of the actors themselves became an audience, inducing the actual audience to believe that they are watching not a play but something closer to real life; paradoxically it produces further realism through further illusion.' Milton A. Levy[2] finds it difficult to answer the question (involving both source- and plot-structure), 'Did Shakespeare Join the Casket and Bond Plots in *The Merchant of Venice*?' *Il Pecorone* he finds to be the immediate source of many unexplained details and allusions but concludes that unless Shakespeare had recourse to a hitherto undiscovered play, he 'substituted the casket device himself and has left some small traces of his handiwork'. Mary Lascelles in an urbane account of Shakespeare's debt to Malory[3] adds a suave footnote to the year's consideration of influences: 'this talk of indebtedness, idle even when scholarship is in question, must always dissolve to absurdity where the subject under discussion is great imaginative art'.

The subject of the Shakespearian theatre has produced a major study of the first importance in a new edition of Henslowe's *Diary*.[4] Greg's edition of 1904 has long been out of print and this transcript, in providing a new text of 'the primary source for the theatrical history of the Elizabethan age', also gives a definitive opportunity of reconsidering some of Greg's assumptions. This is done in a lucid and substantial introduction. The editors question Greg's conclusion that Henslowe was 'an illiterate moneyed man...who regarded art as a subject for exploitation'; with this assumption, Greg endorsed Fleay's argument that 'Henslowe's methods were not those best adapted to the free development of the dramatic energies of the company' and (probably the most misleading of the assumptions) 'that the financial arrangements which we find obtaining in the groups of companies under Henslowe's control were the exception rather than the rule'. Foakes and Rickert find insufficient evidence for this last statement; they find that 'the account book reveals a friendly and, on the whole, harmonious relationship between Henslowe and the players', and conclude that, within the limits of our present knowledge, 'there is little justification for drawing a contrast between Henslowe, as a mercenary capitalist, and the Burbages'. The editors further solve some detailed cruces in the account-book records and demonstrate the value

[1] *Essays and Studies* (1960).   [2] *Shakespeare Quarterly*, XI (1960), 388–91.
[3] 'Sir Dagonet in Arthur's Show', *Shakespeare-Jahrbuch*, 96 (1960), 145–54.
[4] Edited R. A. Foakes and R. T. Rickert (Cambridge University Press, 1961).

of their new edition in making possible a constant re-scrutiny of the transactions which are frequently ambiguous and unexplained. Related material printed in appendices includes letters between Edward Alleyn and his wife, and other documents bring the business items in the *Diary* to vivid actuality; there are deeds of partnership, warrants and petitions relating to the establishment of the Fortune and the temporary closure of the Rose; and finally inventories of costumes in Alleyn's possession and lists of actors in the seven extant dramatic plots associated with Alleyn. The Cambridge University Press has served this rich source-book handsomely.

The editors of Henslowe discuss a drawing[1] in the Henslowe papers (and included in their edition) in *Shakespeare Survey 13*. It is a cryptic little sketch which I suggest may indicate a crudely simplified version of the Serlian 'tragic scene' with superimposed staging, or, more probably, an elaboration of the steps approaching the playing area which Serlio drew before all his scenes, here adapted to make a multi-level set—a curious and singularly modern conception. A. J. Gurr[2] returns to the De Witt sketch, assumes that the obscure lower part of the stage drawing indicates drapes withdrawn to show the understage and concludes that the whole drawing is 'concerned to show the facilities for playing rather than the architecture of the framework'. R. H. Bowers[3] cites parallels between Shakespeare's Autolycus and the Autolicus of the manuscript *Converted Robber* (by John Speed?). E. W. Ives examines in detail (with line and half-tone illustrations)[4] the portraits of Tom Skelton the jester at Muncaster Castle and the Shakespeare Institute (formerly of the Haigh Hall collection). Among much interesting matter, the argument concerning the nature of 'motley' is carried one stage further.

Two articles examine the significance of acting, disguise and feigning in Shakespeare. Charles Brooks[5] discusses with subtlety the male roles played by Julia, Portia, Rosalind, Viola and Imogen and extends the argument to the conclusion: '"acting" involves both "doing" and "pretending". ...The boy actor's playing of a woman who plays a man is a clear instance of Shakespeare's interest in the problem of creating life for an imagined person and in the way the problem mirrors the problems of identity, knowledge, reality, and illusion in the world. The act of acting is a key to the nature of being.' Within a more limited field Hugh Maclean distinguishes the purposes and results of disguise as employed by Kent and Edgar[6] and once more the dramatic intention is seen to go beyond the mere expedience of plot; 'the person best fitted to move through the "tough world" will...recognise the need, from time to time, to conceal his true character from the "wolvish image" of nature turned monstrous'. Further critical implications of costume (as distinct from disguise) in *King Lear* are considered by W. M. Merchant,[7] while Evelyn B. Richmond contributes a 'footnote' on 'Historical Costuming', extending, with illustrations, our detailed knowledge of Planché's notable costumes for Kemble's *King John*.[8]

This year has again seen an important body of studies in Shakespeare's use of music. Richard Hosley[9] considers the stage-directions which contribute to our understanding of the physical

---

[1] 'An Elizabethan Stage Drawing.'   [2] *Notes & Queries* (September 1960), p. 328.

[3] 'Autolycus in 1636', *Shakespeare Quarterly*, XI (1960), 88–9.

[4] *Shakespeare Survey*, XIII (1960) 90–105.

[5] 'Shakespeare's Heroine-actresses', *Shakespeare-Jahrbuch*, 96 (1960), 134–44.

[6] 'Disguise in *King Lear*', *Shakespeare Quarterly*, XI (1960), 49–54.

[7] *Shakespeare Survey*, XIII (1960), 72–80.,   [8] *Shakespeare Quarterly*, XI (1960), 233–4.

[9] 'Was there a Music-Room in Shakespeare's Globe?', *Shakespeare Survey*, XIII (1960), 113–23.

location of music-making in the theatre, particularly those which require a curtained room which could be used in a raised playing-area by both players and musicians. Edward S. Le Comte[1] reinforces the suggestion he made earlier (*E.L.H.* XVII, 1950) that Ophelia's 'Bonny Sweet Robin' is an allusion to Robert Devereux, Earl of Essex. Two notes in *Shakespeare–Jahrbuch*, 96[2] continue the debate between John P. Cutts and Richard Flatter on the stage-direction, *Enter Hecat, and the other three witches*. Andrew J. Sabol[3] prints two songs for *Cynthia's Revels* and *The Dutch Courtesan*, with a valuable examination of their dramatic relevance, and noting that 'in contrast to the popular and familiar tunes of the day...in the closing decades of the sixteenth century, composers of merit such as Richard Edwards, Nathaniel Patrick, and Richard Farrant had written notable dramatic laments for the coterie theater' and that these songs must have provided one of the major attractions in these plays for the trained vocalists of the Children of the Chapel and of Paul's. John P. Cutts[4] proceeds from an examination of Pericles' 'I hear most heauenly musicke' (V, i, 2) to a consideration of the dramatic use of allusions to the music of the spheres as 'resolved disorder in the macrocosm', relating the theme to *The Tempest*. Cutts also[5] prints with comment the words and music of Falstaff's 'Heauenlie Iewel' in *The Merry Wives* (III, 3). Fernand Cosin has a detailed examination of the dirge in *Cymbeline*,[6] with particular reference to theological overtones in the play; and Charles Haywood examines at considerable length William Boyce's 'Solemn Dirge' in Garrick's production of *Romeo and Juliet* in 1750,[7] when the rivalry of Rich and Garrick led to the employing of Arne and Boyce in an effort to make the play more attractive.

There has been an important batch of books and articles on the intellectual background of Shakespeare's age. Curtis Brown Watson analyses the varying and frequently contradictory senses of honour in the Renaissance.[8] His principal thesis is the conflict between the Christian virtues which Shakespeare inherited from the Middle Ages and classical moral philosophy rediscovered at the Renaissance. The plan of the book, both historical and analytic, will be of value to students, particularly the judiciously summarized sources of the concept of honour (though for the more advanced student these will sometimes appear foreshortened to the point almost of travesty, an inevitable defect in so ambitious an undertaking). Least satisfactory is the balance-sheet which Watson attempts to strike between pagan and Christian elements, concluding that Shakespeare's tragedies are more classical and pagan than Christian in temper. Tom F. Driver takes an equally massive intellectual structure as the subject of his analysis in *The Sense of History in Greek and Shakespearean Drama*.[9] The book opens with a close study of the relation of drama to the historical consciousness of each great age of dramatic literature, distinguishing by means of theological and historical categories the 'Hellenic historical consciousness' from the 'Judaeo-Christian'. The second part explains the relation of dramatic form, treated in abstraction, to 'temporal and spatial values', for it is Driver's central assumption that

---

[1] *P.M.L.A.* LXXV (1960), 480.

[2] '"Speak—Demand—We'll Answer"', p. 173, and Professor Flatter's Reply, p. 192.

[3] 'Two Unpublished Stage Songs for the "Aery of children"', *Renaissance News*, XIII (1960), 222–31.

[4] *Notes & Queries* (May 1960), pp. 172–4.

[5] *Shakespeare Quarterly*, XI (1960), 89–92.

[6] *English Studies*, XL (June 1959).   [7] *Shakespeare Quarterly*, XI (1960), 173–88.

[8] *Shakespeare and the Renaissance Concept of Honor* (Princeton U.P.: London; Oxford University Press, 1960).

[9] Columbia University Press, 1960.

'it is the form of the plays, more than the subject-matter, which bears the mark of presuppositions about time'. The third part is the important critical core of the book, in four chapters on juxtaposed pairs of Greek and Shakespearian tragedies: The *Persians* and *Richard III* exemplifying 'nemesis and judgement'; the *Oresteia* and *Hamlet* contrasting 'synthesis and providence' as resolutions of tragedy; *Oedipus Tyrannus* and *Macbeth* in contrasted 'uses of time'; and the *Alcestis* and *The Winter's Tale* as studies in 'release and reconciliation'. In this third section, almost wholly free from the teasing over-abstraction of the introductory matter, Driver develops acute critical insights; the book as a whole is a necessary corrective to the naïvety of much contemporary approach to Elizabethan historiography. W. Schadewaldt, in a brief study,[1] examines some of the same concepts as Driver and has wise things to say about 'character and destiny' and upon later medieval conceptions of 'the Greek'. Still exploring the classical world, John L. Tison Jr. examines[2] the consolations for exile by decree, 'a serious adversity in almost one-third of Shakespeare's plays'. Showing the diverse uses to which Shakespeare puts the tradition derived from Seneca, the Fathers, Boethius, and Renaissance and Reformation treatises, he concludes that Shakespeare, consciously aware of the *consolatio* and its codified system, follows (or breaks) the conventional pattern in order to console, to create dramatic irony, or even to intensify the dramatic suffering of the exiled. Michael Lloyd also demonstrates Shakespeare's exact awareness of classical learning[3] in his free use of 'daemons' (angels, spirits, or geniuses) who take upon them 'God's mysteries', prophetic or retributive, an argument especially relevant to *Lear*, *Julius Caesar* and *Antony and Cleopatra*.

C. J. Sisson, in 'Shakespeare's Helena and Dr William Harvey'[4] enters another field of Shakespeare expertise, the medical. After a brief review of the medical practitioners in the plays he examines suits in the Court of Chancery, with new material concerning Simon Forman, Peter Chamberlain and William Harvey, passing from the latter to a deft-handed defence of Helena's conduct in *All's Well*. Kenneth Muir relates 'Madness in *King Lear*'[5] to contemporary beliefs to show that 'Shakespeare is clinically accurate in the presentation of the symptoms of madness' and that, whatever Shakespeare's private opinions on demonic possession, he never assumed madness to have been caused by possession.

Ernest Schanzer has an especially valuable account of 'Marriage-Contracts in *Measure for Measure*',[6] closely summarizing 'the complex and inherently contradictory nature of the contemporary laws and edicts relating to marriage, which had remained basically unchanged since the twelfth century'. His examination of *de praesenti* and *de futuro* contracts fully justifies his warning that 'of all Shakespeare's plays *Measure for Measure* is the one where ignorance of Elizabethan moral tenets and edicts is likely to lead [the reader] furthest astray'. *Measure for Measure* has also received another distinguished treatment, by Raymond Southall,[7] a close analysis of the themes of supernatural grace and of 'seeming', preserving through its argument a proper critical balance between dramatic values and the treatment of the play as an intellectual thesis,

---

[1] 'Shakespeare und die griechische Tragödie', *Shakespeare-Jahrbuch* 96 (1960), 7–34.
[2] 'Shakespeare's "Consolatio for Exile"', *Modern Language Quarterly*, XI (1960), pp. 142–57.
[3] 'Plutarch's Daemons in Shakespeare', *Notes & Queries* (September 1960), pp. 324–7.
[4] *Essays and Studies*, 1960 (English Association), pp. 1–20.
[5] *Shakespeare Survey 13* (1960), pp. 30–40.   [6] *Ibid.* pp. 81–9.
[7] '*Measure for Measure* and the Protestant Ethic', *Essays in Criticism*, XI (1961), 11–33.

for *Measure for Measure* is no 'partisan tract on the Grace controversy, nor is it simply an attack upon the social designs of the bourgeoisie'. To complete this very eclectic series of 'background studies', G. Monsarrat contributes[1] comprehensive 'Notes sur le Vocabulaire Astronomique et Astrologique de Shakespeare'.

3. TEXTUAL STUDIES

reviewed by JAMES G. McMANAWAY

During the last fifteen years, there has been curiosity about the minutely detailed study of the Shakespeare First Folio by C. K. Hinman and the machine he invented to facilitate his work. From time to time he has published announcements of the discovery of pages bearing the marks of Jaggard's proof-reader; evidence that the Folio was set by formes and not seriatim, page by page; and the characteristics of an apprentice workman who, unfortunately for scholarship, had a large hand in the setting of the tragedies. These fragmentary interim reports have but whetted interest in the *opus magnum* which was in prospect. Now that this is in process of publication, Hinman has decided to give a hint of some of his conclusions.[2] The first reading of the printed version of his lecture—slightly abridged but not altered substantially—may dismay a little those who do not grasp the significance of some of Hinman's comments or who have not heard in private conversation of some of the discoveries that are not even glanced at in this latest report.[3]

What are some of Hinman's conclusions after collating thirty-six plays in fifty of the Folger Shakespeare Library's copies of the First Folio (how fortunate that they are in one place for collation)? And what of the capacity and effectiveness of the collating machine? Of the machine it may be said that optical lenses, unlike human eyes, never tire, and that experienced scholars can multiply their output of collation by ten. They can scan pages and spot variants in less time than is needed to record them. And they may work on the assurance that the machine has not failed to report a variant.

But what of the weightier matters? One result of Hinman's years of study is the discovery that there is no warrant for the confidence, inspired by the discussion of a single page of proof of *Antony and Cleopatra*, that all of the First Folio benefited by careful proof-reading and press-correction. So far as his minute collation has proceeded, he is satisfied that 'only 134 of the nearly 900 pages of the Folio which contain Shakespearian text were proof-corrected; and the average number of changes made even in these 134 was less than four per page. Approximately 750 Folio pages appear not to have been proofed at all' (p. 9). In the comedies, Hinman has recorded about seventy variants that reflect proof-reading; in the histories, about seventy more. The tragedies received more careful attention, but almost half of the some 370 variants in this section 'are confined to a mere 70 pages—the pages which prove to have been set by an apprentice compositor' (p. 9).

When we learn that the proof-reader was more interested in typographical niceties (turned

---

[1] *Études Anglaises*, XIII (1960), 319–30.

[2] Charlton Hinman, *Six Variant Readings in the First Folio of Shakespeare* (University of Kansas Libraries, 1961).

[3] The description of how the collating machine works will make textual editors eager to use one of the dozen or more copies that have been installed in research libraries in the United States and in England.

type, space-types that took ink, etc.) than in errors affecting the sense of the text, and, what is much more serious, that in dealing with substantive errors he relied on native wit instead of consulting his copy,[1] it is tempting to ask, 'Is this the promised end?' And if it be, has Hinman spent his years in much ado about nothing?

The discussion of the six variant readings that Hinman has singled out for comment has less significance than some of the things merely alluded to or assumed silently. How is it possible to prove that the Folio was set by formes, and what are the implications of the discovery, as it may affect lineation, omission of words or lines, verbal substitutions? What kind of evidence enables a man to parcel out the type-setting among five compositors, and ascertain their reliability in transmitting text accurately? With what validity can an editor state that a given play— or even a specified portion of a play—was more than usually difficult for the compositor? The answers to these questions, with supporting evidence, will presumably be found in the eagerly awaited book, with who knows what besides.

Meanwhile, a comment on one small point. Hinman makes the observation (p. 5) that uncorrected impressions of formes of the First Folio eventually found their way into different copies of the finished book. 'Not, however, into any particular copies.... The uncorrected states of the various formes that make up the whole book did not go regularly into the same few copies.' In consequence, no particular copy should be expected to contain an unusually high percentage of uncorrected formes. There is a quarto play in the Garrick collection in the British Museum so made up, and a copy of Spenser's *Faerie Queene* in the Tudor and Stuart Club Library at the Johns Hopkins University. Some of the sheets of the latter are of very thick paper. Probably both of these copies were made up as printers' 'copy books', partly from sheets that would otherwise have been discarded, partly from sheets of paper of different weight and texture surreptitiously slipped into the press in order to increase the number of 'copy books'.[2] Remembering these two books, I am perverse enough to hope that some day a copy of the First Folio will be found in which there is just such an extraordinary percentage of uncorrected formes and imperfect sheets.

Of the text of *Coriolanus*, in Greg's words, 'There can be no doubt that behind F lies a carefully prepared author's manuscript'.[3] Many of the stage directions, as J. D. Wilson pointed out in 1928 and repeats in his New Shakespeare volume,[4] seem intended by the author in Stratford to guide the producer in London, while others, as Greg suggests (p. 406), have nothing to do with performance but look more like information for the reader. 'Holds her by the hand silent' (V, iii, 182) is a fine example of the former, and 'Enter Martius Cursing' (I, iv, 30), of the latter variety. The text of the play is clean, requiring relatively few emendations. As in *Antony and Cleopatra*, there is much mislineation. Wilson thought in 1928 and still believes that much of this is to be charged to the compositor, who was often cramped by the shortness of the Folio typeline and, he now adds, sometimes embarrassed by having to work with counted-off copy.

---

[1] Hinman has found only two indubitable cases of consultation of copy by the proof-reader.

[2] Cf. Francis R. Johnson, 'Printers' "Copy Books" and the Black Market in the Elizabethan Book Trade', *The Library*, 5th series, I, 97–105. Johnson should have included in his discussion the surviving copies of books that have sheets printed on one side only and others in which there are sheets that show the inked impression of one forme superimposed on the blind (uninked) impression of a different forme.

[3] *The Shakespeare First Folio*, p. 407.   [4] *Coriolanus* (Cambridge University Press, 1960).

Greg (p. 404) notes that the reasons for the mislineation are probably the same as for that in *Antony*; namely, that Shakespeare seems to have run on half-lines to save space, and that in his later plays he often renders lineation uncertain by the liberties taken with the normal scansion of blank verse.

A passage in II, iii contains an interesting problem and suggests a clue to the solution of some of the other textual difficulties in the play. Lines 240 ff. appear thus in F:

> Of the same House *Publius* and *Quintus* were,
> That our best Water, brought by Conduits hither,
> And Nobly nam'd, so twice being Censor,
> Was his great Ancestor.

Since the time of Pope, editors have recognized that something has been omitted after line 241 and have supplied the missing words from Plutarch or from North's translation. Wilson believes that the simplest explanation of the gap is the omission of a line.

> Of the same house Publius and Quintus were,
> That our best water brought by conduits hither;
> [And Censorinus that was so surnamed]
> And nobly nam'd so, twice being censor,
> Was his great ancestor.

His emendation, which uses some words taken from North, has the virtue of beginning with the same word as line 243 that follows and thus providing the compositor with an excuse for the omission. What Wilson does not point out, and what other commentators seem not to have observed, is the typographical appearance of page bb 1ᵛ, column A, in which the passage occurs. Column A begins with II, iii, 243 and ends with III, i, 22. The Act heading, *Actus Tertius*, is squeezed in between the horizontal rules with no white space above and very little below, contrary to the practice at the beginning of Acts IV and V, for example, and elsewhere in F. Furthermore, there is no spacing between the lower rule and the initial S.D. of the next scene. Obviously, the compositor, setting from counted-off copy, and working backwards from bb 3ᵛ towards bb 1, has found himself with more text than he can set conveniently in the available space. Whether he deliberately omitted the line naming Censurinus or skipped it by accident, we shall never know. But the mislineation a few lines below at II, iii, 263–4 is surely traceable to the need to save space:

> Repaire to th' Capitoll.
> *All.* We will so: almost all repent in their election.
> > > > > > > > > > > > *Exeunt Plebeians.*
> *Brut.* Let them goe on:

Wilson regularizes this satisfactorily thus:

> Repair to th' Capitol.
> *Citizens.*   We will so: almost all
> Repent in their election.
> *Brutus.*   Let them go on;

There is similar mislineation in F at III, i, 32–3 and again at 48–9, 61–2, and 65–7 in column B. The treatment of half-lines at II, iii, 128–30, 137–40, 151–2, 158–9, 164–5, 187–8, 204–5, and in the last seventeen lines on the page shows that the compositor had to continue compressing his text as much as possible on bb 1, the last page of his stint; and the crowding of centred S.D.'s after ll. 123 and 152 provides additional evidence.

In his New Arden edition of *The Poems*,[1] F. T. Prince reprints the basic texts with spelling and punctuation modernized except where it seems desirable to retain visual rhymes. He argues, at perhaps unnecessary length, that the early reprints of *Venus and Adonis* (1593) and *Lucrece* (1594) have no authority and gives readings to show how the texts were progressively corrupted to the end of the seventeenth century. *The Phoenix and Turtle* provides no textual difficulties because only two copies survive of the only early edition. For *The Passionate Pilgrim*, Prince wisely bases his text on the unique fragment of the first edition, which gives poems I–V, XVI–XVIII, and takes the other poems from the second edition. By so doing, he can give stanzas 3 and 4 of XVIII in the correct order, instead of transposed with stanzas 5 and 6 as in Q 2. In three places that have come to my attention, the editor, rather disturbingly, has introduced silent emendations: (1) *Lucrece* 1252, 'cover them', *Lucrece* 1351, 'us'd no words', where the Huntington copy, Lee's facsimile of a Bodleian copy, and Rollins's Variorum agree in 'cover crimes' and 'laid no words'; and (3) *Passionate Pilgrim*, XIV, 27, 'moon', as required by the context and the rhyme scheme, where the Huntington copy of Q 2 and Rollins's Variorum read 'houre'. In the penultimate line on page xxiii, Y[4] and Z[1] should have been printed Y 4 and Z 1.

Another volume, *The Merchant of Venice*, has been added to the revision of the Yale Shakespeare.[2] Limited by the plan of the series, the editor, A. D. Richardson, III, follows J. R. Brown's New Arden edition rather closely in his treatment of date of composition and Shakespeare's printed sources, but allies himself with J. D. Wilson in the belief that *The Merchant* is Shakespeare's revision of an old play, possibly *The Jew* mentioned in 1578 by Stephen Gosson. He finds positive evidence of revision at four places. In the first passage (I, ii, 122), 'four strangers seek' Portia 'to take their leave'; whereas Nerissa has named suitors from six countries. 'The discrepancy would seem to be evidence that Shakespeare revised an earlier play'(p. 113). In the second (III, ii, 217), Gratiano directs attention to the arrival of 'Lorenzo and his infidel' and of Salerio, but not until line 236 is a word spoken to Jessica, and meanwhile Lorenzo has ignored Portia in his first response to Bassanio's welcome. Is this necessarily evidence of revision of an old play? Jessica is a minor figure, who can wait until someone nearer her in station has opportunity to be gracious. The matter of primary importance is for Bassanio to dominate the stage as the new lord of Belmont. This he does, with proper deference to Portia. Lorenzo's devoirs to her can be paid, either silently at his entrance or when Bassanio names her. It is difficult to see how Shakespeare could have introduced more formalities without slowing the action. The third instance (III, iv, 48), where Portia says 'Mantua' instead of 'Padua', has much in common with the first; both, in my opinion, are to be explained by the nature of the manuscript given to the printer. This important subject is scanted with a reference to 'indications that the copy was close to Shakespeare's manuscript' (p. 119). There is no mention of the fact that the licensed prompt-copy must have been presented at Stationers' Hall on 2 October 1600 ('Entered...

[1] London: Methuen, 1960.
[2] A. D. Richardson, ed., *The Merchant of Venice* (Yale University Press, 1960).

A booke called the booke of the m'chant of Venyce'), no discussion of the probability that the manuscript used in Roberts's shop was not the prompt but Shakespeare's autograph papers, partly annotated by the prompter, no reference to the fact that in other quartos printed from foul sheets there are inconsistencies (six *v.* four suitors), slips of memory (Mantua for Padua), permissive stage-directions ('Enter Marochus..., and three or foure followers'), and inconsistency in the designation of characters ('Shylock' and 'Iew', 'Launcelot' and 'Clowne'). As for the doggerel verses on the three scrolls, which Richardson thinks 'point to a much earlier and far more naïve style, which in this case Shakespeare may well have taken almost verbatim from the earlier play', is it not Shakespeare's custom, when he introduces 'poetry' into his plays —cf. *Hamlet* and *Lear*—to write verses that differ radically in metre and diction from the blank verse which is their setting? The fourth instance (v, i, 33) is the reference to a hermit who accompanies Portia and Nerissa back to Belmont but does not appear on stage—'this may well be the remnant of an earlier play' (p. 116). The hermit's existence may be as fictional as that of the 'holy crosses' where the two promised brides have purportedly been kneeling and praying 'for happy wedlock hours'; but even if Portia had arranged to have such an escort across the countryside, she could readily have dismissed him upon her safe arrival—one more supernumerary means one more costume.

Scholarly reviews of editions of Shakespeare frequently contain statements of principle or criticisms of methods that have substantive importance. Thus Miss Alice Walker is taken to task by J. P. Brockbank[1] for her temerity in emending the text in her edition (New Cambridge) of *Troilus and Cressida*. 'Ought one', he asks, 'to postulate both an error and an oversight in order to enlarge Shakespeare's vocabulary and exempt Ajax from vulgarity?...What is at issue is not our right to assume errors common to Q and F (there must be many) but our right to emend in the confidence that we know what they are.' Again, Miss Madeleine Doran[2] admits the weight of evidence for single authorship (Shakespeare's) of *Henry VIII* that R. A. Foakes collects in his New Arden edition, particularly that to be found in the fact that variant speech prefixes for a single character (e.g. both *Car.* and *Wol.*) cut across the customary authorship division (between Shakespeare and Fletcher) as well as across the presumed compositorial revisions; but she insists that the crucial question is that of style. 'The important thing in *Henry VIII* is that the statistical indications from these several sorts of data [about diction and metre] agree in a remarkable way.' There are non-Shakespearian patterns that cannot be ignored, and Miss Doran finds it difficult to believe that the mature Shakespeare could or would have deliberately imitated Fletcher in serious and moving passages.

The plays in which Shakespeare is often supposed to have had a major or minor collaborator have been re-examined by Kenneth Muir.[3] His attribution to Shakespeare of specified passages in *Edward III* wins the approval of Geoffrey Bullough,[4] who agrees also with Muir's account of *Pericles* and *The Two Noble Kinsmen*. Clifford Leech[5] declares that Muir 'presents a very considerable case for recognizing Shakespeare's hand' in *Pericles*, *Two Noble Kinsmen*, and *Edward III*. The book adds little to what is already agreed upon about *Sir Thomas More* and *The History of Cardenio*. It gives new examples of Shakespearian iterative imagery in *The Two Noble Kinsmen*

---

[1] *R.E.S.*, n.s. XII (1961), 80–3.   [2] *J.E.G.P.* LIX (1960), 287–91.
[3] *Shakespeare as Collaborator* (London: Methuen, 1960).
[4] *English*, XIII (1961), 151–2.   [5] *Notes & Queries*, n.s. VIII (1961), pp. 156–7

and *Edward III* and proposes an ingenious if complicated hypothesis about *Pericles*. There are in George Wilkins's novel, Muir notes, lines that can be read as blank verse—but not Shakespeare's. Perhaps they derive from a play by an unknown dramatist which was revised by Shakespeare about 1607, cursorily in Acts I–III, but extensively in IV–V. Knowing something of this play, Wilkins based his novel upon it, but to bring the narrative closer to the play being acted by the King's Men he adopted the names in Shakespeare's revision. Approaching the problem of collaborative authorship in *Pericles* along a different line, F. D. Hoeniger argues from textual parallels that John Day may have written the non-Shakespearian portion.[1] The much more conservative Paul Bertram promises to present a case for Shakespeare's sole authorship of *The Two Noble Kinsmen*, which he believes was written in the autumn of 1613 (probably in November).[2]

The text of *King Lear* is touched on by two writers. T. B. Stroup gives additional reasons for believing that Shakespeare designed the roles of Cordelia and the Fool to be played by one gifted young actor. He points out that the entrance of Cordelia in IV, iv, after long absence from the stage, is prepared for elaborately in the same way that Shakespeare paved the way for the Fool's first appearance in I, iv. This was done, he believes, because Shakespeare wanted to dissociate the boy's two roles (Cordelia in I, i, Fool in I, iv; the Fool from I, iv to IV, i, Cordelia again from IV, iv to the end). He observes that there is the same interval (357 lines) between Cordelia's exit in I, i and the Fool's entrance as between the Fool's exit in IV, i and Cordelia's return (365 lines later)—sufficient time for the necessary change in costume and for the audience to adjust itself. He suggests further that by about 1620 changes in the personnel of the company may have led to the use of a different boy for each role, thus removing the need for change of costume and for mental adjustment, and permitting the elimination of IV, iii from performance (it appears only in Q). He speculates that Edgar, Cordelia, and the Fool may have been less popular about 1620 than when the play was first performed, for they lose more lines in the F version than any other of the dramatis personae. J. S. G. Bolton argues that *Lear* was printed from a manuscript in Shakespeare's hand (but marked for use as a prompt-book) whose frayed margins often made it necessary to improvise passages of text.[3]

Of conjectural readings and proposed emendations, there is no end. Some are new solutions of old puzzles; others affect lines that have attracted little or no attention. H. W. Jones proposes[4] modestly that when F reads

> I see that men make rope's in such a scarre,
> That wee'l forsake our selves   (*All's Well*, IV, ii, 38)

Shakespeare wrote

> I see y^t men may cõpas's in such a snare
> y^t wee'l forsake our selves

In support of the emendation, he quotes the Edward VI version of Psalm cxvi. 3: 'The snares of death compassed me round about....' It may be objected that though the sense of the

---

[1] 'A New Author for *Pericles*', *Shakespeare Quarterly*, XI (1960), 27–38.

[2] 'The Date of *The Two Noble Kinsmen*', *Shakespeare Quarterly*, XII (1961), 21–32.

[3] 'Wear and Tear as Factors in the Textual History of the Quarto Version of *King Lear*', *Shakespeare Quarterly*, XI (1960), 427–38.

[4] '*All's Well*, IV, ii, 38 Again', *M.L.R.* LV (1960), 241–2.

emendation is good, the line becomes metrically irregular and harsh. Another emendation in the same play is discussed by Richard Hosley in his review[1] of G. K. Hunter's New Arden edition. He supports Hunter's emendation of the S.D. at v, i, 6, 'Enter a gentle Astringer' to 'Enter a Gentleman, a stranger' by citing a direction from Part 2 or Whetstone's *Promos and Cassandra*, II, ii: '*Apio and Bruno, Two Gentlemen straungers, with Rosko.*' And F. S. Hook[2] would revive Theobald's emendation in II, ii, 4–7. F reads:

> *Clown.* ...I know my businesse is but to the Court.
> *Countess.* To the Court, why what place make you speciall, when you put off that with such contempt, but to the Court?

Hook agrees with Theobald that the point of the Countess's speech is sharpened by inserting 'But' at the beginning, so that she starts and ends with a snorted 'But to the Court!' Hook argues also that a fine pun can be recovered at IV, v, 15–19 by the change of one word. F:

> *Clown.* Indeed sir she was the sweet Margerom of the sallet, or rather the hearbe of grace.
> *Lafew.* They are not hearbes you knaue, they are nose-hearbes.
> *Clown.* I am no great *Nabuchadnezzar* sir, I have not much skill in grace.

Alter Lafew's fourth word from *hearbes* to *grass*, Hook urges, and the play of wit is smoother.

The first person to propose that the Quarto's description of Hamlet's flesh as 'sullied' should be changed to 'solid' was Tennyson. M. W. Ware has discovered the expression of the poet's preference in a letter to F. J. Furnivall written in 1883.[3] Richard Flatter finds support[4] for *solid* in *Venus and Adonis*, 1165–6, *Tempest*, IV, i, 148 ff., and *Pericles*, V, iii, 41 ff. In the same play, G. W. Williams finds the reading of Q at III, i, 166 is preferable to that of F (the line is wanting in Q 1).[5] Speaking of Hamlet's reason, Ophelia says that now it is

> Q 2: Like sweet bells jangled out of time, and harsh
> F:　　Like sweet bells jangled, out of tune and harsh

Williams believes that Shakespeare's figure is that of ringing changes on a set of bells. They must be rung in proper order (in time), or there is confusion. He cites Kittredge's use of lines from *The Pilgrim*, IV, III, 4–5, 'Like bells rung backward,They are nothing but confusion and mere noises'.

In the opinion of C. H. Gold,[6] Q 1 has a better reading than F in *King Lear*, I, i, 149. In the quarto, Kent tells Lear that 'To plainnesse honour's bound When majesty falls to folly'. The Folio variant is *stoops*. At this stage, and in his current mood, says Gold, Lear cannot stoop; the preferred reading is 'falls to folly'. It may be so, but some will consider the alliteration in Q objectionable and the line choppy. A weightier matter is discussed by Terence Hawkes.[7]

---

[1] *M.L.R.* LV (1960), 266–7.
[2] 'Two Proposed Emendations in *All's Well*', *Shakespeare Quarterly*, XI (1960), 387–8.
[3] 'Hamlet's *Sullied/Solid* Flesh', *Shakespeare Quarterly*, XI (1960), 490.
[4] '"Solid" or "Sullied", and Another Query', *Shakespeare Quarterly*, XI (1960), 490–3.
[5] 'Hamlet's Reason, Jangled out of Time: III, i, 166', *Notes & Queries*, n.s. VII (1960), pp. 329–31.
[6] 'A Variant Reading in *King Lear*', *Notes & Queries*, n.s. VIII (1961), pp. 141–2.
[7] 'The Fool's "Prophecy" in *King Lear*', *Notes & Queries*, n.s. VII (1960), pp. 331–2.

One of the changes Duthie makes in the New Shakespeare *Lear* is to put lines 91–2 of the Fool's prophecy (III, ii, 81–96) ahead of line 84. Hawkes gives an account of the age and weight of the tradition of Merlinesque prophecies and suggests that Duthie's rearrangement of the lines defeats the poet's intention.

In Q 1 of *Romeo and Juliet*, an exclamation of dismay to be spoken at V, iii, 71 by the Page of County Paris is centred on the page as a stage-direction and printed in italics without a speech heading. Q 2 and F treat it properly as dialogue 'Boy. O Lord they fight, I will go call the Watch' (a difference in the Folio speech prefix is irrelevant). G. W. Williams believes that there is a somewhat analogous situation at III, i, 93.[1]

Q 1:	*Tibalt vnder Romeos arme*	
	thrusts Mercutio, in and flyes.	
Q 2 (centred):	*Away* Tybalt	
Q 3 (in margin):		*Away* Tybalt
F:	*Exit Tybalt*	

Williams argues that Shakespeare wrote the line to be shouted to Tybalt by his companion after Mercutio falls mortally wounded and explains that the memorially reconstructed text of Q 1, which simply describes the action here, has influenced Q 2 and F to treat a line of dialogue as a stage direction.

Remembering that in *Lear well* is printed *will* at I, i, 225 and I, iv, 1 in the Folio, Kenneth Muir proposes[2] a change in *Antony and Cleopatra*, III, xiii, 73–8: Cleopatra is sending a message to Octavius:

> there to kneele.
> Tell him, from his all-obeying breath I heare
> The doome of Egypt.

The sense is much improved, Muir thinks, if the lines are changed thus:

> there to kneele,
> Till, from his all-obeying breath, I heare
> The doome of Egypt.

He supposes that in F 'Tell him' has been brought over from line 77 and that it was easy to misread *e*'s and *i*'s in the F copy.

---

[1] 'A New Line of Dialogue in *Romeo and Juliet*', *Shakespeare Quarterly*, XI (1960), 84–7.
[2] '*Antony and Cleopatra*, III, xiii, 73–8', *Notes & Queries*, n.s. VIII (1961), p. 142.

BOOKS RECEIVED

[Inclusion of a book in this list does not preclude its review in a subsequent volume.]

BAYLEY, JOHN. *The Characters of Love* (London: Constable, 1960).

BRYANT, J. A. *Hippolyta's View* (University of Kentucky Press, 1961).

BULLOUGH, G. *Narrative and Dramatic Sources of Shakespeare*, vol. III (London: Routledge and Kegan Paul, 1960).

DRIVER, T. F. *The Sense of History in Greek and Shakespearean Drama* (Columbia University Press, 1960).

FISHER, S. T. *Letter to a University Librarian on Sir John Falstaff* (Montreal: Redpath Press, 1960).

FOAKES, R. A. and RICKERT, R. T. (editors). *Henslowe's Diary* (Cambridge University Press, 1961).

GITTINGS, R. *Shakespeare's Rival* (London: Heinemann, 1960).

GOMES, E. *Shakespeare No Brasil* (Ministério de Educação e Cultura, 1960).

HALLIDAY, F. E. *Life of Shakespeare* (London: Duckworth, 1960).

KNIGHTS, L. C. *An Approach to 'Hamlet'* (London: Chatto and Windus, 1960).

MAITRA, SITANSU. *Shakespeare's Comic Idea* (Calcutta: Mukhopadhyay, 1960).

ROSSITER, A. P. *Angel with Horns* (London: Longmans, 1961).

ROUSE, W. H. D. (editor). *'Shakespeare's Ovid': Golding's translation of the Metamorphoses* (London: Centaur Press, 1961).

SHAKESPEARE, WILLIAM
 (The Yale Shakespeare)
  The Merchant of Venice, edited by A. D. Richardson (Yale University Press, 1960).

 Meri, G. *Komoodiad II* (Eesti Riiklik Kirjastus, 1960).

 Hugo, F-Victor, *Théâtre Complet de Shakespeare* (Paris: Garnier, 1961).

STRATFORD-UPON-AVON STUDIES (General editors: John R. Brown and Bernard Harris), vol. 3. *Early Shakespeare* (London: Arnold, 1961).

WATSON, C. B. *Shakespeare and the Renaissance Concept of Honor* (Princeton University Press; London: Oxford University Press, 1960).

WELCH, C. *Lectures on The Recorder* (London: Oxford University Press, 1961). (Reprinted from *Six Lectures on the Recorder*, 1911.)

INDEX

INDEX

INDEX

Henriksson, Alf, 138
Henslowe, Philip, 172
    See also Foakes, R. A.
Hepburn, Katharine, 139
Hepton, Bernard, 144
Herbert, George, 92
Herbert, William, Third Earl of Pembroke, 12
Herford, C. H., 26, 40 n.
Herodotus, 102
Hesiod, 102
Hewitt, Douglas, 114
Heywood, Thomas, 8
    The Rape of Lucrece, 40 n., 91
Highway to Heaven, The, 66
Hinkle, G. K., 12
Hinman, Charlton K., *Six Variant Readings in the First
    Folio of Shakespeare* reviewed, 175–7
Histriomastix, 63
Hobson, Harold, 147
Hoeniger, F. David, 124 n., 169, 180
Holbein, Hans, 127
Homer, 96
Hook, F. S., 181
Horace, 64
Hosley, Richard, 172, 180
Hotson, Leslie, 10, 12, 112
Hovenden, Valery, 145
Howard, Frances, 168
Hubaux, Jean, 109 n., 110 n.
Hubler, E., 16, 124 n.
Hughes, Peter, 146
Hugo, F-Victor, 168
Hungary, Report on Shakespeare in, 135
Hunter, G. K., 181
Hutton, James, 9
Hyde, Isabel, 165
Hyman, Stanley E., 123 n.

Iljovski, V., 142
India, Report on Shakespeare in, 135
Ing, Catherine, 8
Irving, Washington, 136
Isaacs, J., 8
Isherwood, Millicent, 144
Italy, Report on Shakespeare in, 136
Ives, E. W., 172

Jackson, Vincent, 3
Jackson, William A., 128
Jacquot, Jean, 9, 138
James, D. G., 121
James I, King, 1, 125
    Daemonology, 112
Jarvis, William, 136
Jauneau, René, 133
Jerome, 90, 97 n.

Johnson, Ewart, 145
Johnson, Francis R., 176 n.
Johnson, Richard,
    Golden Garland of Princely Delight, 40 n.
    Choyce Drollery; Songs & Sonnets, 40 n.
Johnson, Richard, 147
Johnson, Robert, 6
Johnson, Samuel, 28, 33, 136
Jones, H. W., 180
Jones, M. W., 169
Jones, Robert, 6
Jonson, Ben, 3, 8, 27, 62, 99, 102
    Cynthia's Revels, 173
    Epicoene, 40 n.
    Poetaster, 65
Jorgensen, Paul A., 10
Josephson, Lennart, 138
Jovanović, Lj., 141
Jovanović, Ž., 142
Joyce, James, 30 n.

Kapoor, Kiran, 136
Keats, John, 22, 41, 50, 74, 79 n., 80 n., 108
Kemble, John Philip, 172
Kempe, William, 62
Kenya, Report on Shakespeare in, 137
Kernodle, George F., 113
Kettle, A., 140
Kiasashvili, Nico, 168
Kirschbaum, Leo, 159
    Two Lectures on Shakespeare reviewed, 164
Kitto, H. F. D., 163
Kittredge, George L., 5, 15, 181
Knight, Charles, 2, 5
Knight, G. Wilson, 7, 16, 17, 20, 26, 28, 100, 102, 103, 105,
    108 n., 109 n., 113, 114, 115, 116, 120, 121
Knights, L. C., 11, 17, 80 n.
    An Approach to Hamlet reviewed, 163–4
Knijiga, Narodna, 142
Knuth, Gustav, 138
Koneski, B., 142
Kortner, Fritz, 134
Ković, P., 142
Koźmian, Stanisław, 137
Kreft, B., 141, 142, 143
Krushelnitzkii, M., 140
Kuhl, E. P., 23
Kuruç, Bozkurt, 138
Kyd, Thomas, *The Spanish Tragedy*, 113

Labé, Louis, 98 n.
Lactantius, 100, 102, 106, 107, 109 n., 110 n.
    De Phoenice, 29
Laevius, 109 n.
Lamson, Roy, 40 n.
Landino, Christophe, 95, 96

189

INDEX

Mirandola, Pico della, 95
Mirror for Magistrates, A, 24, 169
Molinet, Jean, 93
Monsarrat, G., 175
Montgomerie, William, 112
Montmorency, J. E. G., 16
Moore, J. R., 5
Moore, K. V., 146
Morgann, Maurice, 33
Mori, Masayuki, 137
Morley, Thomas, 6, 9, 10 n.
Motley, 147
Moudouès, Rose-Marie, 133
Muir, Kenneth, 20, 23, 24, 26, 27, 28, 29, 30, 140, 165, 174, 179, 180, 182
    Shakespeare as Collaborator reviewed, 169
Muller, Herbert, 113
Mullins, Ian, 144
Munday, Anthony, *John a Kent,* 170
Murdock, George P., 123 n.
Murray, Gilbert, 111, 115
Murrie, E. B., 7
Murry, J. Middleton, 26, 79 n.

Nashe, Thomas, 63, 72 n., 126, 128
    Summer's Last Will and Testament, 40 n.
Naylor, Edward Woodall, 1, 3, 4, 5, 7, 8, 9
Nedić, B., 142
Nejgebauer, Aleksander, 164
Nels, S., 140
Neville, John, 141, 145
Newdigate, Bernard H., 27
Newton, 10
Nichols, John, 1, 2
Nicoll, Allardyce, 7, 9, 11, 168, 170, 171
Noble, Richmond, 5, 6, 7
Noli, F. S., 142
North, Sir Thomas, 177
Norton, Thomas and Sackville, Thomas, *Gorboduc,* 142, 170
Nosworthy, J. M., 9, 12
Nowottney, Winifred, 17, 159

Oakeshott, Walter, 72 n.
Obey, André, 133
Occhini, Maria, 136
Ogle, M. B., 15
Okhlopkov, N., 140
Olivier, Sir Laurence, 141, 147, 150
O'Loughlin, Sean, 20, 23, 24, 26, 27, 28, 29, 30
Olson, Paul A., 112
Ong, Walter J., 27
Onions, C. T., 6
Ord, H., 15
Ortelius, Abraham, 128
Ost, Geoffrey, 144
Otway, Thomas, 153

Overbury, Sir Thomas, 168
Ovid, 20, 23, 24, 26, 29, 62, 81, 82, 84, 88 n., 90, 93, 99, 115, 169
    Amores, 29, 93, 98 n., 108 n.
    Ars, 98 n.
    Fasti, 29, 92, 94, 97 n.
    Metamorphoses, 14, 28

Pafford, J. H. P., 9
Painter, William, *Palace of Pleasure,* 29
Palingenius, Marcellus, *Zodiacus Vitae,* 14, 17
Pandurović, S., 140
Paolucci, Anne, 166
Papp, Joseph, 139
Parigot, Guy, 133
Parrott, Kenneth, 144
Parrott, Marc, 40 n.
Partridge, A. C., 30, 160 n.
Partridge, Eric, 40 n.
Pasternak, Boris, 136
Pater, Walter, 19
Patrick, Nathaniel, 173
Pattison, B., 7, 8
Paul, David, 146
Paul, Henry, 111
Paul, St, 96
Paulsen, Carl, 146
Pawlo, Toivo, 138
Payne, R. J. G., 144
Pearson, Lu Emily, 20, 21
Peele, George, 63, 113, 114
    Old Wives' Tale, 113
Peguilhan, Aimeric de, 98 n.
Pembroke, Third Earl of, *see* Herbert, William
Percy, Bishop Thomas, 1, 7
Petrarch (Francesco Petrarca), 43, 95, 98 n., 101, 106, 109 n.
Phillips, G. W., 14
Pinto, V. de Sola, 7
Piper, David, 130 and n.
Pistoia, Cino da, 98 n.
Planché, J. R., 172
Planchon, René, 138
Planchon, Roger, 133
Plaović, R., 141
Plato, 21, 96, 143
    Phaedrus, 81, 83
Plautus, 98 n.
Playford, J., 3
Plotinus, 105
Plutarch, 170, 177
Poe, Edgar Allan, 109 n.
Poel, William, 5
Poland, Report on Shakespeare in, 137
Pollock, Ellen, 145
Pontanus, Jacobus, 98 n., 101, 106

INDEX

Ponz de Capduelh, 93
Pooler, Knox, 11, 12, 18, 19, 22
Pope, Alexander, 177
Popović, V., 140
Potter, Frank H., 3
Prager, Leonard, 165
Prakash, Nigram, 136
Prange, Gerda, 9
Praz, Mario, 9
Price, Hereward T., 20, 24, 29
Price, R. T., 17, 109 n.
Prince, F. T., 18, 22, 24, 25, 99, 107, 108 n., 167, 178
Prior, R., 144
Probus, 97 n.
Propertius, 97 n.
Prouty, C. T., 170
Pulver, Jeffrey, 4
Purcell, Henry, 5, 9
Pushkin, Alexander, 143
Putney, Rufus, 20, 21, 27
Pythagoras, 96

Quasimodo, Salvatore, 136

Raglan, Lord, 124 n.
Raimon de Toulouse, 93
Raleigh, Sir Walter (1861–1922), 6, 19
Randolph, Thomas, *The Drinking Academy*, 40 n.
Rang, F. C., 16
Ransom, J. C., 16, 17
Rappoport, R., 137
Ravenscroft, Thomas, 1, 6
Raymond, M., 109 n.
Reed, E. B., 8, 13
Reed, Robert R., 170
Return from Parnassus, The, 62, 71 n., 72 n.
Reusner, Nicholas, 97 n.
Reynolds, George F., 139
Rich, John, 173
Richardson, A. D., 178–9
Richardson, Anthony, 145
Richardson, Tony, 151
Richmond, Evelyn B., 172
Rickert, R. T., *see* Foakes, R. A.
Ridley, M. R., 26
Rimbault, Edward Francis, 2
Ringler, W. A., 8
Ritson, Joseph, 1
Roberts, James, 179
Robertson, J. M., 12
Rollins, Hyder E., 6, 11, 13, 17, 19, 20, 26, 30 n., 34, 40 n., 61 n., 98 n., 109 n.
Romano, Giulio, 94
Ronconi, Luca, 136
Ronsard, Pierre de, 29, 81, 82, 84, 85, 86, 98 n., 105, 106, 109 n.

Rosen, William, *Shakespeare and the Craft of Tragedy* reviewed, 161–2
Ross, William, 12
Rosseter, Philip, 6
Rossiter, A. P., 118, 119, 159, 160, 164, 165, 167
Rothe, Hans, 134
Rougemont, Denis de, 122
Royden, Matthew, 26, 29, 30, 100, 101
  Elegy for Astrophil, 100, 109 n.
Rubens, Peter Paul, 19
Ruggeri, Osvaldo, 136
Russell, Lucy Harrington, Countess of Bedford, 27
Rylands, George, 23
Rylskii, M., 140

Sabol, Andrew, 8, 9, 173
Sabuncu, Nur, 139
Sackville, Thomas, *see* Norton, Thomas
Şahinbaş, Irfan, 139
Saint-Denis, Michel, 133, 147
Saint-Hilaire, De Queux de, 97 n.
Saintsbury, George, 19, 22, 26
Saliceto, Bartolomi di, 97 n.
Salusbury, Sir John, 25, 27, 99
Salutati, Collucio, 95
Samarin, R., 140
Santuccio, Giacomo, 136
Sartain, Donald, 144
Sauget, Henri, 133
Sbragia, Giancarlo, 136
Scaliger, J. C., 97 n.
Scase, David, 144, 146
Schaap, K., 128
Schadewalt, W., 174
Schalla, Hans, 138
Schaller, Rudolf, 134
Schanzer, E., 167, 170, 174
Schell, Maximilian, 134
Schilders, Richard, 128
Schlegel, A. W. von, 15, 132, 134
Schlegel, F. von, 15
Schlosser, A., 140
Schneider, Romy, 133
Scholes, Percy, 4, 5, 7
Schreyvogel, F., 132
Schröder, F. L., 132
Scott, J. G., 11, 14
Scott, Nathan, 123 n.
Sehrt, Ernst T., *Der dramatische Auftakt in der elisabethanischen Tragödie* reviewed, 171
Selden, Samuel, 117, 118
Semmelroth, Wilhelm, 134
Seneca, 23, 88 n., 169, 174
  Hippolytus, 83, 84
Seng, Peter J., 9
Serban, M., 140

INDEX

INDEX